PART TWO
A HISTORY SINCE 1939

AMERICA IN THE TWENTIETH CENTURY

PART TWO

A HISTORY SINCE 1939

AMERICA IN THE TWENTIETH CENTURY

JAMES T. PATTERSON

Brown University

Under the General Editorship of

JOHN MORTON BLUM

Yale University

HARCOURT BRACE JOVANOVICH, INC.

NEW YORK   CHICAGO   SAN FRANCISCO   ATLANTA

Library of Congress Catalog Card Number: 76-1448

ISBN: 0-15-502223-7

Acknowledgments for illustrations appear on page xviii

COPYRIGHTS AND ACKNOWLEDGMENTS

For permission to use the selections reprinted in this book, the author is grateful to the following publishers and copyright holders:

IRVING BERLIN MUSIC CORPORATION for excerpts from lyrics of "This Time" by Irving Berlin on page 316. © Copyright 1942 Irving Berlin. © Copyright renewed 1969. Reprinted by permission of Irving Berlin Music Corporation.

DOUBLEDAY & COMPANY, INC. for "The Reckoning," copyright 1941 by Theodore Roethke, from the book *The Collected Poems of Theodore Roethke*. Reprinted by permission of Doubleday & Company, Inc.

FARRAR, STRAUS & GIROUX, INC. for "When I get to the other side" from *Anyplace But Here* by Arna Bontemps and Jack Conroy. Reprinted with the permission of Farrar, Straus & Giroux, Inc., from *Anyplace But Here* by Arna Bontemps and Jack Conroy, Copyright © 1945, 1966 by Arna Bontemps and Jack Conroy.

MARCUS GARVEY, JR. for "Black queen of beauty, thou hast given color to the world" by Marcus Garvey, Sr. Reprinted by permission of Marcus Garvey, Jr., literary executor of the estate of Amy Jacques Garvey.

HARPER & ROW for "Superman" from *The Carpentered Hen and Other Tame Creatures* by John Updike. Copyright © 1955 by John Updike. Reprinted by permission of Harper & Row, Publishers, Inc.

HOUGHTON MIFFLIN COMPANY for "When the organizers needed dough" from *Coming of the New Deal* by Arthur M. Schlesinger, Jr. Reprinted by permission of the publisher.

EILEEN LAMB for "Where are You, God?" from *So Far, So Good! An Autobiography* by Elsie Janis. Reprinted by permission of Eileen Lamb.

MACMILLAN PUBLISHING CO., INC. for "The Leaden-Eyed" by Vachel Lindsay. Copyright © 1914 by Macmillan Publishing Co., Inc., renewed 1942 by Elizabeth C. Lindsay.

SANGA MUSIC for "I don't want your millions mister" by Jim Garland. © Copyright 1947 by Stormking Music Inc. All rights reserved. Used by permission.

CHARLES SCRIBNER'S SONS for "Richard Cory" by Edwin Arlington Robinson. Reprinted by permission of Charles Scribner's Sons from *The Children of the Night* by Edwin Arlington Robinson.

TWAYNE PUBLISHERS, INC. for "If We Must Die" from *Selected Poems of Claude McKay*; copyright 1953 by Twayne Publishers, Inc., and reprinted by permission of Twayne Publishers, a Division of G. K. Hall & Co., Boston.

To Nancy, Steve, and Marnie

A note on the two-part edition

This volume is part of a variant printing, not a new or revised edition, of *America in the Twentieth Century: A History*. Many instructors may find that a two-volume version will enable them to fit the text into the particular patterns of their teaching and scheduling. To meet their needs, the publishers have prepared this printing, which consists of two separate volumes that exactly reproduce the text of the one-volume version. The first of these volumes starts at the beginning of the century and continues through World War II. The second volume repeats the chapter on World War II (chapter 10), and carries the account forward to the present. The variant printing, then, is intended as a convenience to those instructors and students who have occasion to use either one part or the other of *America in the Twentieth Century: A History*. Consequently, the pagination and index of the one-volume version, as well as its illustrations, maps, and other related materials, are retained in the two-volume printing. The difference between the one-volume and the two-volume versions of the book is one of form.

Preface

America in the Twentieth Century brings together my thoughts concerning
United States history from about 1900 to the present, a field in which I have
taught for some twelve years. Although the book pays due attention to the
traditional areas of political and diplomatic history, it also focuses on areas of
increasing interest to students and scholars: black history, women's history,
urbanization, the role of ethnic groups, the rise of presidential power and of
the federal bureaucracy, the power of corporations and the conflict of economic groups, changing sexual mores, and trends in regional and national
values.

I have tried to give pace to the narrative by including anecdotes and
quotations, by describing key personalities, and by setting aside selections
from primary sources that illuminate passages in the text. I hope, however,
that readers will not conclude that my purpose is to entertain or to avoid
serious issues. On the contrary, I have tried to offer up-to-date interpretations
and to state my conclusions on major questions. Without sacrificing my own
viewpoint, I have also tried to present various sides of controversial issues.
My aim is to stimulate the thinking of college-level students in survey courses
and in courses dealing with twentieth-century American history.

Many people helped me during the writing and production of this book.
These include Thomas A. Williamson and William J. Wisneski, my editors at
Harcourt Brace Jovanovich, and Carla Hirst Wiltenburg, who did an excellent
job of finding pictures and cartoons. I am also indebted to Alexandra Roosevelt for her careful attention to the details of the manuscript. Sidney Zimmer-
man of HBJ was an especially intelligent, well informed, and thought-provok-
ing manuscript editor. Professor John Thomas of Brown University helped
greatly by reading early drafts of two chapters, as did Daniel Fischel, a Brown

graduate student. Professor John Morton Blum of Yale University criticized the entire manuscript with great care and discrimination, and Professor Lawrence Veysey of the University of California, Santa Cruz, also read the whole manuscript and offered extensive and extremely valuable criticism of it. Both scholars immeasurably improved the book.

James T. Patterson

Contents

12
The Middle-class world of the 1950s
371

13
The 1960s:
from altruism to disenchantment
411

14
Turmoil, 1965–1968
449

15
The unsettled 1970s
485

The Constitution of the United States of America
521

Presidential elections, 1900–1972
534

Index
537

Tables

Maps and Graphs

Illustration Credits

295, Library of Congress; 300, United Press International; 302, The Franklin D. Roosevelt Library; 311, Culver; 314, Kaiser Industries Corporation; 317, (top right) Culver; (bottom) Library of Congress; 302, U.S. Department of Labor; 324, Wide World; 325, Wide World; 327, Wide World; 328, U.S. Army Photo; 339, United Press International; 352, Eve Arnold, Magnum; 361, John Dominis, Time-Life Picture Agency; 362, Carl Mydans, Time-Life Picture Agency; 365, Cornell Capa, Magnum; 366, United Press International; 370, Bill Owens, Magnum; 373, Arthur Tress, Magnum; 374, Drawing by Claude, © 1956 The New Yorker Magazine, Inc.; 391, © 1956, Cartoon from *Herblock's Special for Today,* Simon & Schuster, 1958; 398, © 1956, Cartoon from *Herblock's Special for Today,* Simon & Schuster, 1958; 404, Elliott Erwitt, Magnum; 410, Flip Schulke, Black Star; 412, Hank Walker, Time-Life Picture Agency; 418, Charles Moore, Black Star; 419, *Ebony Magazine;* 423, Wright, *Miami News;* 431, Bruce Davidson, Magnum; 434, Richard Bellak, Black Star; 448, Wide World; 452, (both) Bob Adelman, Magnum; 455, Wide World; 460, Philip Jones Griffiths, Magnum; 463, Brooks, *Birmingham News;* 465, Wide World; 468, Bonnie M. Freer, Photo Trends; 474, NOW Legal Defense/Education Fund; 477, (top) Charles Harbutt, Magnum, and (bottom) Roger Malloch, Magnum, both from *Crisis in America,* published by Ridge Press and Holt Rinehart & Winston; 479, Roger Malloch, Magnum; 484, Wide World; 487, Bettye Lane; 490, B. Curtis, Black Star; 496, *Valley Daily News,* Tarentum, Pa.; 497, John A. Darnell, Time-Life Picture Agency; 505, United Press International; 507, United Press International; 511, © 1973 by Herblock in the *Washington Post;* 512, Editorial Cartoon by Bill Sanders, courtesy of Field Newspaper Syndicate; 515, Wide World; 518, © 1975 by Herblock in the *Washington Post.*

PART TWO
A HISTORY SINCE 1939

AMERICA IN THE TWENTIETH CENTURY

10

SOLDIERS *without guns*

World War II: the great divide

Beginning around 1939, the social historian John Brooks concluded, America began a "Greap Leap" toward the future. The critic Irving Kristol added that the 1930s were the "last amateur decade." Both writers properly stressed the incalculable impact of World War II on American life. In every area—military and diplomatic affairs, politics, social and economic relations—the war greatly accelerated the processes of economic change, political centralization, and international involvement that were the grand themes of American twentieth-century life. More than ever before, there was no turning back.

The military effort

America's primary task after the attack on Pearl Harbor was of course to settle on the quickest, most effective way of defeating the enemy. This problem, in turn, raised four major questions, all of which had profound long-range implications.

295

Which adversary, Germany or Japan, was to be concentrated on first? Should the enemy be totally defeated or, as in 1918, be permitted to reach an armistice? What emphasis should Britain and the United States place on strategic bombing, thought by some to be a way of avoiding the bloodbath of World War I? Where, and when, should Allied ground forces actually attack Germany and Japan?

The answer to the first question aroused little controversy at the time. At least as early as the fall of France, Roosevelt and his advisers considered Germany the number one enemy, and in March 1941 British and American military leaders agreed. After the attack on Pearl Harbor, Prime Minister Winston Churchill came to the United States for the first of many summit conferences, and the agreement became official policy.

At times during the war Roosevelt appeared to depart from this position. In mid-1942, American naval forces scored unexpectedly quick victories at the battles of Midway and Coral Sea, and Admiral Chester Nimitz, commander in the central Pacific, was authorized to mount offensives against Japanese-held islands. By October America had more forces deployed against Japan than against Germany; by the spring of 1943 Nimitz's forces had captured the Solomon Islands; and by October 1944, after desperate island battles, American soldiers were invading the Philippines. This military progress in the Pacific caused a few critics to argue later that America should have concentrated its efforts against Japan, thereby leaving Hitler and Stalin to destroy each other in the West.

Roosevelt refused to go that far. The offensives against Japan were expropriating landing ships needed for a full-scale amphibious assault on the European continent. Roosevelt recognized that any American invasion of Japan's home islands would encounter fanatical resistance. He also had to

Whether nations live in prosperity or starve to death interests me only so far as we need them for slaves for our Kultur; otherwise it is of no interest to me. Whether 10,000 Russian females fall down from exhaustion while digging an anti-tank ditch interests me only in so far as the anti-tank ditch for Germany is finished. We shall never be rough and heartless when it is not necessary, that is clear. We Germans, who are the only people in the world who have a decent attitude toward animals, will also assume a decent attitude toward these human animals. But it is a crime against our blood to worry about them and giving them ideals, thus causing our sons and grandsons to have a more difficult time with them. When someone comes to me and says: "I cannot dig the anti-tank ditch with women and children, it is inhuman, for it will kill them," then I have to say "You are the murderer of your own blood, because if the anti-tank ditch is not dug German soldiers will die, and they are the sons of German mothers. They are our own blood."

Heinrich Himmler, head of the Nazi SS, explains the nature of modern war.

respond to the incessant pleas of Josef Stalin, his wartime ally, for aid against Germany. And like most of his contemporaries, the President was anxious to destroy the scourge of Hitler first and forever. For all these reasons he paid little attention to the "Asia-firsters" (whose counsel might have left Stalin free to overrun all of Europe). Under the circumstances Roosevelt's decision for "Europe first" was both unavoidable and sensible.

The second question was answered formally at the Casablanca conference in January 1943, at which Roosevelt, with Churchill's apparent approval, proclaimed the policy of unconditional surrender. Later, America deviated slightly from it: Italy was permitted to lay down its arms in 1943, and Japan was ultimately allowed to retain its emperor. But the total defeat of the enemy remained at the heart of Roosevelt's thinking. "I do not want them to starve to death," he said of the Germans, "but, as an example, if they need food to keep body and soul together, they should be fed three times a day with soup from army soup kitchens." In late 1944 he even initiated the unrealistically harsh Morgenthau Plan aimed at "converting Germany into a country primarily agricultural and pastoral in character." Though he quickly dropped the plan, he adhered consistently to the central goal, that of beating the enemies so thoroughly that they could never again threaten the peace.

To many postwar critics the policy of unconditional surrender seemed a tragic mistake. Supposedly, it steeled the resolve of the enemies, discouraged leaders of the resistance in Germany and Japan, and practically invited Russia to move into the power vacuum in central Europe and Manchuria. Roosevelt, it appeared, forgot the fundamental maxim that wars are fought for political as well as military objectives.

Some of these criticisms were well taken. American insistence on Japan's unconditional surrender proved a stumbling block (though not the only one) to peace in July 1945, before the dropping of the atomic bombs on Hiroshima and Nagasaki. Otherwise, however, the critics were unfair. No policy, no matter how generous, could have swayed the leaders of Germany and Japan from their destructive course. The threat of unconditional surrender did not prevent dissidents in Germany from attempting to overthrow Hitler—an officers' plot almost succeeded in 1944. And Russia charged into central Europe because its armies were powerful, not because of the policy of unconditional surrender. If Roosevelt had shown the slightest tendency to negotiate a truce with Hitler—which he did not—Stalin would probably have kept on fighting—and have ended up with more territory than he did.

The critics of unconditional surrender also forgot the ruthless nature of modern war. In 1917 it was possible for "Yanks" to believe that they were fighting a war to save democracy; there were ideals to be achieved. In 1941, however, American soldiers were "GIs"—"government issued" machines sent abroad by a much more organized society that remembered Pearl Harbor and loathed Hitler. Like Willie and Joe, cartoonist Bill Mauldin's dirty, unshaven infantrymen, they fought because they had to, and they had few aims save destroying the enemy quickly and coming home. General Lesley J.

McNair, director of the training program for all American ground forces, put it this way to a radio audience in 1942: "We must lust for battle; our object in life must be to kill; we must scheme and plan night and day to kill." What McNair meant, and what every American understood, was that Germany and Japan must be totally defeated. No Allied leader in World War II could have pursued a policy that promised otherwise.

The quest for total victory helps explain Roosevelt's support of scientific research into the development of atomic weaponry. This effort began in October 1939, when Leo Szilard, Enrico Fermi, and other emigré scientists, worried about Nazi progress in the field of atomic physics, persuaded Albert Einstein to write a letter to Roosevelt. The letter urged the President to engage the United States in the race to harness atomic energy. Though responsive to the scientists' pleas, the President moved slowly, and it was not until the summer of 1941 that the administration established a "uranium section" in the National Defense Research Committee.

The attack on Pearl Harbor gave renewed urgency to the program, and in 1942 Secretary of War Henry Stimson placed General Leslie Groves, a tough, secretive administrator, in charge of the Manhattan District Project, code name for bomb development. The project's purpose was to beat the Nazis. Japan, concentrating on more conventional weapons, was never seriously engaged in the race.

From 1942 on, American and emigré scientists working on the program received more than $2 billion in federal funds. All of it was appropriated for unspecified military purposes by a Congress that heeded Stimson's requests not to probe closely into how it was going to be used. Top military leaders, including generals Douglas MacArthur and Dwight Eisenhower, America's army commanders in the Pacific and Atlantic, were kept almost as much in the dark. Working rapidly, scientists at the University of Chicago succeeded in setting off a controlled atomic reaction in December 1942. Other scientists and technicians at secret places like Oak Ridge, Tennessee, and Hanford, Washington, prepared material to be used in the bombs, while J. Robert Oppenheimer headed a bomb manufacture laboratory at Los Alamos, New Mexico. In all, some 540,000 people worked on the project during the war.

This incredibly vast, secret operation enabled the United States to pass Germany, which diverted much of its expertise to jet planes and rocketry and failed to test a bomb before the end of the European war in May 1945. The Manhattan project also testified amply to America's desire to win the war by whatever means necessary, and to the willingness of the nation's elected representatives to turn over authority, no questions asked, to the executive branch. This delegation of responsibility, justified at the time by the need for security, was both unprecedented and frightening.

The passion for total victory also helped to sustain the argument for strategic bombing—mass raids against enemy cities, factories, storage facilities, military bases, and transportation complexes. Theoretically, these raids would do such a thorough job of weakening enemy strength (and morale) that ground forces could complete the job with minimal loss of American life. "Strategic air power," General Henry ("Hap") Arnold claimed, "is a war-winning weapon in its own right, and is capable of striking decisive blows far behind the battle line, thereby destroying the enemy's capacity to wage war."

Though Arnold did not get all the planes he wanted until late in the war, he could hardly complain about the administration. As early as 1940 Roosevelt astounded Congress by asking for production of 50,000 planes per year. By 1942, B-17's and B-24's were already being flown over to Great Britain; by 1943 they were taking off on steady raids against the enemy; and by late 1944 they were smashing the Japanese home cities. Before the end of the war the strategic bombing attacks had leveled many industrial cities in both nations.

Whether strategic bombing was as effective as Arnold claimed was another matter. Undoubtedly, it forced the enemy nations to divert manpower and equipment to reconstruction. In crowded, urban Japan it was so effective that neither the atomic bombs nor an invasion may have been necessary. But until late 1944 it was also terrifically costly to the United States. Only 28 of 120 bombers that took off for a raid on Berlin in July 1943 made it to the target. A month later 60 of 560 B-17's were destroyed in the course of an attack on Regensburg and Schweinfurt. Between February 20 and 26, 1944, America lost 226 bombers, 28 fighter planes, and 2600 crewmen. Only in the last year of the war, when American fighter planes finally gained air supremacy, did these raids become reasonably safe for planes and crew.

Strategic bombing enthusiasts were also far too optimistic about the possibility of "pinpoint" bombing. The British bombed mostly at night and could not be too precise about their targets. Americans were scarcely more accurate. Often it was too overcast to see much; often German fighters or antiaircraft artillery forced American pilots to hurry in and off. Either way, the bombs all too frequently blasted civilian areas. And the British and Americans sometimes resorted to indiscriminate firebombing. One raid against Tokyo killed an estimated 84,000 people and left a million homeless. The city, said one observer, was a "midden of smoking flesh." Another attack by the British and Americans, against nonindustrial Dresden in 1945, killed more than 100,000 people.

Even when the bombs hit their targets, they caused much less disruption than many strategists supposed. Against Japan in 1945 they were devastating, for by then many key targets were defenseless. Germany, however, always maintained surplus factory space and labor, and the bombers caused more inconvenience than crisis. Die-hard enthusiasts of bombing argued later that America's mistake was only in not staging enough raids against German oil reserves, necessary for most forms of production. Perhaps so. But because that was not done, it cannot be proved that bombing the oil reserves would have made a significant difference. What is known is that Germany's productive capacity increased until the last weeks of the war.

These limitations of bombing should have suggested that modern war requires great flexibility in response, that not only bombers but also fighters,

Dresden, Germany, after Allied bombing.

tanks, and—as ever—infantry are essential to victory. Unfortunately, however, strategic bombing continued to offer an almost fatal allure after the war. To many people anxious for quick solutions to complex international problems it seemed a "surgical" way to dispose of troublesome opponents. So President Truman thought in authorizing the incineration of Hiroshima; so General Douglas MacArthur thought in advocating the blasting of Manchuria in 1951; so Secretary of State John Foster Dulles thought in talking about "massive retaliation" against Russia in 1954; and so America's "best and brightest" leaders thought during a decade of war in Vietnam.

The fourth military question—where and when to attack the enemy—was ultimately avoided in the Asian theater, where a land invasion of Japan's home islands proved unnecessary. Regarding Europe, however, it sparked heated debate.

At first it was assumed that Britain and the United States would attack Germany's western front as soon as possible. Stalin, whose people were suffering horribly, insisted on help right away. He was supported by American army leaders like Marshall and Dwight D. Eisenhower, commander of the war plans division. "We've got to go to Europe and fight," Eisenhower said in

January 1942, "and quit wasting resources all over the world—and still worse, wasting time."

With men like Marshall so optimistic, Roosevelt led Stalin to believe that America would stage a second front before the end of 1942. But he then had to confront Churchill, whose cooperation was essential to the success of a cross-Channel invasion. Churchill vividly remembered the frightful British losses in World War I, especially in the disastrous amphibious assault at Gallipoli, which he had engineered himself. He was also persuaded, probably correctly, that the Allies lacked sufficient men and equipment, especially landing ships for vehicles. Accordingly, he insisted on smaller attacks against Germany's periphery in the Mediterranean. Roosevelt had no choice but to postpone the invasion to 1943.

Churchill's stand infuriated American army leaders. Stimson dismissed it as "pin-prick warfare," and Eisenhower suggested concentrating on Japan. Roosevelt, however, replied no—"that would be like taking up our dishes and going home." FDR realized that Stalin, to say nothing of the American public, would expect the army to fight somewhere against the Germans in 1942. So he accepted Churchill's plan for an offensive in November in North Africa, where Britain had historic interests. "In wartime," Marshall observed sourly, "the politicians have to do *something* important every year. They could not simply use 1942 to build up for 1943 or 1944: they could not face the obloquy of fighting another 'phony war.'"

When the North African campaign proved successful, Marshall and Eisenhower hoped for a cross-Channel invasion in 1943. Churchill, however, still posed objections, and at Casablanca in January he persuaded Roosevelt to agree to "pin-prick warfare" against Sicily and Italy. Marshall observed angrily that "we lost our shirts . . . we came, we listened, and we were conquered." Moreover, the Italian campaign proved costly: at war's end in 1945 Allied troops were still battling their way up the peninsula. So the months slipped by without the long-anticipated invasion. Not until the Teheran summit conference of November 1943 did the Russians receive a guarantee for an attack early in 1944.

Churchill's fear of an English Channel "running red with the blood of British and American boys" also caused him to suggest the so-called soft-underbelly strategy. This called for an Allied invasion of the Adriatic coast, to be followed by an offensive into southeastern Europe, where Stalin's onrushing armies would join in the attack. To this idea, however, Americans sensibly objected. Such an invasion would have been difficult to stage so far from the main Allied bases in Britain. It would have committed soldiers to very difficult mountainous terrain that was not "soft" at all. At war's end it might have given Russia some claim to occupy parts of western Europe. Churchill's advocacy of the soft-underbelly idea revealed him to be an imaginative but not very sound armchair strategist.

Churchill was probably right in arguing that a second front in 1943, when the Allies lacked full control of the air, would have been costly. But the

FDR visits Sicily in late 1943 accompanied by his commander of the European theater of operations, General Dwight D. Eisenhower.

political ramifications of postponing "D day" to June 1944 were equally unfortunate, for Stalin, having been assured of aid in 1942 and again in 1943, grew ever more suspicious of his English-speaking allies. And when the front finally materialized, his armies were already poised on Germany's eastern borders. At war's end he had little reason to be trustful of the "friends" who were so slow to help in his time of trial.

Roosevelt's handling of these military questions subjected him later to complaints that he was the same short-sighted opportunist during the war that he had sometimes been during the New Deal. If he had thought more often about the postwar world, critics argued, he would have insisted on a second front in 1943 and done all he could to build up ground forces capable of getting into eastern Europe before the Russians. Barring that, he should have agreed to a conditional surrender before the Russians moved into Germany. These arguments ask the impossible. Neither the American public nor Roosevelt's allies would have tolerated conditional surrender, and Churchill stood in the way of a harmoniously organized invasion prior to 1944. In acting to safeguard military victory and to keep the voters behind him in a long and bloody struggle, FDR did what any democratic leader in war has to do.

Wartime diplomacy

Complaints about Roosevelt's military leadership were but part of broader attacks on his diplomacy. Left-wing critics later charged him with refusing to stand up to imperialists like Churchill and with cooperating with decadent forces in China and France. Right-wingers countered by accusing him of naiveté concerning the Soviet Union. Whatever he did, it seemed he could not win.

The left-wing critics focused first on Roosevelt's dealings with Vichy France, the pro-Nazi collaborators who controlled much of France following Hitler's victory in 1940. First he recognized the puppet regime. Then, in planning the North African invasion he (and Eisenhower) worked carefully with Admiral Jean Darlan, head of the Vichy fleet. The "deal" secured Darlan's noninterference with the Allied invasion. But it also annoyed General Charles de Gaulle, the super-sensitive leader of the French resistance forces, and it outraged many American progressives. The United States, they thought, was tainted by association with fascists.

The American Left also disliked his handling of China. During the war Chiang Kai-shek, the Nationalist leader, antagonized American officials by fighting harder against the communist Chinese than against the Japanese. Corruption and mismanagement within Chiang's regime were undermining what little hold he retained on the peasantry. By 1943, General Joseph ("Vinegar Joe") Stilwell, America's military commander in China, was so disgusted that he referred to Chiang as "Peanut." Roosevelt urged Chiang to mend his ways. Chiang, however, ultimately responded by demanding Stilwell's recall. Roosevelt acceded. When he named General Patrick Hurley, a Republican anticommunist with little knowledge of China, as ambassador in 1944, he played further into Chiang's hands.

Other liberals grumbled that FDR failed to appreciate the anticolonial stirrings of the nonwhite world. Why didn't the President make it clear to Churchill, who had been so anxious for American aid in 1941, that the price was surrender of India, Malaya, and other colonial possessions? Roosevelt did not, his biographer James MacGregor Burns concluded, because he was too "soft and pasty" to risk unpleasantness in negotiations, and because he was content to let occasional rhetorical outbursts against colonialism substitute for the effective use of American power.

These critics agreed with spokesmen of the Right (and the center) that Roosevelt possessed many traits ill suited for the business of diplomacy. One of these was his legendary reliance on his own charm. Though very effective in his early dealings with Congress, it failed to impress no-nonsense administrators such as Stimson, who described wartime Cabinet meetings as "solo performances by the President interspersed with some questions and very few debates." It led him, critics charged, to jolly his way through conferences instead of standing up to Stalin or Churchill. Worst of all, FDR's detractors pointed out, it caused him to rely on summit meetings and on personal emissaries like Hopkins instead of on briefings by experts. "I know you will not mind my being brutally frank," he told Churchill in 1944, "when I tell you that I think I can personally handle Stalin better than either you or your Foreign Office or my State Department. Stalin hates the guts of all your top people. He thinks he likes me better, and I hope he will continue to do so."

These habits appeared to make Roosevelt into a Great Procrastinator who preferred to keep everyone happy by committing himself to nothing. Unlike Wilson, he gave little encouragement before 1945 to supporters of a United Nations organization. He refused to be specific about America's postwar commitments, except to imply that the United States would win the war and go home. At the Teheran conference he even told Stalin that the American people would chafe at stationing soldiers in Europe after 1947. And in early 1944 he wrote, "I do not want the United States to have the post-war burden of reconstituting France, Italy, and the Balkans. This is not our natural task at a distance of 3500 miles." Attitudes such as these caused some observers to wonder if the President had any purposeful postwar goals at all.

Critics on the Right insisted that Roosevelt's desire to avoid unpleasantness led him to be "soft on the Soviets." If Roosevelt had not been such a procrastinator, they argued, he could have exacted promises from the Russians in 1942, when they were calling anxiously for American assistance. If he had understood the peculiar ruthlessness of Stalin's regime, he would have seen the futility of dealing with him. If he had not been so anxious to win friends at the conference table, he would have refused to make damaging and unnecessary concessions.

In making such criticisms Roosevelt's foes on the Right pointed out that Averell Harriman, America's ambassador to Russia during the later years of the war, had given ample warning of Soviet postwar ambitions. In January 1945 Harriman wrote, "the Soviets are employing the wide variety of means at their disposal—occupation troops, secret police, local communist parties, labor unions . . . and economic pressure . . . to assure the establishment of regimes which, while maintaining an outward appearance of independence and broad popular support, actually depend for their existence on . . . the Kremlin." Instead of heeding Harriman's advice, Roosevelt supposedly went on his feckless way. "Stalin doesn't want anything but security for his country," FDR said, "and I think if I give him everything I possibly can and ask for nothing from him in return, *noblesse oblige,* he won't try to annex anything and will work with me for a world of democracy and peace."

The culmination of this foolish approach, critics grumbled, was at the Yalta Conference of February 1945. There, Roosevelt allegedly betrayed American interests by permitting Russia three seats in the UN General Assembly, by settling for a vague agreement on reparations (which later permitted Russia—when denied American economic aid—to paralyze eastern Germany), by doing nothing to assist Polish boundary claims, and by failing to secure a noncommunist Polish government. Without consulting China, Roosevelt also reached a secret accord with Stalin that gave the Soviets Southern Sakhalin, the Kurile Islands, joint operation of the Chinese-Eastern and Southern Manchurian railways, and which recognized Russia's "preeminent interests" in Manchuria. In return for these concessions Roosevelt secured only the vague Soviet promise to hold free elections in eastern Europe, and the assurance that Russia would enter the war against Japan within three months of Germany's surrender.

Many of these complaints, from both the Left and the Right, were partly justified. Roosevelt placed far too much faith in Chiang Kai-shek, and he overestimated the value of personal diplomacy. His hopes for the democratic governments in eastern Europe were misplaced: by 1948 all of them had fallen under the thumb of the Kremlin. His failure to secure precise guarantees of access routes to western zones in postwar Berlin caused no end of conflict later on. And successful development of atomic energy later made the Asian deal at Yalta unnecessary.

But FDR's options were restricted. As commander-in-chief his first concern, properly enough, was to win the war with as little suffering to America as possible. The deal with Darlan, therefore, seemed necessary; the alternative might have subjected Allied forces to substantial fighting against the French. Playing along with Chiang was less wise. But cutting off aid to Chiang, who threatened to quit the war unless America kept the dollars flowing, would have been politically hazardous. The middle of a world war, in any event, was no time to attempt the impossible task of "saving" China. And what was the President to do with Churchill, who proudly proclaimed, "I did not become the King's first minister in order to preside over the liquidation of the British empire"? If preserving wartime unity was the primary goal—as it had to be—it made little sense for America to issue demands on such a cooperative ally. In assuming that the United States could have forced its will,

Roosevelt's detractors presumed an omnipotence that America has never possessed.

Complaints about the President's Russian diplomacy falsely assumed that Soviet designs were both evil and clear at the time. In fact, Roosevelt heard not only from hard-liners like Harriman but from much more conciliatory men like Hopkins, Hull, and Eisenhower, who reported that "nothing guides Russian policy so much as a desire for friendship with the United States." The critics also exaggerated America's potential to influence events. The Soviets overran eastern Europe by force of arms, just as the United States and Great Britain took France and the low countries. Recognizing the American sphere of influence, Stalin expected the United States, which had historically shown little concern for the fate of eastern Europe (witness the Munich accord, or the division of Poland in 1939) to leave him alone in his sphere of interest. This meant letting Russia protect itself against unfriendly governments on its borders. And it meant permitting Stalin to subjugate the East Germans, who had invaded Russian territory twice since 1914. In this sense Roosevelt did well to get Russia to make any "promises" whatever about eastern Europe. Americans at the time applauded his "success" at Yalta.

Roosevelt was right also in recognizing that America could secure free elections in eastern Europe only by force, which he had neither the will nor the power to apply. His attitude was best expressed in an exchange with Admiral William Leahy, his top military aide. Leahy complained that the Polish accord was so vague that Russia could "stretch it all the way from Yalta to Washington without ever technically breaking it." Roosevelt nodded, but replied, "I know it, Bill—I know it. But it's the best I can do for Poland at this time." This was not naiveté, but an accurate appreciation of military reality in Europe.

Roosevelt could even be forgiven his concessions to the Soviet Union in Asia. In February 1945 the Japanese were obviously doomed, with or without Russian intervention. But no one could be sure at the time that the atomic bomb, untested until July 1945, would work. What Roosevelt did know was that Japan was fighting fanatically to hold all its possessions. He was further advised (probably wrongly) that America might suffer as many as a million

We really believed in our hearts, that this was the dawn of a new day we had all been praying for and talking about for so many years. We were absolutely certain that we had won the first great victory of the peace, and by 'we' I mean ALL of us—the whole civilized human race. The Russians had proved that they could be reasonable and farseeing, and there wasn't any doubt in the minds of the President or any of us that we could live with them and get along with them peacefully for as far into the future as any of us could imagine.

Harry Hopkins reflects American hopes for postwar cooperation, after Yalta (1945).

casualties in an invasion of the home islands. To avoid such a catastrophe he determined to secure Russian help, which Stalin would have given grudgingly, if at all, without securing concessions for himself.

In these ways Roosevelt's Russian diplomacy revealed not softness but the realism born of perceived military necessity. Despite strains over the second front (and over the Russian use of lend-lease supplies), his policies managed to sustain Allied cooperation. Roosevelt may also have been correct in assuming that Stalin was more concerned for his nation's security (and for traditional Russian territorial gains) than in fomenting world-wide communist revolution. Stalin gave little support to communist forces under Marshal Tito of Yugoslavia; he recognized Chiang in China (then, as always, Stalin was ambivalent about Mao Tse-tung); and he kept a bargain made with Churchill in the fall of 1944, by which Britain recognized Russia's paramount interests in much of southeastern Europe in return for a Soviet hands-off policy in Greece (which became scarcely more "democratic" than Poland). Stalin also cruelly disappointed the communist parties in Italy and France, which had hoped for Russian postwar aid in the West.

All these Soviet actions suggested that Stalin's ambitions—at least to 1945—were limited, and that postwar cooperation was possible. In making such assumptions FDR took risks. But he was operating according to a higher realism, which perceived that Soviet-American détente in the postwar world was a *sine qua non* for world peace. Compared to Wilson's milennial visions, this faith struck many Americans as amoral and unfeeling, but it was in fact responsible, flexible statesmanship.

The expansion of government

FROM WELFARE PROGRAMS TO WARTIME POWERS

In December 1943 Roosevelt explained that he was no longer "Dr. New Deal," but "Dr. Win the War."

His remark confirmed that the exciting days of domestic reform were past. Though Roosevelt continued to work for his programs, he was necessarily preoccupied with military problems. And Congress grew even more obstructive than it had been in his second term, especially after the Republicans made further inroads in 1942. The conservative coalition of Republicans and rural Democrats killed the WPA, the CCC, and the National Resources Planning Board. It defeated bills for federal aid to education, national health insurance, and public power development, and it ignored groups crusading for civil rights. As responsive as ever to well-organized interest groups, it approved legislation granting farmers 110 percent of parity and exempting many agricultural laborers from the draft.

The conservatism of the wartime Congresses was most pronounced in the areas of labor legislation and taxation. In 1943 Congress approved, over Roosevelt's veto, the Smith-Connally Act, which authorized the President to seize strike-bound defense plants and to impose thirty-day "cooling off" periods before labor could go on strike. In the same year it enacted a plan that introduced the principle of withholding taxes, but at the cost of forgiving taxpayers an estimated 75 percent of 1942 taxes. The plan especially benefited high-income people in the good year of 1942. Then in 1944 Congress passed a tax bill that raised only $2 billion more than before. FDR, who had called for an increase of $10 billion, snapped publicly that it was "not a tax bill, but a tax relief bill providing relief not for the needy but for the greedy." His blunt remark angered even his congressional supporters, who helped to pass the bill over his veto. Long before FDR's death in 1945, relations between Capitol Hill and the White House were cold indeed.

The balance of power within the parties also shifted toward the Right during the war. In 1944 the GOP nominated New York governor Thomas E. Dewey as its presidential candidate. Though Dewey accepted much of the New Deal, he waged an abrasive campaign. Other Republican orators engaged in a demagogic effort to link the Roosevelt administration with communism. The Democrats, meanwhile, refused to renominate the liberal Henry Wallace for the vice-presidency. Instead, Harry Truman, a dependable middle-of-the-roader from Missouri, received the prize. Thanks to the power of the Democratic voting coalition, and especially to the efforts of organized labor (which provided $2 million to party funds), Roosevelt and Truman won handily. But their margin of 3.6 million votes fell well short of the Democratic lead of 5 million votes in 1940 and 11 million in 1936. Republicans understandably looked forward to 1948, when they expected to triumph at last.

Despite these blows against the New Deal, the war years did not witness any triumph for reaction. Many of the defeated programs, such as the WPA or the CCC, truly seemed unnecessary in the midst of a revived wartime economy. More important reforms—TVA, social security, the minimum wage, even the NLRB—emerged intact. Nondefense spending actually increased during the war from $7.2 billion to $17 billion, thus remaining at about 8 percent of the Gross National Product. Having helped to build a partial welfare state, Congress was not about to dismantle it.

The growth in domestic expenditures was but one manifestation of a virtual explosion in the size of government during the war. Thanks primarily to defense spending, the federal budget jumped from $9 billion in fiscal 1940 to $98 billion in 1945, or from 9 percent to 46 percent of the GNP. The number of civilian employees of the federal government increased during the same period from 1 to 3.8 million. Federal taxes leaped ahead from $5 billion to $44.5 billion, and millions of Americans felt the bite of the Internal Revenue Service for the first time. With so much money at its command, and with virtual armies of bureaucrats staffing such new agencies as the Office of Price Administration, the War Production Board, the War Labor Board, and Selective Service, the federal government enjoyed more power than the most avid New Dealers ever envisioned in the 1930s.

The impact of this expansive fiscal policy was little short of revolutionary. By increasing federal spending more than tenfold within six years, the government ran up deficits averaging more than $30 billion per year, or ten times the average deficits during the New Deal. Chiefly because of this spending, the economy finally surged back. Unemployment virtually disappeared (thanks in part to the draft), and the GNP (in 1929 prices) shot forward from $121 billion in 1940 to $181 billion in 1945. Few politicians dared to endorse this Keynesian approach as a matter of regular policy, and deficits were modest (except during war) from 1946 through 1963. Still, the power of public spending had been demonstrated beyond doubt. Thereafter all but the most hardened fiscal conservatives admitted that a little pump priming in times of recession was desirable.

The war witnessed an almost equally revolutionary growth in the power of the presidency. Only the White House seemed able to carry on the war and manage the nation's more complex international responsibilities. As Professor Edward Corwin noted ruefully, phrases describing the presidency as the "great engine of democracy" and "the American people's one authentic prophet" began appearing in textbooks. The diplomatic historian Thomas Bailey spoke for many scholars in 1948 by stressing the need for a strong presidency. "Just as the yielding of some of our national sovereignty is the price we must pay for effective international organization," he wrote, "so the yielding of some of our democratic control of foreign affairs is the price we may have to pay for greater physical security." If TR began the twentieth-century American infatuation with the presidency, World War II transformed it into a long-lived affair.

BIG GOVERNMENT: BLESSING OR CURSE?

Most reformers welcomed this explosion in the power of the presidency. Congress, after all, was in the hands of conservatives, and the Court had until

1937 stood in the way of social legislation. By 1945 belief in an activist central administration was a cardinal tenet of modern American liberalism.

Even during the war, however, some people worried about the concentration of enormous power in the hands of a few. One concern was the Office of War Information, which was formed to apprise the public of the course of the war. The *New York Times* observed that it was "feeding us bad news when it was thought we could stand it and good news when it was thought we needed it." Even Elmer Davis, the experienced newsman who headed the agency, fought regularly with military brass who refused to give him accurate, up-to-date information. Admiral King's idea of war information, Davis complained, "was that there should be just *one* communique. Some morning we would announce that the war was over and that we won it." Though these charges were a little exaggerated, they were accurate in complaining about the government's close-mouthed monopoly on sources of important news. They suggested also that Americans had become more conscious of the damages of government manipulation—and of the need to protect civil liberties—than they had been during the days of the Committee on Public Information in World War I.

The administration's handling of civil liberties during the war was equally unsettling. The 12,000-odd conscientious objectors who refused to accept noncombatant military service were placed in so-called Civilian Public Service camps, where the courts refused to extend the protection of the first and fifth amendments. They did not receive pay. The administration imprisoned some 5500 other conscientious objectors, including Jehovah's Witnesses, who claimed exemptions as ministers. Roosevelt also showed himself capable of harshness in handling allegedly profascist dissenters. In 1942 the Justice Department charged twenty-six "native fascists" with conspiring against the government. The accusations were based in part on the arbitrary Smith Act of 1940, which made it an offense even to advocate the overthrow of the government. After much legal wrangling, which revealed no evidence of conspiracy, the government finally had to drop the cases in 1944.

Defenders of the administration rightly pointed out that Roosevelt treated dissenters more even-handedly than Wilson had in World War I. But this improvement did not necessarily signify that America was growing more tolerant or more mature. Rather, it reflected the relative absence of dissent in a war precipitated by the "sneak attack" on Pearl Harbor. As one congressman phrased it a week after the attack, "This war had to come. It is a war of purification in which the forces of Christian peace and freedom and justice and decency and morality are arrayed against the evil pagan forces of strife, injustice, treachery, immorality, and slavery. . . ."

This kind of passion erupted quickly in open racism against Japanese-Americans. A California barber advertised "free shave for Japs," but "not responsible for accidents." A funeral parlor proclaimed, "I'd rather do business with a Jap than with an American." A poll in 1944 that asked Americans

Japanese-Americans start the relocation process at detention camps in World War II.

to say which enemy, Germany or Japan, the United States could "get along with better after the war" revealed that only 8 percent picked Japan.

This kind of thinking led to unjust policies. Though the government treated German- and Italian-Americans well, in 1942 it began systematically to round up Japanese-Americans and to place them in detention centers. These were really concentration camps guarded by soldiers and situated in remote areas of the West. In all, they contained some 112,000 people for the duration of the war. Most of these (perhaps 70,000) were second-generation Nisei who were American citizens. Though a few brought suit, the Supreme Court sanctioned the government's action (during wartime) in 1944. Only later, when passions had subsided, did Americans realize the truth of Justice Frank Murphy's dissent labeling the evacuations "one of the most sweeping and complete deprivations of constitutional rights in the history of this nation."

Those who feared the excesses of big government could content themselves with the hope that ominous wartime developments like the Office of War Information and detention centers were temporary phenomena. The administration's handling of defense contracting, however, led first to bureaucratic confusion and then to the development of a military-industrial complex. Together these exposed the dangers of the governmental expansion produced by modern war.

Bureaucratic confusion began as early as 1939, when Roosevelt created the War Resources Board to oversee defense needs. It received only limited support from the administration before being replaced after the fall of France by the Advisory Commission of the Council of National Defense. This, in turn, gave way in 1941 to the Office of Production Management. All these agencies had to contend with other sources of power, such as Secretary of the Interior Harold Ickes, who was also oil administrator, and Jesse Jones, the imperious banker who headed the Reconstruction Finance Corporation. Critics demanded that Roosevelt create a more permanent agency and give it real authority.

When the President established the War Production Board in January 1942, it appeared that he recognized the need for centralization. But he still refused to make Donald Nelson, the WPB chief, a "czar" over production. His stand was deliberate. As he told Labor Secretary Frances Perkins, "there is something to be said . . . for having a little conflict between agencies. A little rivalry is stimulating. . . . the fact that there is somebody else in the field who knows what you are doing is a strong incentive to strict honesty." The President also did not want to turn over such power to someone else. So he gave only sporadic support to Nelson's efforts at concentrating authority in the WPB. Important pricing matters were handled by Chester Bowles, head of the Office of Price Administration, while James Byrnes, who ran yet another agency, the Office of Economic Stabilization, possessed more power than Nelson himself. From the beginning Nelson, like almost all later civilian officials in charge of defense planning, was unable to override the military whom Roosevelt permitted to control the crucially important matter of procurement.

The WPB needed most the authority to establish priorities for the allocation of scarce commodities. Without such power, it could not assure that contractors and subcontractors would receive necessary supplies. The result was shortages, serious delays in production, and, most ominously, so-called priorities unemployment. In 1943 the WPB at last began applying the Controlled Materials Plan, which required defense contractors to submit quarterly estimates of their needs. This plan removed bottlenecks, but it came too late to help businessmen who, for lack of materials, had been unable to convert to war production. It also led many producers to exaggerate their needs and forced the government to supervise more closely the manifold activities of American manufacturing. The process created considerable bureaucratic growth, red tape, and hard feelings.

Despite these problems, American production leaped ahead with astonishing speed. Confusion, in fact, was less prominent than it had been in World War I. After procrastinating in 1940 and 1941 to assure themselves of markets, American manufacturers converted rapidly to war production. Many assumed direction of plants built almost overnight with public funds. The enormous airplane manufacturing facilities at Willow Run, Michigan, were larger than the combined prewar plants of Boeing, Douglas, and Consolidated Aircraft. More than a mile long, they included 1600 machine tools and 7500 jigs and fixtures. The story of rubber production was equally amazing. The government built fifty-one synthetic rubber making plants, which by 1944 made close to a million tons per year. (The German peak, in 1943, was 109,000 tons.) These fantastic increases in output created a virtual overabundance of weaponry by late 1943. Thereafter many contractors began scrambling for the privilege of reconverting to civilian production.

The production miracle unfortunately led many people to believe that America was all but omnipotent, that it could move with lightning speed to demolish enemies all over the world. It also caused businessmen to praise

A ship is launched at one of Henry Kaiser's seven shipyards. At its peak, this yard turned out a ship a day.

themselves for accomplishing so much. Conveniently overlooking the role of government spending, they extolled the virtues of capitalistic free enterprise, and they rejected arguments that more government supervision might have secured better results. To a degree this claim may have had merit, for even a "czar" might have found it impossible to manage an economy so huge and complex as America's. Businessmen may have been equally correct in asserting (Roosevelt agreed) that a degree of voluntarism was necessary for morale in such a long war. For social reformers, however, the self-assured hostility of many businessmen to government "interference" proved a formidable obstacle to change in the 1940s and 1950s.

Reformers worried also about the lasting connections developed in wartime between big business and the military. For it was the big operators to whom the army, the navy, and the newly created Office for Scientific Research and Development turned for help. These large organizations had the capital, the research potential, and the equipment to produce quickly. They could free middle management specialists and white-collar workers to handle government red tape. Above all, big institutions could be dealt with quickly. Government officials liked to work with a handful of experienced operators instead of with a host of smaller entrepreneurs unfamiliar with the labyrinth of federal bureaucracy.

Top government officials made sure that big business was at home in its developing relationship with Washington. Many of them had been recruited, by the supposedly "radical" New Deal, from corporations, and they agreed that producing for defense ought to bring a handsome profit. "If you are going to . . . go to war, . . . in a capitalist country," Stimson observed, "you have got to let business make money out of the process." Stimson and others offered contractors cost-plus contracts and generously renegotiated deals when businesses complained. The government also provided low-interest federal loans for plant expansion and easy tax write-offs. Patents for processes developed with government aid generally reverted to the manufacturer. Such massive assistance assured big corporations of commanding positions in areas formerly handled by subcontractors. Similarly, scientists engaged in practical military research, especially in atomic physics, reaped great rewards from government grants while scholars in the humanities and social sciences had to plug away as in the past.

There was no easy way for government to reverse the long-range movement toward concentration, whether in business or in universities. Still, progressives correctly complained about government's enthusiastic hand on the tiller. They astutely observed that big business and the military, eclipsed by other contenders for federal favor in the 1930s, had now surpassed in influence other interest groups like big labor and big agriculture. They prophesied also that the military-industrial complex, as it came to be known, could lock the nation on a martial course. Among the baneful results of political centralization, the military-industrial nexus perhaps was the most frightening of all.

The war and American society

Stuart Chase, a liberal economist, surveyed American society at the end of the war and concluded that prosperity had worked wonders that all the measures of the New Deal had failed to bring about. "The facts," he said, "show a better break for the common man than liberals in 1938 could have expected for a generation."

Almost every economic indicator supported Chase's conclusion. Despite rationing of gasoline, coffee, tin, and other goods, few Americans suffered much at home. National income jumped from $81 billion in 1940 to $182 billion five years later, or from $573 to $1,074 per capita. Improvements in diets and health care during the same period caused life expectancy to increase by three years to sixty-six. (However, poor teeth and eyes, symptoms of malnutrition, still caused more than 50 percent of young men in some regions to fail preinduction physicals.) Thanks in part to the GI Bill, 8 million young people learned a trade or attended college after the war, while bonuses for American veterans totaled more than $2 billion.

The war even improved the distribution of income. This was not because the rich were getting poorer, but because workers were regularly employed and drawing extra pay for overtime. Accordingly, the share of income earned by the bottom fifth of wage-earners rose during the war by 68 percent, compared to 20 percent for the top fifth. These modest gains in income redistribution were the only such advances in modern American history.

Important social changes accompanied this return to prosperity. One was even greater movement of an already mobile people. Those who moved included 12 million men in uniform, dependents who pulled up roots to follow, and millions more who left their homes to work in war plants. Though it is impossible to know exactly how many people moved, the migrations clearly accelerated the trend toward urbanization, which had slowed during the depression years. The number of people living in urban areas increased from 74 million in 1940 to 89 million in 1950, while the total classified as "rural farm" actually decreased during the decade, from 30 to 23 million. A few states, well-favored in the granting of war contracts, virtually exploded in population. California alone gained 2 million people during the four years of war.

The status of women also changed considerably during the war. In 1940 only 14 million American women (26 percent of the total work force) were employed; by 1945, 19 million (or 36 percent) were. Moreover, 22 percent of these working women in 1945 were married, as opposed to 15 percent five years earlier. Contemporaries thought these trends were temporary, for the numbers of regularly employed women dipped in 1946. Polls also suggested that Americans considered it unnatural for women to enter the labor force: a

This is the last time
This time we will all make certain
That this time is the last time!
> *For this time we are out to finish*
> *The job we started then*
> *Clear it up for all time this time*
> *So we won't have to do it again*

The words to a wartime song by Irving Berlin suggest the no-nonsense thoroughness with which Americans approached the war.

The home front. Above, a massive bond drive in Times Square, New York. Above right, ration stamps restricting consumption. Bottom right, a woman contributing a garment to the war effort.

woman's place, the ladies' magazines added, was at home. But increasing numbers of women disagreed, and by 1951 the number of women in the work force was already higher than at any time in World War II. These trends provided an economic underpinning to movements for women's liberation in the late 1960s.

Wartime developments led to yet other changes in the American family. Thousands of young people who had postponed marriage or family in the depression refused to wait in the 1940s. Thousands more, confronted with the draft and overseas service, did the same. The result was a trend toward younger marriages and a baby boom that began in 1940 and rose irregularly throughout the war. Demographers who assumed the increase in birth rates would end with the war were wrong, for the baby boom lasted until the mid-1950s. Rising birth rates helped stimulate demand in a host of consumers goods industries; they prompted great growth in home-building and in suburban development; and they all but swamped educational institutions until the 1970s. By 1965, when these war and postwar babies had reached their late teens or early 20s, the baby boom culminated in the growth of a "youth culture," which baffled and frightened older generations.

To many observers during the war (and since) these developments were unfortunate. Young people, it seemed, were hurrying irresponsibly into marriage and parenthood. They were pulling up roots to live in ill-constructed housing developments without proper socializing institutions for children. Some women were "abandoning" their children in order to enter the work force, while others—"allotment Annies"—deserted their soldier husbands as soon as their dependence allowances stopped coming. A rapidly increasing divorce rate appeared to be one unhappy result of these patterns of behavior. Juvenile delinquency involving "wolf packs" in housing developments and "zoot suit" gangs in large cities appeared to be another. Some people foresaw a new "Lost Generation."

These Cassandras oversimplified a complex set of developments. The increase in divorce, for instance, was assisted by more tolerant attitudes and by more permissive legislation. The rise in juvenile crime is harder to explain, or even to document, because statistics for the period are not very reliable. But it seems to have stemmed from a variety of causes: increasing racial tensions; laws that banned child labor and required bored young people to stay in schools until the age of sixteen; and the broadening areas for petty crime, especially car theft, available in an urban, technological society.

Above all, the war prompted anxieties about the future. Having survived ten years of depression, Americans entered the 1940s already searching for security. With regular employment, they seemed at last to have found it. But would it endure? Many felt certain that depression would recur, that hard-earned gains would be wiped out, that the status of other groups would rise at the expense of their own. The writer Bernard de Voto observed that this anxiety rarely received "public expression, and little direct expression even in private." But "it exists and it may well be the most truly terrifying phenomenon of the war. It is a fear of the coming of the peace."

One group that clearly displayed this anxiety was organized labor—in part because it had gained so amazingly much. In a strong bargaining position at the start of the war, unions received government support of a "maintenance of membership" clause in contracts. This required members to stay in the union for the duration of the war. Unions then drove ahead to recruit the seven million new workers who found jobs between 1940 and 1945. Accordingly, union membership increased from 9 million in 1940 to almost 15 million in 1945, a growth more rapid than at any time in American history. Management generally acquiesced in this union activity: with great profits to be made and a war to be won, it did not seem wise to goad militant workers into strikes. This relative harmony between labor and management foreshadowed a development that was later to become an exploitative reality: both sides cooperating to raise wages and prices, while nonunion wage earners (who still comprised 65 percent of the nonagricultural work force in 1945) paid the bills.

Despite these gains, unions remained uneasy about the future. John L. Lewis and other leaders led dramatic walkouts for better pay during the war. Work stoppages, though usually short-lived, increased from 2,968 in 1942 to 4,956 in 1944. In 1945, 4,750 stoppages affected 12.12 percent of the labor force and involved 3.4 million workers. And 1946, when wartime frustrations could finally be expressed, witnessed a record 4,985 stoppages involving 4.6 million laborers. Unionists, having begun to taste power and increased income, were insisting upon more in the future.

A similar revolution in expectations affected blacks, who made unprecedented gains during the war. Some of these advances were essentially symbolic—in 1943 the first black joined the American Bar Association; in 1944 the first black was admitted to a presidential press conference. Other changes were vitally important. The number of blacks who secured jobs in the federal government increased from 50,000 in 1939 to 200,000 six years later, and the appeal of jobs in northern and western cities pulled more than a million blacks out of the South. This mass migration, one of the greatest of its kind, persisted in the postwar period.

As in the years between 1914 and 1919, this combination of migration and relative prosperity created mounting militancy among black leaders. The Congress on Racial Equality, an interracial organization devoted to pacifism as well as to civil rights, was founded in 1942. The NAACP, the largest of the interracial organizations, increased its membership during the war from 50,000 to 500,000. Most alarming of all to whites was the black power shown by A. Philip Randolph, the porters' union leader who threatened to call for a mass march on Washington in 1941 unless Roosevelt acted to prevent racial discrimination in employment. After much procrastination (for Roosevelt still hesitated to offend southern Democrats), the President relented far enough to issue an executive order setting up a Fair Employment Practices Commission. Easily his most significant contribution to racial justice, it stemmed entirely from black pressure. The lesson was not lost on later leaders of the black cause.

These advances merely reminded blacks how far America had to go. The poorly financed, understaffed FEPC was able to resolve only one-third of the 8000 complaints it had time to hear. Of its forty-five compliance orders, thirty-five were ignored. Despite a Supreme Court ruling against white primaries,

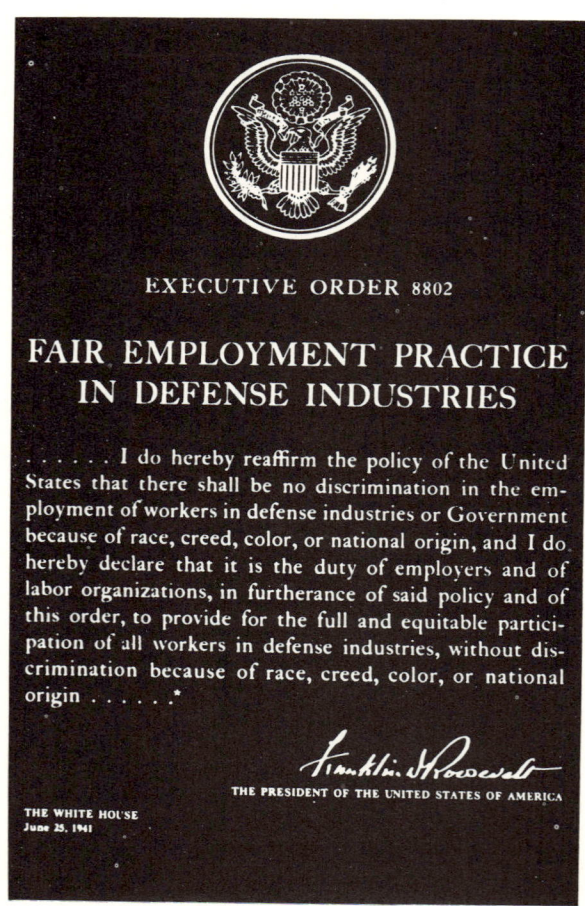

EXECUTIVE ORDER 8802

FAIR EMPLOYMENT PRACTICE IN DEFENSE INDUSTRIES

. . . . . . I do hereby reaffirm the policy of the United States that there shall be no discrimination in the employment of workers in defense industries or Government because of race, creed, color, or national origin, and I do hereby declare that it is the duty of employers and of labor organizations, in furtherance of said policy and of this order, to provide for the full and equitable participation of all workers in defense industries, without discrimination because of race, creed, color, or national origin . . . . . .*

Franklin D Roosevelt
THE PRESIDENT OF THE UNITED STATES OF AMERICA

THE WHITE HOUSE
June 25, 1941

> While the March on Washington Movement may find it advisable to form a citizens committee of friendly white citizens to give moral support . . . it does not imply that these white citizens . . . should be taken into the March on Washington Movement as members. The essential value of an all-Negro movement such as the March on Washington is that it helps to create faith by Negroes in Negroes. It develops a sense of self-reliance with Negroes depending on Negroes in vital matters. It helps to break down the slave psychology and inferiority-complex in Negroes which comes and is nourished with Negroes relying on white people for direction and support. This inevitably happens in mixed organizations that are supposed to be in the interest of the Negro.
>
> A. Philip Randolph promotes black power, 1942.

most blacks in the South continued to be disfranchised through poll taxes, literacy tests, and other ruses. Jim Crow laws segregating southern blacks in trains, buses, hotels, schools—even bathrooms and drinking fountains—were daily reminders of injustice. The armed forces, which were under federal control, flagrantly discriminated against blacks. The marines and army air corps simply excluded them, the navy gave them menial tasks, and the army segregated them under white officers. "Leadership," Secretary of War Stimson explained, "is not imbedded in the negro race yet, and to try to make commissioned officers to lead men into battle—colored men—is only to work a disaster to both." It was not until 1944 that the navy integrated the crews of a few of its ships or that the army sent blacks into combat.

Though most blacks supported the war, these humiliations inevitably created conflicts. In 1943 blacks in Harlem rioted against discrimination. A race riot in Detroit the same year killed 34 and injured more then 700. The antiwhite Black Muslims began to make modest gains among the dispossessed. CORE leaders experimented with sit-ins (only in the North) and other forms of direct action. And countless blacks expressed themselves bitterly against a society that fought fascism abroad while ignoring injustice at home. One told Gunner Myrdal, the Swedish social scientist investigating race relations, "just carve on my tombstone, here lies a black man killed fighting a yellow man for the protection of a white man." A "Draftee's Prayer" in a black newspaper added,

> Dear Lord, today
> I go to war:
> To fight, to die,
> Tell me what for?
> Dear Lord, I'll fight,
> I do not fear
> Germans or Japs;
> My fears are here.
> America!

Such attitudes among organized workers and blacks captured one essential aspect of life on the home front. So long as the enemy fought on the field, Americans would try to suppress their frustrations and concentrate on winning the war: The common fear of fascism promoted more unity than in World War I. But it was an increasingly impatient, factious unity. Blacks and workers, like farmers, businessmen, veterans, even specialized groups like educators, had caught the scent of prosperity, and they wanted desperately to taste it once the war was over. More organized than ever, they sought to advance their own interests with the same grim single-mindedness that they showed in battle. This militancy amid plenty, this revolution of expectations, this scramble not only for security but for slices of an ever larger pie—all these were among the major social developments of the ''Great Leap'' of World War II.

Suggestions for reading

The key books covering American politics and diplomacy in World War II are James M. Burns, *Roosevelt: Soldier of Freedom** (1970); and A. Russell Buchanan, *The United States and World War II*, 2 vol.* (1964). See also W. H. McNeill, *America, Britain, and Russia* (1953); Gaddis Smith, *American Diplomacy During the Second World War, 1941–1945** (1965); John Snell, *Illusion and Necessity: The Diplomacy of World War II** (1963); Herbert Feis, *Churchill, Roosevelt, Stalin** (1957); and the revisionist account by Stephen Ambrose, *Rise to Globalism: American Foreign Policy Since 1938** (1971). Gabriel Kolko, *The Politics of War: The World and U. S. Foreign Policy, 1943–1945* (1969) stresses economic motives.

Other relevant studies are Raymond O'Connor, *Diplomacy for Victory: FDR and Unconditional Surrender** (1971); Trumbull Higgins, *Winston Churchill and the Second Front, 1940–1943* (1957), and *Soft Underbelly: The Anglo-American Controversy over the Italian Campaign, 1939–1945* (1968); Diane Shaver Clemens, *Yalta* (1970); and Robert Divine, *Second Chance: The Triumph of Internationalism During World War II* (1967). Important books on military policy are Kent Roberts Greenfield, *American Strategy in World War II: A Reconsideration** (1967); and Louis Morton, *Strategy and Command* (1962). For science policy consult James P. Baxter, *Scientists Against Time** (1946); Richard G. Hewlett and Oscar E. Anderson, *The New World* (1962), and *The Atomic Shield* (1969), on atomic development; and the highly readable narrative by Robert Jungk, *Brighter Than a Thousand Suns: A Personal History of the Atomic Scientists** (1958).

Books dealing with Asia are John Toland, *The Rising Sun** (1970); Robert Butow, *Japan's Decision to Surrender* (1954); Tang Tsou, *America's Failure in China, 1941–1950** (1963); and Barbara Tuchman, *Stilwell and The American Experience in China, 1911–1945** (1971). Important books on wartime sources of the Cold War include John Gaddis, *The United States and the Origins of the Cold War, 1941–1946** (1972); and George C. Herring, Jr., *Aid to Russia, 1941–1946* (1973).

The starting point for life in the United States during the war is Richard Polenberg, *War and Society: The United States, 1941–1945** (1972). See also John M. Blum, *V Was for Victory* (1976). Other surveys are Richard Lingeman, *Don't You Know There's a War On?* (1970); Geoffrey Perrett, *Days of Sadness, Days of Triumph* (1973);

and William Ogburn, ed., *American Society in Wartime* (1943). For economic policy consult Eliot Janeway, *Struggle for Survival* (1951); John M. Blum, *From the Morgenthau Diaries: Years of War, 1941–1945* (1967); and Bruce Catton, *War Lords of Washington* (1948). See also David Ross, *Preparing for Ulysses* (1969), which deals with manpower and military policies; Walter Wilcox, *The Farmer in the Second World War* (1947); and Joel Seidman, *American Labor from Defense to Reconversion* (1953). Useful biographies of labor leaders include Saul Alinsky, *John L. Lewis* (1949); and Matthew Josephson, *Sidney Hillman* (1952). William Chafe's book on American women, cited in the bibliography for chapter 6, is indispensable.

The experiences of blacks during the war is detailed in Richard Dalfiume, *Desegregation of the Armed Forces, 1939–1953* (1969); August Meier and Elliott Rudwick, *CORE . . . 1942–1968* (1973); Robert Shogan and Thomas Craig, *The Detroit Race Riot* (1964); and Gunnar Myrdal, *An American Dilemma** (1944, rev. ed. 1962), a classic sociological account. The fate of Japanese-Americans is well told in Jacobus ten Broek, et al., *Prejudice, War, and the Constitution* (1945); and in Roger Daniels, *Concentration Camps** (1971). Lawrence S. Wittner, *Rebels Against War: The American Peace Movement, 1941–1960* (1969) covers its subject sympathetically. For constitutional developments see Edward S. Corwin, *Total War and the Constitution** (1947); Francis Biddle, *In Brief Authority* (1962), by Roosevelt's wartime attorney general; and J. Woodford Howard, *Mr. Justice Murphy* (1968).

11

Acrimony, home and abroad

1945 - 1952

When Roosevelt died in April 1945, liberals were distraught. TVA director David Lilienthal shuddered to think of "that Throttlebottom Truman. The country and the world doesn't deserve to be left this way." Worrying about Truman's rise in the corrupt politics of Kansas City, the journalist Max Lerner asked, "can a man who has been associated with the Pendergast machine be able to keep the panting politicians and bosses out of the gravy?"

Millions of Americans appeared to share this anxiety. After all, Roosevelt had been president for as long as many people could remember. Yet now, with the Germans still fighting, with Japan to be invaded, and with postwar problems yet to be tackled, the country was saddled with an uninspiring border state senator whom the party had plucked from relative obscurity. Even Truman himself seemed frightened about the responsibilities ahead. "Boys," he told reporters, "if you ever pray, pray for me now. I don't know whether you fellows ever had a load of hay fall on you, but when they told me yesterday what had happened, I felt like the moon, the stars, and all the planets had fallen on me."

Actually, people worried too much, for past events—assassinations, divisive wars, corruption in high office—had demonstrated, as they would again, that the American political system was stable enough to withstand sudden shocks to the presidency. While Truman groped to master his office, delegates in San Francisco completed the task of devising a United Nations charter, which the Senate adopted by a vote of eighty-nine to two in July. In Europe, Allied forces mopped up the Germans, who surrendered on May 8. And in Asia, Americans pressed forward into Iwo Jima and Okinawa. The country's awesome military-industrial machine surged ahead, largely unaffected by personalities in the White House.

Truman also showed himself capable of acting firmly when necessary. His most far-reaching decision in these early months was to authorize the dropping of atomic bombs on Hiroshima (August 6) and Nagasaki (August 9). Later, critics argued persuasively that in reaching this decision he did not ask advice on *whether* the bomb should be used but *how,* and that he listened only to scientists and government officials who could have been expected to favor its use in war. In the process he ignored the pleas of scientists who urged him to warn the Japanese or to demonstrate the bomb in an uninhabited area. Instead, Truman merely told the Japanese on July 26 to surrender unconditionally or face "prompt and utter destruction." Since this was what they had already been receiving from fire raids, it was not surprising that they kept on with the war.

The use of the bombs may have been unnecessary. By July 1945 the Japanese knew they were doomed, and their moderates were exploring avenues to peace. If Truman had told them that they could retain their emperor, they might have agreed to surrender, particularly after Russia joined the war against them on August 8. At least, he could have awaited the impact of the Russian declaration, and of further fire bombings, which many later observers felt would have won the war without an American invasion. He definitely should have paused after incinerating close to 100,000 people in Hiroshima, instead of authorizing the air force to go ahead on its own and kill 40,000 to 75,000 more at Nagasaki. Truman's actions showed that he was more decisive—more impetuous, even—than reflective.

Truman never wavered in defending his decision. Warning the Japanese or demonstrating the bomb seemed risky. The Japanese, he reasoned, would ignore the warning and concentrate their remaining defenses against air

Victims of the atomic blast at Hiroshima await aid a few hours after the explosion.

Seven weeks later I returned to Alamogordo after I had watched the same model of the A-bomb devastate the city of Nagasaki. On that return visit I saw for the first time what the bomb had done to the desert. Over a radius of four hundred yards the ground had been depressed to a depth ranging from ten feet at the periphery to twenty-five feet in the center. All life within a mile, vegetable as well as animal, had been destroyed. There was not a rattle-snake left in the region, nor a blade of desert grass. The sand in the depression had been fused into a glasslike substance the color of jade, all of it radioactive. Eight hundred yards away a steel rigging tower weighing thirty-two tons had been turned into a twisted mass of wreckage. The one-hundred-foot-high steel tower at the top of which the bomb was exploded was completely vaporized. A herd of antelope that had been grazing several miles away had vanished. It was believed they had started on a mad dash for the wilds of Mexico. A number of cows at a similar distance developed grey spots from deposits of radioactive dust. These radioactive cows and their progeny became the nearest equivalent to "sacred cows" in the United States, being carefully studied for the effects of radiation.

William Laurence, a leading American reporter, recalls the power of the first atomic bomb, detonated in Alamogordo, New Mexico, in July 1945.

attacks. Japan might even succeed in shooting down the plane carrying such a bomb. Moreover, there was the chance that a bomb dropped in a demonstration might not work. How foolish the United States (and Truman) would look if that happened, especially as there were only two bombs to go in early August! For Truman, therefore, the decision involved little soul-searching. The United States had spent six years and billions of dollars developing the weapon, and once it had been successfully tested, he thought, it was silly not to use it.

A few later critics contended that Truman authorized use of the bombs to demonstrate America's power to the Soviet Union and to end the war before the Russians could join it. Such concerns did influence men like James Byrnes, who became secretary of state in 1945. They also moved General Leslie Groves, head of bomb development, who recalled, "Russia was our enemy . . . and the project was conducted on that basis." But if America had wanted to keep Russia from entering the war, the most direct way would have been to negotiate in earnest for Japan's conditional surrender in June and July. Moreover, Truman himself was focusing single-mindedly on Japan, not on the Soviet Union. Like Roosevelt, he was more preoccupied with short-run military necessity than with postwar diplomacy. At the time, the Japanese seemed prepared to fight to their last man, and in Okinawa they lost 110,000 men in eighty-three days, while killing 12,500 Americans, or 150 per day.

American soldiers celebrate V-J Day, the day Japan surrendered, in 1945.

(Later, in Vietnam, it was a bad *week* when 200 Americans died.) It was primarily to stop such losses as these, and to prevent the still more unthinkable bloodletting anticipated in an invasion of the home islands, that Truman did what he did.

At the time, Americans had no chance to debate the alternatives and no idea of Truman's options. But they did know that the bombs had worked and that Japan had finally surrendered. So they reacted not with horror at what had been done but with profound relief that the war was over. In this way Truman's popularity was further enhanced, his judgment seemingly vindicated. For the time being, there appeared little question of Truman's capacity to rule.

Domestic controversies

1945–1946

With characteristic briskness, Truman wasted little time after Japan's surrender before turning to problems at home, and on September 6, four days after V-J Day, he asked Congress to enact a "second Bill of Rights" for the American people. Among these rights, Truman declared, were "useful and remunerative" jobs for all, government assistance to farmers, protection for small businessmen against monopoly, decent housing for every family, "adequate medical care," "protection from the economic fears of old age, sickness, accident, and unemployment," and the "right to a good education." These rights, he said, echoing Roosevelt, "spell security."

Truman's requests, to be known as the Fair Deal, aimed at consolidating the partial welfare state built during the Roosevelt years. Indeed, in calling for such measures as national health insurance he went beyond the New Deal. Inevitably his requests provoked controversy. To secure them from a conservative Congress the new president would need all the skill he could muster.

As the struggle developed, it was clear that Truman possessed some of the qualities necessary to win. One of these was his awareness that the president must lead. As he liked to say, "the buck stops here." Another was his initially friendly relations with congressmen of both parties. A senator for ten years, he had pleased New Dealers by supporting most of Roosevelt's policies, while his impartial chairmanship of a wartime committee investigating defense contracting had made him acceptable to moderates and conservatives.

Truman made gestures to improve congressional-executive relations, which had deteriorated badly under Roosevelt. To placate the GOP he named Senator Theodore Burton, an Ohio Republican, to the first vacancy in the Supreme Court. He resurrected Herbert Hoover by having him head a commission studying governmental reorganization. His appointment of Byrnes, a former congressman and senator from South Carolina, as secretary of state and of Fred Vinson, a popular Democratic congressman from Kentucky, as secretary of the treasury (and in 1946 as chief justice) were especially well received on the Hill. More than FDR, Truman appeared to appreciate congressional advice and counsel.

But Truman also left himself open to criticism. In making lesser appointments he showed a tendency to favor old friends from his days in the national guard (he had been a captain in World War I) and in Missouri politics, where he had moved forward through the malodorous Pendergast machine of Kansas City. Most of these appointees, like his military aide Harry Vaughn, enjoyed no real power. But to observers used to the intellectuals and brain trusters who had flourished under Roosevelt they seemed an undistinguished lot. "The composite impression," the journalist I. F. Stone wrote, "was of big-bellied, good-natured guys who knew a lot of dirty jokes, spent as little time in their offices as possible, saw Washington as a chance to make 'useful' contacts, and were anxious to get what they could for themselves out of the experience. . . . The Truman era was the era of the moocher. The place was full of Wimpys who could be had for a hamburger."

The liberal admirers of FDR were especially offended by some of Truman's conservative appointees to important positions. These included Charles Snyder, a Missouri banker who held several major jobs before becoming secretary of the treasury in 1946, and Tom Clark, a conservative Texan who became attorney general and then a Supreme Court justice. By the end of 1946 almost all the important New Dealers whom Truman had inherited—Frances Perkins, Harold Ickes, Henry Wallace, Attorney General Francis Biddle— had resigned or been fired.

These changes were not wholly surprising. The new president, after all, was entitled to his own team of advisers. But Truman alienated many people, who wondered—with good reason—if he was really a sincere New Dealer. Roosevelt's intimates, he told a friend, were "crackpots and the lunatic fringe." He added, "I don't want any experiments; the American people have been through a lot of experiments, and they want a rest." Harry Dexter White, assistant secretary of the treasury under FDR and Truman, explained that when Roosevelt was alive, "we'd go over to the White House for a conference on some particular policy, lose the argument, and yet walk out of the door somehow thrilled and inspired to go on and do the job the way the Big Boss had ordered." Now, he added, "you go in to see Mr. Truman. He's very nice to you. He lets you do what you want to, and yet you leave feeling somehow dispirited and flat."

In addition to discouraging imagination, Truman failed to maintain order within his administration during his first two years in office. Perhaps no one could have done so very well, for the transition from war to peace inevitably caused confusion. But Truman, still feeling his way, too often failed to let conflicting bureaucrats know where he stood. Internal battles, which might have been cleared up quickly, were allowed to fester. Wilson Wyatt, his expeditor for housing, fought a host of rival agencies in his efforts to get much-needed building materials and finally resigned in disgust at the end of 1946, never having received the backing he had been led to expect from the White House. Chester Bowles, who was supposedly in charge of price control, faced the similarly discouraging task of getting presidential support against more conservative competitors in government. He too failed and finally resigned. Harold Smith, Truman's budget director, expressed the dismay of many government officials. "I don't know what goes on around here," he confided to his diary in February 1946, "and that is a rather dangerous situation for all of us to be in. . . . The top people in government are solving problems in a vacuum, and the vacuum is chiefly in their heads."

Moreover, Truman's approach to Congress lacked finesse. Instead of working purposefully for one or two goals at a time, he outlined grandiose programs and left Congress to its devices. "What the country needed in every field," he said, "was up to me to say . . . and if Congress wouldn't respond, well, I'd done all I could in a straight-forward way." To conservatives like House Minority Leader Joseph Martin, however, Truman was "out New Dealing the New Deal." Offended by his demands, they sat back and picked off his programs one by one.

Liberals became even more disenchanted. Truman, they said, should devote less rhetoric to demanding the impossible and more time to working hard behind the scenes. One advocate of civil rights complained that Truman's strategy was "to start with a bold measure and then temporize to pick up the right-wing forces. Simply stated, backtrack after the bang." TRB, the progressive columnist for the *New Republic,* later saw a disturbing pattern: "Truman would ask Congress for about 120 percent more than he expected. Congress, with a great show of indignation, would slash it to 75 percent. Truman would smile his little-man smile and bounce back with something else. It's a funny way to run a country."

Piecing these criticisms of Truman together made a most unflattering portrait. The new president, it appeared, was a poor judge of people, an anti-intellectual, a sloppy administrator, a rhetorical liberal, a heavy-handed manager of Congress. Possibly, he felt unprepared and insecure in the White House and overcompensated by sounding tough and decisive. Perhaps so. In any event, he possessed little of the deftness and none of the charisma that had characterized Roosevelt at his best.

In retrospect it is equally clear that Truman (like most of his contemporaries among leading politicians) lacked vision. Though he carried liberalism slightly beyond the bread and butter issues of the Roosevelt era—as in his support of civil rights—he was blind to the prevalence of poverty and the continuing maldistribution of income. Instead, he concentrated on meeting the presumed threat from the Soviets. To a degree, of course, any president in the late 1940s would have had to do the same. With Truman, however, the focus on foreign affairs meant that many domestic problems received low priority.

But most of the progressives who blamed Truman for the nation's troubles had to concede that he faced formidable obstacles. By 1945 the Democratic party was almost as sharply divided between its northern-urban and southern-

America's mood:
the public's view
of the most important problem
facing the country,
according to Gallup Poll results,
1949–1952

1949	High cost of living
1950	War and the threat of war
1951	War and foreign policy
1952	Korean War

SOURCE: Marian Irish and Elke Frank,
U. S. Foreign Policy (New York, 1975), p. 107

western-rural wings as it had been in the 1920s. Though outnumbered, the rural wing, which opposed the urban liberalism of the New Deal, coalesced successfully with Republicans to dominate both houses of Congress. For example, Joseph Martin and Charles Halleck, his right-hand man from Indiana, worked closely with southern conservatives like Howard Smith of Virginia, a rural reactionary who was a power on the House Rules Committee. The Senate was dominated by southern conservative Democrats, among them Harry Byrd of Virginia and Richard Russell of Georgia, and by Republican leaders like Robert Taft of Ohio.

A still greater barrier to domestic reform was the national mood. Having sacrificed during four years of war (and ten years of depression), Americans demanded the good life. They chafed at shortages, and they yearned for material goods. In doing so they helped build up enormous demand for a host of products that had barely existed, if at all, in 1940: television, heat-and-serve dinners, automatic transmissions, tubeless tires, airconditioning, hi-fis, filter cigarettes, dishwashers, freezers, detergents, tape recorders, and fiberglass. Americans began to fly in four-engine planes, to drive on superhighways, to live in ranch-style homes, to shop in supermarkets. With such a shiny, packaged world spreading out before their eyes it was easy, as it had been in the 1920s, for Americans to turn to their own private concerns.

This mood, however, was different from the "normalcy" of the 1920s, when people praised the virtues of rugged individualism. By 1945 the modest welfare state of FDR had come to stay, and special interest groups fought single-mindedly to broaden their share of it. Veterans demanded benefits, farmers higher prices, unions better wages and working conditions, consumers more goods and lower prices. Where Harding and Coolidge could win acclaim by leaving people alone, Truman (and his successors) had to act to sustain these groups in a standard of living that no society in world history had ever enjoyed before. He was confronted with the full force of the revolution in expectations.

Like Roosevelt, Truman had to rely on an essentially nonideological, indeed almost apathetic, electorate. As studies of voters were beginning to show, most Americans did not act as "liberals" or as "conservatives." Rather, they voted as their parents or their peers did. Millions (some 40 percent of the eligible electorate) failed to vote at all even in presidential elections. It was therefore difficult for Truman (and for reformers in the next fifteen years) to mobilize a mass following or a Democratic party that would consciously demand enactment of a "liberal" program. Instead, he had to work with constituency-oriented congressmen and senators, few of whom felt much pressure from home for progressive legislation.

THE ISSUES

These obstacles, with Truman's own limitations, combined to defeat all of the Fair Deal goals in 1945–46. Congress brought an end to the wartime Fair Employment Practices Commission and filibustered to death efforts to create a new one. It failed to pass measures against poll taxes. It ignored or defeated bills for public housing and federal aid to education. It passed the antilabor Case bill, which was vetoed by Truman. Though it approved the Employment Act of 1946 (which established a Council of Economic Advisers and proclaimed the government's responsibility to step in against economic declines), it rejected amendments that would have committed the government to using Keynesian fiscal policies.

The most pressing issues of Truman's first two years barely touched on his Fair Deal proposals. Rather, they concerned the economic consequences of the war. In trying to deal with them Truman received little but blows for his pains.

The pressures for a return to civilian life were overwhelming by mid-1945. Business interests demanded lower taxes, immediate demobilization, and the end of lend-lease and other measures assisting other foreign competitors in international markets. Soldiers insisted on being allowed to come home, and office-holders were swamped with postcards from Asia labeled, "No boats, no votes." Under such pressure the politicians of both parties simply collapsed. In November 1945 Congress approved a $6 billion tax cut, even though it would obviously contribute to inflation. The administration quickly disposed of most of its war plants, usually by turning them over to private interests on very generous terms. It let business move ahead quickly into civilian production. Given no choice by Congress, it cut lend-lease shipments. And—feeling secure with an atomic monopoly—it brought the boys home. The armed forces, 12 million strong in 1945, had only 3 million by mid-1946 and but 1.6 million by mid-1947.

This rapid demobilization was popular enough at first. But by the end of 1945 its costs were already becoming apparent The return of so many soldiers to the domestic scene created great competition for jobs and enormous demand for housing. One veteran complained, "six months ago I was piloting a B-29 against the Japs. Now I am trying to build a home in my home town. The first fight was easier. . . .'' Though the economy opened up quickly enough to provide most veterans with jobs, the housing market, depressed since 1928, fell far short of demands, and Americans crowded into urban slums or shacks scattered in the countryside.

Truman tried to alleviate the housing shortage. Through existing agencies such as the Federal Housing Agency he (and his successors) helped millions of Americans get government-insured mortgages at moderate rates of interest. He also called for more generous appropriations for public housing, but even the backing of Robert Taft failed to stop a predominantly rural coalition from blocking the proposal until 1949. Meanwhile, Truman made matters worse by authorizing John Snyder, his director of reconversion, to remove federal controls on building materials. This action, one of many that attempted to placate private interests, made it impossible for Wyatt and other experts to offer central direction to housing policy. It also meant that materials flowed into the areas that would bring builders immediate profit. These areas, as often in the construction business, were commercial, not residential or industrial.

The housing crisis, though serious, seemed almost trivial compared to the problem of inflation. To a large degree this too was inevitable after the war, because demand for consumer goods had been pent up since 1941, during which time Americans had saved unprecedented sums. The baby boom and the sudden return of so many soldiers made this demand still more formidable. Following the end of the war in September 1945, the consumer price index jumped almost 25 percent in the next year and a half. This was a rate of increase greater than at any time since World War I. It seemed destined to wipe out all the hard-earned gains of war.

Truman, of course, could hardly bring prices down. That would happen on a broad front only when supply caught up with demand—in 1948. Moreover, he was again stymied by the conservative coalition in Congress, which passed a law extending price controls in only very weak form after June 30, 1946. Truman vetoed the measure, and the country was without controls at all. Congress then passed another weak bill, but the damage had already been done, and prices rose almost uncontrollably during the summer. By November 1946 Truman removed the few controls that remained.

Truman's handling of inflation made this difficult situation worse. Instead of demanding strong controls from the start, he did little to assist Bowles's congressional supporters. Then, belatedly, he stepped in with a ringing veto of the price control bill. This procedure revealed him to be better at rhetorical outbursts than at the necessary process of day-to-day congressional bargaining. It angered not only conservatives but some of his own party leaders, who had advised him to accept the bill as the best to be had under the circumstances. "The government's stability policy," Bowles complained, "is not what you have stated it to be, but is instead one of improvising on a day-to-day, case-by-case method, as one crisis leads to another—in short . . . there is really no policy at all."

In dealing with labor–management problems Truman again helped exacerbate an already acrimonious situation in which unions tried to make up for wartime restraint by demanding sizeable wage increases. Management refused, and millions of American workers went out on strike in late 1945 and early 1946. Both sides then turned to Truman, who had the power (stemming from the war) to authorize price increases. After a show of firmness, Truman gave way under business pressure by permitting price hikes of approximately 19 percent. Management then granted workers pay increases of 18 to 19 percent. Truman's actions settled some of the strikes, but only by encouraging the first of many postwar rounds of inflationary wage-price agreements between powerful interest groups. Nonunion workers and their families, a majority of Americans, paid the bill in higher prices for basic consumer goods.

John L. Lewis then led the soft coal miners out on strike April 1, 1946. American industry, very dependent on coal, seemed threatened by what promised to be a long and divisive confrontation. At the same time railway engineers and trainmen also served notice of their intention to strike. Furious, Truman went before a joint session of Congress to demand emergency powers. As he was reading his message, he was handed a note advising him that the railwaymen had come to terms. But he went on with his address, which

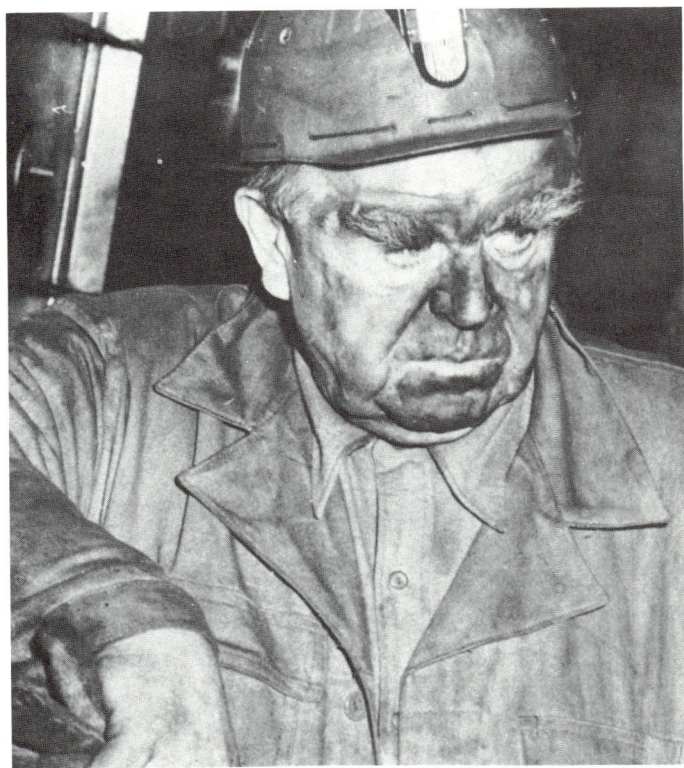

John L. Lewis, the defiant,
outspoken leader
of the
United Mine Workers,
inspecting
mine conditions.

called on Congress to give him power to order federal troops into strike-bound industries, and even to draft strikers into the armed services.

It was a sign of the hysteria of the times that the House quickly approved this violation of labor's civil liberties. The Senate, however, ultimately listened to calmer men like Taft, the supposed enemy of organized labor, and rejected Truman's appeal. The episode showed how hard it was for Truman (and later presidents) to impose their will on organized labor. It revealed that he could be hot-tempered to the extent of endangering the liberties of working people. Few of his actions were more ill-considered or counterproductive.

By the fall of 1946 these struggles over reconversion, controls, and labor policy had badly damaged Truman's standing with the voters. Gleeful opponents circulated cruel jokes about the President's blundering. One conjectured how Roosevelt would have handled matters by asking, "I wonder what Truman would do if he were alive." Republicans proclaimed that "to err is Truman" and repeated, "Had Enough?" In November, with meat shortages provoking fury among consumers, they succeeded in winning control over Congress for the first time since 1930. With liberals in disarray and with the conservative coalition riding high, Truman seemed doomed to electoral extinction in 1948.

THE 80TH CONGRESS

During the 1948 campaign Truman sounded one theme almost endlessly: the Eightieth Congress of 1947–48 had been "good-for-nothing." Like most politicians at election time, he distorted the past, for the Congress had actually compiled a significant list of foreign policy legislation, including military assistance to Greece and Turkey, the Marshall Plan of foreign aid to Europe, and the National Security Act, which attempted to reduce interservice rivalries by setting up the Joint Chiefs of Staff and the Defense Department. The law also established the National Security Council and the Central Intelligence Agency. These agencies vastly increased the role the military and intelligence services would play in subsequent decision-making.

In giving the impression that the Eightieth Congress was totally obstructive, Truman also distorted the truth. What he should have said was that the majority of congressmen opposed labor union power, deficit spending, high taxes, and wage and price controls—that is, progressive fiscal policy and state regulation of private enterprise. Otherwise, they were often conciliatory. In the 1940s and 1950s most of them supported, though often belatedly, increases in social security and the minimum wage. In battling for tax cuts many of them were in effect conservative Keynesians who agreed that federal policies could and should promote consumer spending. Taft, the conservative leader, spearheaded the battle for aid to education and public housing, both of which passed the Republican Senate in 1948, only to fail in the House. Not just a brave and lonely Harry S. Truman but also conservatives and moderates helped sustain the partial welfare state of the New Deal in the 1940s: it offered too much to too many groups to be abolished.

Truman also conveniently overlooked his own equivocations in 1947–48. After doing little for civil rights in the first two years of his presidency, he used the election campaign to outline (but not work hard for) a broad program which he knew Congress would never pass. He demanded national health insurance, which he had said little about during Democratic control of Congress in 1946. To appear forceful concerning inflation he called for presidential power to control prices—authority he did not really want and knew he could not get. Overreacting to fears about communist subversion, he established loyalty boards, which had the power to ignore civil liberties of governmental employees. It was not surprising that many people thought that Truman cared less about broadening human rights than about getting himself reelected in 1948.

Still, Truman was correct in claiming that the Eightieth Congress was both conservative and partisan. Among its new members—the "infamous class of '46"—were such Red-hunters as Richard Nixon of California and William Jenner of Indiana, opportunists like Joseph McCarthy of Wisconsin (who replaced Robert La Follette, Jr.), and conservatives like John Bricker of Ohio and William Knowland of California. Led by Taft, one of the hardest-working, best-prepared Senate leaders of the postwar era, they were formidable foes to the administration.

In this frame of mind they joined with conservative Democrats to defeat the entire Fair Deal program. The Eightieth Congress rejected public housing, aid to education, and Truman's appeal for universal military training. It refused to relax immigration quotas or to aid displaced persons. Though it did not challenge well-established interest groups such as farmers or veterans or dismantle the social welfare programs of the New Deal, it complained loudly (and most unfairly) about Truman's "lavish" spending. To insure there would be no more four-term presidents, as Roosevelt had been, it set in motion a constitutional amendment limiting presidents to two terms that was later ratified in 1951.

Congress reserved its heaviest ammunition for tax and labor policies. Twice in 1947 it passed tax cuts, only to watch Truman veto them with the claim that they favored the wealthy and imperiled the budget. In the election year of 1948, however, enough of Truman's supporters deserted him to override a third presidential veto. In the area of labor law Congress approved, again over Truman's veto, the Taft-Hartley Act of 1947. The measure enumerated unfair labor practices, outlawed the closed shop, required union officers to sign noncommunist oaths to secure access to the NLRB, and authorized the president to impose eighty-day "cooling off" periods before workers could start strikes threatening national health or safety. Furious, the unions called the act a "slave-labor law."

Neither the tax cut nor the Taft-Hartley law was as retrogressive as Truman and his supporters claimed. The tax cut, which administration economists had thought would be inflationary, helped sustain purchasing power during a recession in 1949, while the labor law proved a workable, if clumsy, measure that Truman himself employed in attempts to head off strikes in key industries. For all their complaints, unions were able to live with Taft-Hartley for decades thereafter. The limited impact of both statutes suggests that the conservatives in Congress were unable (and in part unwilling) to alter the basic realities of income distribution or labor-management relations. Federal legislation, it appeared, made less difference than the politicians claimed.

But the struggles of the Eightieth Congress, and especially over Taft-Hartley, did make a difference in American politics. In 1945–46 Truman had often seemed aimless and complacent. In battling against Taft-Hartley and the tax bills, his combative, partisan spirit arose. Progressives, though remaining suspicious of his motives, cheered him on. "Let's come right out and say it," one exulted. "We thought Truman's labor veto message thrilling." If it did nothing else, the strife of the Eightieth Congress enabled Truman to strike a pose—for that in part is what it was—for the "people" against the "interests." This fighting image, which gained him the support of many New Dealers, was valuable in an election year.

Cold war, 1946–1948

The closing months of 1945 brought no respite from the tension that had been gathering between the United States and the Soviet Union. For the next three years, indeed for the next two decades, this Cold War, as it became known by 1947, was the paramount issue not only of international relations but of domestic politics.

Of the many forces that helped to foment tensions, the most important was Stalin's determination to safeguard Russian interests. By the end of 1945 it was clear that he had no intention of relinquishing his hold on eastern Europe. At the same time he systematically stripped East German industrial potential, and shipped thousands of German citizens—Nazis, Stalin claimed—to forced labor camps in Russia and its "satellites." He pressured Turkey for control of the straits leading from the Black Sea to the Mediterranean, and Iran for oil rights in Azerbaijan. In February 1946 he alarmed American observers by proclaiming that communism and capitalism were incompatible. Eric Sevareid, a progressive journalist, concluded that the speech made it "clear as daylight that the comintern, formalized or not, [was] back in effective operation. If you can brush aside Stalin's speech . . . you are a braver man than I."

These events led western leaders to stiffen their response to Stalin. In a timely cable sent two weeks after Stalin's speech, George Kennan, a top American diplomat in Moscow, argued that Stalin was "only the last of that long succession of cruel and wasteful Russian rulers who have relentlessly forced their country on to ever new heights of military power. . . ." Churchill,

Churchill, Truman
and Stalin
at Potsdam, Germany,
July 1945.

out of power but widely admired in America, spoke two weeks later in
Missouri of an "iron curtain" descending around eastern Europe. The Soviets, he declared, sought the "indefinite expansion of their power and doctrines." An approving Truman sat on the platform as Churchill delivered this
speech. The President also acted firmly. By dispatching an American battleship to the eastern Mediterranean, he warned against further Russian pressure
on Turkey, and by sending stiff notes protesting against Soviet behavior in
Iran, he helped stave off Russian encroachment. The American people
obviously supported this get-tough policy: 71 percent said they disapproved of
Russia's international conduct, and 60 percent thought America "too soft" in
dealing with Moscow.

American leaders reflected this hardening of opinion in 1946. In September
Secretary of State Byrnes proclaimed that the United States would henceforth
forget about trying to secure Russian cooperation in the occupation of Germany. America would unilaterally strengthen its own zone. Russia, with good
reason to fear a revitalized Germany, was understandably alarmed. Within a
year and a half of the end of the European war, Germany, once the scourge of
the world, was becoming the front line of western defense, while Russia, one
of the Big Three, became the enemy.

In the same month Truman blundered into an impasse that resulted in the
firing of Secretary of Commerce Henry Wallace. While Byrnes was negotiating with the Soviets in Paris, Wallace gave a speech that said the Russians

Legend:
- Areas annexed by USSR
- Areas controlled by Poland
- Allies of U. S., 1955
- Allies of USSR, 1955
- Independent communist states, 1955

Division of Europe, 1945–1955

were trying to "socialize their sphere of interest just as we try to democratize our sphere of interest. . . . Only mutual trust would allow the United States and Russia to live together peacefully, and such trust could not be created by an unfriendly attitude and policy." Truman had looked at the speech beforehand, but too perfunctorily to realize how sharply it contradicted his own position. Senator Arthur Vandenberg, with Byrnes in Paris, cabled "we Republicans can cooperate with only one secretary of state at a time." Having maneuvered himself clumsily into a corner, Truman thereupon fired Wallace. In so doing he cut an important tie with left-wing American opinion on foreign policy.

Truman proved especially unbudging on the crucial question of atomic energy. Moderates such as former Secretary of War Stimson had been arguing that Russia would soon be able to develop the bomb on its own and that America ought to earn Soviet good will by sharing scientific secrets. Having done so, the United States and the Soviet Union could develop plans for international supervision and inspection. "The chief lesson I have learned in a long life," Stimson said, "is the only way you can make a man trustworthy is to trust him; and the surest way you can make a man untrustworthy is to distrust him and to show your distrust."

Even during the war, however, America had withheld atomic secrets not only from Russia but from England—in part to secure industrial advantages in the postwar world. Truman, who reflected this attitude, ignored Stimson and listened instead to anticommunist advisers like financier Bernard Baruch and future Secretary of State Dean Acheson. They called for international inspection and for the gradual sharing of scientific information (which could not be kept secret anyway). But they opposed letting the Soviet Union in on American technical expertise. Russia, in short, was to be subjected to prying into her military installations while the United States retained a monopoly of bomb manufacture. Stalin, demanding that America begin by destroying its stockpile, rejected the American proposal, and by the end of 1946 chances for international control of atomic weapons had disappeared.

A series of crises in the next year and a half intensified the Cold War. Indigenous communist guerillas in Greece threatened British influence in the eastern Mediterranean, and communist parties capitalizing on severe economic discontent seemed about to gain office in France and Italy. Responding quickly, Truman called in March 1947 for $400 million in military aid to Greece and Turkey. This Truman Doctrine stated that "it must be the policy of the United States to support free peoples who are resisting subjugation by armed minorities or by outside pressures. . . . we must assist free peoples to work out their own destinies in their own way." In May the same Republican Congress that was blocking Truman's domestic program granted his request.

A month later George Marshall, who had replaced Byrnes as secretary of state in January, called for massive aid to Europe. Seeking to deflect criticisms that America focused on providing military aid to shore up nations against communism, Marshall explained that his aid program was "directed not against any country or doctrine but against hunger, poverty, desperation, and chaos.'' But the President admitted that the Truman Doctrine and the Marshall Plan (both of which bypassed the United Nations) were ''two halves of the same walnut.'' Marshall himself observed that American economic aid was aimed at permitting the ''emergence of political and social conditions in which free institutions can exist.'' He also made European cooperation (and sharing of information about resources) a condition of getting aid—a requirement that inevitably discouraged Russian and eastern European participation in the plan. And Kennan, whose memorandums had influenced Marshall's thinking, published an article in July (written in January) that urged America to embark on ''long-term, patient but firm and vigilant containment of Russia.'' The Marshall Plan, like the Truman Doctrine, embraced this doctrine of containment.

Congress moved slowly in considering Marshall's request, but the Soviets played into the administration's hands by communizing Czechoslovakia in early 1948. In June they reacted to western plans to create a more autonomous Federal Republic of Germany by blockading West Berlin. Truman, Secretary of Defense James Forrestal, and other ardent hawks in the administration responded with alarmist talk about a Russian takeover of western Europe— and with an airlift to relieve West Berlin. Congress then acquiesced by approving a peacetime draft—which lasted until 1973—and by passing the first of many authorizations for foreign aid.

These grants, so sharp a contrast to America's stinginess after World War I, helped restore European economic health. They showed how far the Cold War had dragged the country from isolation. But they were not altruistic. On the contrary, recipients of aid (which totaled some $100 billion in the next quarter century) were required to buy American goods in return. For Truman and his successors, preserving ''free'' institutions meant assisting American ''free'' enterprise. It also meant circling the Soviet Union with military force to ensure that such ''freedoms'' would thrive.

THE SOURCES OF AMERICAN ANTICOMMUNISM

To a degree, Russian-American rivalry was inevitable. As Alexis de Tocqueville had pointed out more than a century earlier, Russia and the United States were becoming the ''two great nations in the world. . . . each seems marked out by the will of heaven to sway the destinies of half the globe.'' By 1945, with power vacuums in Europe and Asia, Tocqueville's prophecy came true, for the two superpowers found themselves head-to-head for the first time in history. Conflict between such different societies was to be expected.

As Wallace pointed out at the time, however, America's attitude toward the Soviet Union after 1945 was unusually truculent, especially in contrast to its patience with Hitler from 1933 to 1940. Though dictatorial, suspicious, often ruthless, Stalin was not bent on world conquest, or even (as French and Italian communists discovered to their dismay) on controlling western

American enterprise abroad, 1925–1955

| | FOREIGN TRADE (In millions of current dollars) | | | | | INTERNATIONAL INVESTMENTS (In billions of current dollars) | | |
| | EXPORT | | IMPORT | | | | | |
	AMOUNT	% OF GNP	AMOUNT	% OF GNP	BALANCE (+ OR −)	U. S. INVESTMENTS ABROAD	FOREIGN INVESTMENTS IN U.S.	NET INVESTMENT POSITION (+ OR −)
1925	5,272	5.4	4,419	4.6	+ 852	10.9[a]	3.9[a]	+ 7.0
1930	4,013	4.2	3,500	3.4	+ 514	17.2	8.4	+ 8.8
1935	2,304	3.1	4,143	5.7[b]	−1,839	13.5	6.4	+ 7.1
1940	4,030	4.0	7,433	7.4[b]	−3,403	12.3	13.5	− 1.2
1945	10,097	4.9	4,280	1.9	+5,816	16.8	17.6	− 0.8
1950	10,816	3.6	9,125	3.1	+1,691	32.8	19.5	+13.3
1955	15,563	3.9	11,562	2.9	+4,001	44.9	29.6	+15.3

SOURCE: Adapted from *Historical Statistics of the United States*, pp. 537, 542, 564
[a]Data for 1924   [b]Percentages recomputed from Census data

Europe. Despite Truman's assertions, the USSR did little to assist the Greek communists. Rather, Stalin seems—Soviet secrecy makes his ambitions unclear—to have sought traditional Russian goals: expanded influence in Iran to the south, in Manchuria to the east, in Turkey in the southwest. Above all, he hoped to preserve Russian power in eastern Europe as protection against a rearmed Germany. In this sense Wallace was probably correct in stating that Russia wished to protect and communize its sphere of influence in much the same way that the United States wished to expand its interest in Latin America and western Europe.

Why then did America act with such a show of energy and determination against the Soviet Union? The answer lay not only in Russian behavior, but also in domestic tensions and pressures within the United States.

Some of these stemmed from America's historical experience as the world's leading democratic nation. Until 1917, when Lenin led the Bolshevik revolution, Americans had confidently cherished their experience; it was their "manifest destiny" to serve as an example to the world. The rise of communism in Russia, however, was a frightening specter—so much so that America refused even to recognize the new regime until 1933. Like fascism, communism threatened democratic government and individual freedom. It also struck at private property. It possessed a prophetic strain in its ideology—worldwide proletarian revolution—which lent credence to the notion that communism and aggression were much the same. Americans, once so sure of their revolutionary appeal, now felt insecure and defensive, for they had to contend not only with Russian power but with a rival ideology of enormous appeal. Insecure nations, as both Russia and the United States revealed, often act impatiently and provocatively.

Americans especially feared communism's threat to capitalism. Already, it had cut off the markets (such as they were) of eastern Europe. What would happen if it crept into Asia, Latin America, or—as seemed possible in 1947—into Greece and western Europe? The answer, Truman's advisers thought, was that America's exports would suffer. A communistic world would therefore undermine America's dearly loved standard of living. This is not to say that economic motives dominated Truman's policies. But it was true that Truman, his advisers, corporate leaders, labor unions, Americans generally, sought the widest possible "Open Door" for American enterprise abroad. After all, capitalism and democratic government had expanded almost as one; the decline of one might mean the ultimate collapse of the other.

The presumed threat from Russia also aroused what Kennan later called the "American urge to the universalization or generalization of decision." By this he meant that the United States, with a history of relative security, had frequently talked in sweeping, moralistic terms. Now that America had the power to gain its goals, its leaders argued that cherished principles—of constitutional government, individual liberty, and capitalistic free enterprise—were universally good. From this perspective communism was universally evil, and Stalin loomed as the head of a united, worldwide conspiracy against the visions of the Founding Fathers. It followed that the United States must think in equally cosmic ways and spread the blessings of capitalism and democracy around the world. This "globalism" was at the root of Truman's doctrine supporting all "free peoples." By late 1948 it virtually silenced people who sought a more sensitive, limited response to international problems.

As in the past, the "lessons" of history affected policy. In the 1930s, Truman now thought, appeasement had encouraged aggressors to provoke a war. There must be no more "Munichs." Moreover, World War II had disposed people to think in all-or-nothing terms. Coexistence, to use a term the hard-liners hated, had been impossible with Hitler; Stalin, too, had to be battled at every turn until he was driven from the world stage. Some Americans even demanded a "preventive war" with the Soviet Union. Though responsible leaders never endorsed such a plan, their rhetoric grew almost as apocalyptic by the mid-1950s.

Domestic politics in America added to these pressures for firmness. Many of the most outraged anticommunists, including Polish-Americans, were Democrats whom Truman had to satisfy. So were many Catholics, who loathed the atheistic anticlericalism of bolshevism. Moreover, isolationalism virtually vanished, a casualty of war. German-Americans, silenced by Hitler's atrocities, were anxious to prove their patriotism by standing up to the Bolsheviks. Republicans like Vandenberg wondered if America could be isolated in the age of air power. Others feared to sound like appeasers. And conservative Republicans were quick to oppose left-wing ideologies whether at home or abroad. The defection of such groups from the isolationist cause meant that Truman, unlike Roosevelt in the 1930s, was safer politically when he struck back at the Soviet Union than he was when he turned the other cheek.

But Truman was no simple prisoner of public opinion. On the contrary, he had displayed his feelings toward Stalin as early as July 1941, when he said, "if we see that Germany is winning we ought to help Russia, and if Russia is winning we ought to help Germany." In office only a few weeks in 1945, he took such a firm line that Foreign Minister Molotov complained that he had never been spoken to so harshly in all his life. "Carry out your agreements," Truman snapped undiplomatically, "and you won't get talked to like that." Once America became the sole possessor of the A-bomb, he felt safer than ever in adopting an unbending line. Thereafter Truman made little effort to carry on Roosevelt's earlier policy of cooperating with the Russians.

These preconceived notions helped Truman to talk tough without qualms. They made him unreceptive to Soviet requests for economic aid. They enabled him to talk of "saving" eastern Europe, an area traditionally outside America's national interest. They induced him to overlook the fact that the bomb, which was of limited value except to blast Soviet cities, was not a credible deterrent in case of military clashes in western Europe. As the historian John Gaddis put it, the bomb represented the Impotence of Omnipotence. Truman's anticommunism also led him deliberately to exaggerate the Soviet threat. This was the approach—"scaring hell out of the country," Senator Vandenberg said approvingly—that he used in 1947 in getting Congress to approve the Truman Doctrine. Far from trying to change the contours of public opinion, Truman exploited the prevailing anticommunist fears of most Americans. In so doing he helped escalate the Cold War.

Truman could have employed much subtler ways of serving his ends. Indeed, the containment policy of the world's only nuclear power made Stalin even more suspicious than he already was. If Truman had really hoped to defuse the Cold War (and after 1946 there is no evidence that he did), he might have spent less time in futile talk about getting the Russians out of eastern Europe. He might have recognized the foolishness of trying to keep knowledge of atomic energy from Russian scientists. He might have conceded the truth of the argument that the Truman Doctrine shored up undemocratic regimes in Greece and Turkey.

America might also have made better use of economic policy. This would have involved providing Stalin with aid as a carrot to induce Soviet cooperation. Because World War II had devastated Russia, Stalin very much wanted such help. Considering Russian sacrifices, he felt he deserved it. If he had gotten it, he would still have insisted on controlling eastern Europe: there was no way to avoid tensions altogether. But economic assistance might have made him feel more secure, less suspicious, much less resentful. It might even have induced him to moderate his pillage of East Germany—one of the most divisive issues of the Cold War. In any event, the carrot of economic assistance would have been better than no carrot at all.

Truman's failure to follow these potential avenues to détente attracted relatively little notice at the time. Instead, he and his fellow warriors struck most Americans as patriots combatting a worldwide communist conspiracy that was as "immoral" as that of fascism a few years before. Blunt, moralistic, and anticommunist, Truman reflected the sentiments of most of his countrymen. As the election campaign approached, his determined foreign policy was an asset, not a liability.

Truman's second term

TRUMAN IN 1948

In early 1948 many liberal Democrats rebelled at the thought of renominating Truman for the presidency. Franklin D. Roosevelt, Jr., Hubert H. Humphrey, the young, progressive mayor of Minneapolis, and others backed General Eisenhower. The *New Republic* editorialized, "As a candidate for President Harry Truman should quit." "If Truman is nominated," the columnists Joseph and Stewart Alsop wrote, "he will be forced to wage the loneliest campaign in history."

After the conventions Truman's chances seemed little better. Though he secured the Democratic nomination (Eisenhower refused to be considered), many left-wing leaders gave their support to Henry Wallace, who broke away to form the Progressive party. Their defection appeared likely to hurt Truman in key urban areas. In addition, Truman had to contend with southerners who bolted in protest against a liberal Democratic civil rights plank. They named Governor J. Strom Thurmond of South Carolina as their candidate on the States Rights Democratic (Dixiecrat) ticket. And Republicans, rejecting Taft, named what appeared to be a strong ticket composed of the popular vote-getting governors Thomas Dewey of New York and Earl Warren of California. The derisive slogan "We're Just Mild About Harry" appeared an accurate description of Truman's appeal to voters.

Until election day the public opinion polls showed Dewey with a strong lead. But it turned out they were wrong. The Dixiecrats failed to gain much support outside the Deep South. Indeed, their very presence in the campaign forced blacks and other civil rights advocates to recognize Truman's efforts, however limited, in their behalf. In November Thurmond won only four states, while Truman ran up large margins in black wards in the North.

Wallace's campaign disintegrated just as rapidly. Some observers, including many who backed his policies, found him vague and mystical. Others worried that he had become a tool of the communists and that many top Progressives were party members or fellow travelers. Labor leader Walter Reuther, a committed reformer, spoke for many anticommunist liberals in concluding that "Henry is a lost soul. . . . Communists perform the most complete valet service in the world. They write your speeches, they do your thinking for you, they provide you with applause, and they inflate your ego." Wallace's pro-Soviet line at the height of the Cold War ultimately left most liberals with no one to turn to save Truman.

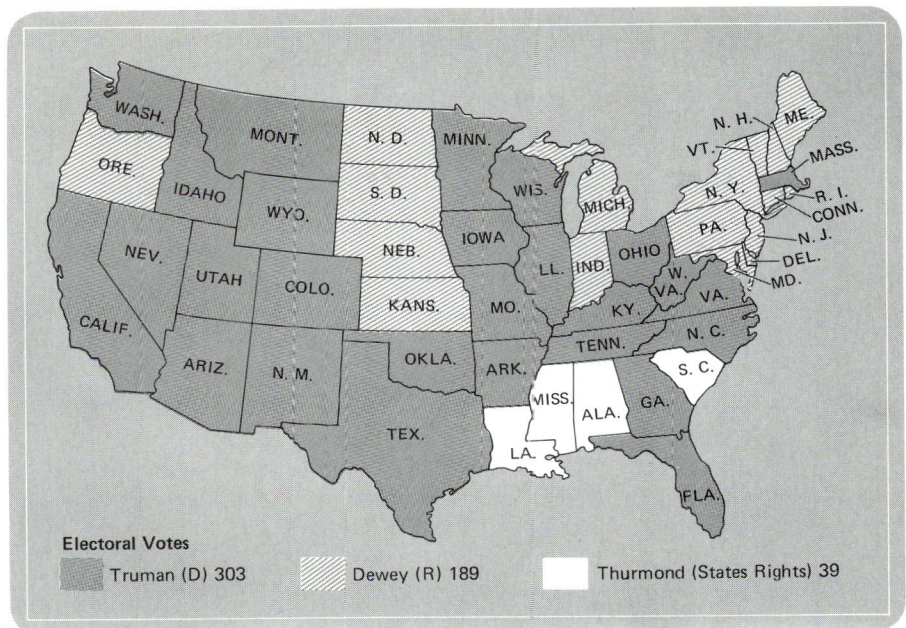

Electoral Votes
Truman (D) 303   Dewey (R) 189   Thurmond (States Rights) 39

Election, 1948

Dewey, too, failed to excite the voters. A trim, dapper little man, he struck one critic as a "certified public accountant in search of the Holy Grail." Others found him cold, curt, and aloof—it was said that "you have to know him really well to dislike him." Certain of victory, Dewey ran a bland campaign aimed at offending the smallest possible number of people. In the process he was vague and unclear on the issues, and he ignited little grass roots enthusiasm. Fewer Republicans came to the polls in 1948 than in either 1940 or 1944.

Finally, Truman himself proved a feisty, opportunistic campaigner. At the convention he electrified the faithful by calling the "do-nothing" Eightieth Congress back into special session to act on Fair Deal legislation. His motives

No presidential candidate in the future will be so inept that four of his major speeches can be boiled down to these historic four sentences. Agriculture is important. Our rivers are full of fish. You cannot have freedom without liberty. The future lies ahead. (We might add a fifth . . . the TVA is a fine thing and we must make certain that nothing like it ever happens again.)

The Louisville *Courier Journal* (November 1948) ridicules Dewey's passive campaign.

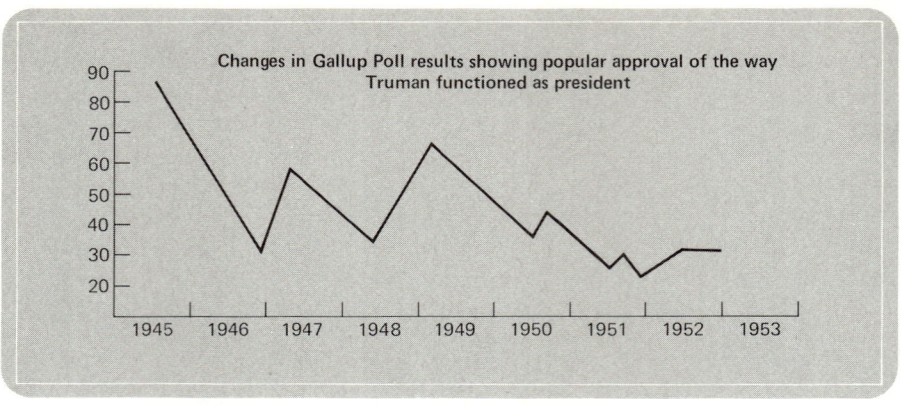

Changes in Gallup Poll results showing popular approval of the way Truman functioned as president

SOURCE: Adapted from Irish and Frank, *U.S. Foreign Policy*, p. 104

Truman started out at the peak of his popularity in 1945, when 87 percent of respondents approved of his presidency, and he consistently moved downward in popular esteem to reach a low in late 1951 when only 23 percent approved of the way he was handling the presidency.

kept up the offensive. Republicans, he charged, were "just a bunch of old mossbacks . . . gluttons of privilege . . . all set to do a hatchet job on the New Deal." He then set off on a series of whistle-stop tours, always on the attack. This partisan strategy developed by his aide, Clark Clifford, was both abrasive and extreme, but it had the virtue of placing the GOP on the defensive. It exploited to the most Democratic ties with labor and the "have-not" coalition that had four times elected Roosevelt.

For all these reasons Truman surprised almost everyone by winning in November, with 24.1 million votes to Dewey's 22 million. Thurmond got less than 1.2 million, and Wallace only 1,157,000 and no electoral votes. Perhaps because of his liberal record as governor of New York, Dewey actually did better in urban states than the Republicans had in 1944, carrying New York, Pennsylvania, Michigan, and New Jersey. But Truman scored well in farm areas, where he had misleadingly accused the Republican Congress of withholding funds for storage facilities. He did sufficiently well in other urban states—narrowly carrying California, Illinois, and Ohio—to pile up a substantial margin in the electoral college of 303 to 189 and to carry with him Democratic majorities in both houses of Congress. Among those who were elected for the first time to the Senate were such important liberal Democrats as Hubert Humphrey of Minnesota, Paul Douglas of Illinois, and Estes Kefauver of Tennessee, as well as the more conservative Lyndon Johnson, who won in Texas. The remarkably low turnout, more than a million less than in 1940, suggested that voters did not find either Truman or Dewey particularly attractive. Truman, in fact, failed to get 50 percent of the vote. But it also showed that the Democratic voting coalition forged during the depression remained intact and that the reforms of the New Deal were safe from attack.

These were impressive reminders of the chronic weakness of the GOP and of the stability of American politics.

PROBLEMS, HOME AND ABROAD, 1949

President in his own right, Truman determined to make up for lost time, and in January 1949 he called on Congress to enact a broad-ranging program. It included health insurance, repeal of Taft-Hartley, extension of social security, increases in the minimum wage, civil rights legislation, federal aid to education, and larger appropriations for public housing. In foreign policy he broached the idea of supplying underdeveloped nations with technical assistance. Point Four, as it was called, suggested that the administration was beginning to worry not only about communism in western Europe but throughout the uncommitted world.

Truman also lent his support in 1949 to the Brannan Plan for farmers. Named after Charles Brannan, his progressive secretary of agriculture, the plan was a dramatic effort to revise the New Deal farm program. Brannan argued correctly that price supports were expensive to the government and a burden on consumers. He insisted that they helped a few large farmers at the expense of small producers, that they encouraged overproduction in crops eligible for federal subsidies, and that other produce—including meat and dairy goods—was often so short in supply that prices escalated and diets suffered. Brannan's answer to these problems was complex. To assist consumers he demanded an end to price supports. Farmers would sell their goods for whatever price they commanded in the open market—prices that would ordinarily be considerably lower than in the past. To help farmers who suffered from the withdrawal of price supports, he called for income supports instead. These income supports, available only in limited amounts per crop, would provide a basic floor under income for all farmers. The package, Brannan thought, would limit the power of agribusiness, assist small farmers, rescue consumers, and save the government money.

During the next two years Truman secured a few of these goals. Some of them, such as progress toward desegregation of the armed forces, came by executive order. Truman also strengthened the Civil Rights Division of the Department of Justice, which brought important suits against Jim Crow practices in education, transportation, and housing. Other reforms actually broke through the bottleneck on Capitol Hill. Congress passed a housing act including funds for public housing. It increased the minimum wage from forty cents to seventy-five cents, extended rent controls through 1950, and approved a displaced persons act admitting some 400,000 refugees to the United States. It raised social security benefits and broadened the program to cover 10 million new Americans. These were the most liberal measures passed by any Congress since 1935.

But the conservative coalition, though weaker than at any time since 1938, still held its own. It fought Truman's requests for civil rights legislation, health insurance, and federal aid to education. It proved slow in providing funds for Point Four. It showed itself willing to revise Taft-Hartley, but when Truman insisted on repeal, Congress balked, and the act remained as it was. After 1949 it proved very stingy in appropriating funds for the public housing program, which never even approached the expectations of reformers. And the Brannan Plan fell under the onslaught of well-organized interest groups. Business people opposed the very idea of income supports, which they insisted would drain the Treasury. Labor unions, seeing nothing in the plan for themselves, were lukewarm. Large commercial farmers opposed the abolition of price supports. Like any proposal lacking the endorsement of entrenched groups, the Brannan Plan was doomed to defeat.

In the area of foreign policy Truman secured a major goal when Congress approved American participation in the North Atlantic Treaty Organization, a mutual defense pact that bound twelve signatories to fight against aggression. It was the first time in American history that Congress had ratified a military alliance with European nations. Later in 1949 Congress added teeth to the pact by authorizing money for military aid to member nations. Because Stalin had no plans to attack western Europe, the NATO pact was of questionable military value. The military assistance plan, still more provocative, propelled America further into the business of supplying arms to other nations. At the time, however, both NATO and military aid were described as essential to sustain the morale of western Europe. They proved highly popular measures during the struggle to win the Cold War.

Events in Asia all but obscured Truman's successes in Europe. Since 1945, when American marines had helped Chiang Kai-shek strengthen his claims on North China, Truman had pursued Roosevelt's illusory hope for a peaceful, noncommunist China. But Chiang's corruption, and his failure to fight hard against the Japanese during the war, had already damaged his claim to rule, and Communist forces under Mao Tse-tung pressed forward. In 1946 Truman dispatched General George C. Marshall to China in an attempt to bring American influence to bear on the situation. Marshall, like other emissaries before him, sought to reconcile Chiang and Mao. When the two sides agreed to a truce, it seemed that his patient efforts had succeeded. But by late 1946 the truce had broken down. Mao's forces pushed on, and Marshall returned home to become secretary of state.

Truman then requested a report from General Albert Wedemeyer, America's chief military emissary in China. Wedemeyer's advice, to escalate aid to Chiang and to send 10,000 American military "advisers" to China, received a cool reception from Marshall and others in the State Department, and Truman not only rejected Wedemeyer's report but kept it from Congress. Within a year and a half, in 1949, Chiang's forces collapsed, and in December he fled to Formosa. China, land of more than 500 million people, was now a communist country.

Truman responded calmly to the "fall of China." His secretary of state after 1948, the tough, aristocratic Dean Acheson, spoke for the administration in defending what had been America's policy since 1945. Sending in "advisers," he pointed out, would lead only to unnecessary loss of American life. Defeating Mao would require a major land war on the Asian continent, a war that the United States had neither the men nor the will to fight, especially at a time when Stalin seemed to pose a threat in Europe. Chiang's own maladministration, not American neglect, had led to the Communist victory. "Nothing this country did or could have done within the reasonable limits of its capabilities," Acheson argued, "would have changed the result, nothing that was left undone by this country has contributed to it."

The Truman-Acheson argument was irrefutable. Few Americans before 1949 had demanded any sizeable commitment to Chiang, and the administration, which was focusing its attention on Europe, would have had serious trouble trying to mobilize support for massive aid in China as well. Moreover, almost no one at the time expected economic or military aid to do much good. Even Wedemeyer had conceded that Chiang was losing because of corruption and "lack of spirit, primarily lack of spirit. It was not lack of equipment. In my judgment they could have defended the Yangtze if they had had the will to do it." In opting for limited aid to Chiang between 1945 and 1949 the Truman administration followed Roosevelt in backing the wrong horse. But it had sense enough not to waste more money than it did (perhaps $2 billion by 1949), and to keep American men out of what would have been an endless bloodbath.

The fall of so much territory to communism was not easy for Americans to accept. The United States, the history books said, had never lost a war. It had beaten both the Germans and the Japanese. It had sole possession of the bomb. Why then had it "lost" China? Why had it not acted to preserve the Open Door policy? Sensible observers replied that China was an ancient civilization that had never been America's to lose. They explained that the Open Door doctrine did not apply, for Mao had triumphed on his own, with little aid indeed from Stalin. But many people refused to listen to reason. Deluded by the illusion of American omnipotence, they continued to ask where and how Truman had gone wrong.

Some of Truman's critics concluded that he had merely made mistakes. Others were "Asia-firsters" or members of the so-called China lobby. Many of these people, especially partisan Republicans, grew nasty. Truman, they charged, had been duped by procommunist sympathizers in the State Department. Moreover, the Russians exploded their own atomic bomb in September 1949: perhaps procommunist scientists working for America had turned over secrets to help Stalin on his way? By 1950, Truman had to confront a resurgence of popular fears about the spread of communism.

MC CARTHYISM

Senator Joseph McCarthy of Wisconsin, the demagogue who capitalized on these fears, began his Red-hunting campaign in February 1950 by claiming in a speech in Wheeling to hold in his hand the names of 207 (or 57—he was not clear) communists in government. Though few people paid him much notice at first, he repeated, expanded, and varied his charges in succeeding speeches, and by March he was front-page news across the country. At last, it seemed to Truman's critics, a responsible person had evidence not only of procommunist sympathy in high places but of disloyalty and treason.

Before McCarthy and fellow Red-haters overreached themselves in late 1954 they broadened their cause into a powerful witch hunt that swept into every corner of American life. McCarthyism destroyed morale in the State Department, cowed the Department of the Army, and exposed America's hysterical anticommunism to the scorn of civilized people throughout the world.

McCarthyism reached deeply into the fabric of American government. The Supreme Court in 1951 upheld the Smith Act of 1940, which had made it a crime even to advocate revolution. Its decision, in *Dennis* v. *U. S.*, resulted in the conviction and imprisonment of eleven top Communists and encouraged the Justice Department to proceed with further prosecutions. Ordinarily decent conservatives, such as Taft, also jumped on the anti-Red bandwagon.

Senator Joseph McCarthy with his aide, Roy Cohn, on his right and Cohn's friend G. David Schine, on McCarthy's left.

ACRIMONY, HOME AND ABROAD 1945–1952

*What the phenomenon of McCarthyism did . . . was to implant in my con-
sciousness a lasting doubt as to the adequacy of our political system. . . . A
political system and a public opinion, it seemed to me, that could be so
easily disoriented by this sort of challenge in one epoch would be no less
vulnerable to similar ones in another. I could never recapture, after these
experiences of the late 1940s and early 1950s, quite the same faith in the
American system of government and in traditional American outlooks that I
had had, despite all the discouragements of official life, before that time.*

One veteran diplomat (George Kennan) recalls the devastating impact of Mc-
Carthyism on American life.

McCarthy, he said, was a "fighting Marine who risked his life to preserve the
liberties of the United States." If accusations proved unfounded, Taft
advised, McCarthy should keep trying. Liberals joined conservatives to
approve the Internal Security Act of 1950. It required Communists to register
with the Attorney General, and it set up the Subversives Activities Board to
review the loyalty of government employees. In vetoing it Truman correctly
contended that the act was obscure, unfair, and unworkable. But 1950 was an
election year, and practically no one dared to oppose the anticommunist
onslaught. Congress quickly passed the act over Truman's veto.

Heartened by such responses, the Red-baiters became almost unbelievably extreme in 1951–52. McCarthy charged that the Democratic party was
"the property of men and women . . . who have bent to the whispered pleas
from the lips of traitors . . . who wear the political label stitched with the
idiocy of a Truman, [and] rotted by the deceit of a Dean Acheson." Marshall,
he added, was "a man steeped in falsehood . . . who has resorted to the lie
whenever it suits his convenience . . . [and who was part of a] conspiracy so
immense and an infamy so black as to dwarf any previous venture in the
history of man." Not to be outdone, Senator William Jenner of Indiana
concluded that America was "in the hands of a secret inner coterie which is
directed by agents of the Soviet Union. . . . Our only choice is to impeach
President Truman and find out who is the secret inner government."

These statements were wholly undocumented. The Red-baiters produced
no evidence to support their accusations, and they never exposed a communist in government. Indeed, McCarthy himself made little effort to follow up
his scattershot accusations. On the contrary, he remained a profane, often
unshaven, half-sober individualist whose crusade against communism was
aimed at securing the recognition he would need for his reelection campaign in
1952, and for higher political ambitions to follow. "That's it," he told friends
who suggested anticommunism as an issue. "The government is full of
communists. We can hammer away at them."

McCarthy's charges were as unnecessary as they were irresponsible, for
Communists in America were weaker in 1950 than at any time since the 1920s.

Anticommunist labor leaders had deprived them of positions of strength that they had enjoyed in the CIO. The government, especially after Truman created loyalty boards in 1947, had launched systematic (and often unconstitutional) security checks on federal employees. Russian moves such as the coup in Czechoslovakia and the blockade of West Berlin had driven all but the avid Stalinists out of the party. By the time McCarthy started his crusade the Communist party had already fallen into the decline that cut its membership from a high of around 80,000 in 1945 to less than 3000 in the late 1950s.

Because McCarthy himself was so crude and reckless, and because communism at home was dwindling, it was hard for contemporary defenders of civil liberties to explain his appeal. In retrospect, however, it is clear that several forces combined to make him the dangerous demagogue that he was.

Among these was McCarthy himself. His very irresponsibility made him a frightening foe, for he thought nothing of charging his critics with communist sympathies. Politicians, therefore, were careful not to antagonize him. McCarthy was also a master at using the press, which had treated his sensational charges as page-one news. Shrewdly, he would call press conferences early in the morning to tell reporters that earth-shaking disclosures were soon to be announced. Alerted, the afternoon papers would print banner headlines, "McCarthy New Revelations Expected Soon." Newsmen for morning papers would then besiege him for the latest developments, and McCarthy obliged by leading them to believe a key witness was about to be found. Hence the morning headlines, "Delay in McCarthy Revelations: Mystery Witness Sought." Tactics such as these brought McCarthy maximum publicity.

McCarthy was also fortunate in his timing. Just as he inaugurated his campaign, Alger Hiss, a former State Department offical accused of espionage, was convicted of perjury—after two widely publicized trials. His conviction, which followed on a congressional investigation spearheaded by Representative Richard Nixon of California, appeared proof that communists infested the government. McCarthy was further helped by the revelation that Klaus Fuchs, a British physicist, had passed American atomic secrets to the Soviets. Legal proceedings stemming from the Fuchs case culminated three years later in the conviction and execution for espionage of Julius and Ethel Rosenberg, American Communists allegedly involved in the atomic plot. Actually, these cases did not prove much. If Hiss was a communist agent— which he steadfastly denied—he appears to have given the Russians nothing of value. Fuchs helped the Russians along on research that they were mastering on their own. The Rosenbergs, whose guilt was still being hotly debated many years later, were in no way associated with the government. Still, the Fuchs case was proof of the need for security. McCarthy, many Americans told themselves, might be a little rough in his methods, but his goals were noble. If permitted to continue, he would uncover the "traitors" in government.

Powerful interest groups further assisted McCarthy's campaigns. Among these were defense contractors and the military forces that had suffered from demobilization. Not all these groups thought well of McCarthy's methods—indeed, he later infuriated the army brass by accusing it of harboring Communists. But his virulent campaign obviously assisted their demands for defense spending. With such potent forces supporting McCarthy's goals, or at least acquiescing in them, he had advantages lesser demagogues would have lacked.

McCarthyism also seemed to offer simple answers to the complex questions of the Cold War. China went Communist, he explained, because State Department "traitors" willed it so. Russia developed the A-bomb because people like Fuchs told them how to do it. Capitalism and democracy would have nothing to fear if the "commies" were rooted out of American life. This conspiratorial approach to the world prevented the country from engaging in the debate necessary to develop flexible policies. But because McCarthy's road to salvation seemed so quick and easy, it exercised an appeal that more complex, more accurate explanations failed to provide.

This conspiracy theory appealed in particular to superpatriotic Americans who responded warmly to McCarthy's attacks on intellectuals, left-wing sympathizers, New Dealers, and well-educated, upper-class easterners like Acheson. "I watch his smart-aleck manner and his British clothes and that New Dealism," Senator Hugh Butler of Nebraska exclaimed of Acheson, " . . . and I want to shout, Get out. Get out. You stand for everything that has been wrong with the United States for years." Butler, a Republican, had partisan reasons for welcoming assaults on the "striped-pants boys" in the State Department. An economic conservative, he would have shuddered at the thought of being linked with populism or with Nebraska's "Great Commoner," William Jennings Bryan. But like many Americans he was at one with Bryan in suspecting the worst of the Eastern Establishment. In this way McCarthy had the best of two worlds: by hammering at communism he could appeal to conservatives, and by slashing at intellectuals and the Eastern Establishment he could win the approval of ordinary people.

Others who reacted positively to McCarthy included many ethnic Americans, especially blue-collar Catholics. By 1950 most of these people were second- or third-generation Americans. Many had fought in World War II. But as ethnics and Catholics they frequently suffered discrimination, and they were rarely accepted as "100 percent Americans." McCarthy, himself a Catholic, seemed one of them. By supporting his movement, ethnics could prove their patriotism, indeed their super-patriotism. Catholics could demonstrate their support of a movement directed against atheistic communism. For these reasons McCarthyism was strong in many heavily Catholic urban areas and in Catholic states like Massachusetts, where some politicians shared his concerns. "McCarthy," said John F. Kennedy, "may have something."

Not all political figures acted like Kennedy. Some, especially those who represented rural, Protestant states, felt freer to speak out in defense of civil liberties. These included senators George Aiken, a Vermont Republican, Margaret Chase Smith, a GOP colleague from Maine, and J. William Fulbright, a Democrat from Arkansas. But most office-holders, including many liberals, were almost as anticommunist as McCarthy himself. They might deplore his methods, but they were committed to a hard-line Cold War policy. This is not to suggest, as some historians have, that Truman's exaggerations about Soviet designs made McCarthyism inevitable. But it is to say that the Cold War that the administration waged after 1945 helped sustain the atmosphere of fear in which McCarthy thrived. To this extent McCarthyism was a broad-based (though unorganized) phenomenon, urban-ethnic as well as rural, and promoted by the rhetoric of liberals as well as conservatives.

In this sense McCarthyism was but the latest of many eruptions of intolerance in American history. Federalists had tried to silence their "radical" Jeffersonian foes by introducing the Alien and Sedition acts of 1798. Know-Nothings, nativist politicians of the 1850s, had developed considerable support in their campaign against Catholics and foreigners. Waves of prejudice against aliens had swept the country in tense periods since the 1870s. The Red Scare of 1919, the sharpest explosion of all, had broken out against foreigners as well as leftists. By the early 1950s the "hyphenated-Americans" no longer seemed much of a threat. But the communists did. In such turbulent times, it was easy to make them a scapegoat for the nation's problems.

McCarthyism was above all the product of partisan politics at midcentury. For years American politicians had courted favor by preaching against the evils of communism. Some, such as Nixon, had built political careers by doing it. Like McCarthy, these people wanted desperately to run the Democrats out of the White House, and anticommunism, by 1950, seemed the most effective issue to employ to that end. Thus it was that when McCarthy ran again in 1952 he scored best in areas that had traditionally been Republican. This connection between McCarthyism and Republicanism was important in giving purpose and direction to the anticommunist crusade.

To counter such implacable opposition Truman might have been well advised to take it seriously. This would have involved giving a bipartisan congressional committee access to classified executive documents concerning alleged security risks. Without publicizing information about individuals, the committee might have established the facts concerning McCarthy's charges. Deprived of the claim that Truman was hiding pertinent data, McCarthy would have had to quiet down, or to watch his accusations be torn to shreds.

Truman, however, hardly considered such a strategy. McCarthy, of course, would have insisted on being named to such a committee. If Democrats in Congress had refused to grant his demand, McCarthy would have shouted that he had been excluded. If they had agreed to it, they chanced having McCarthy give classified (and probably misleading) evidence to the press. Either way, the administration—to say nothing of the alleged security risks—might suffer.

Accordingly, Truman resorted to the doctrine of executive privilege: McCarthy would get no documents from him. He stepped up his campaign to rid the government of alleged security risks. Henceforth employees had to furnish proof, beyond a "reasonable doubt," of their loyalty. He encouraged Democrats in Congress to pursue their own counter-investigation of McCarthy's charges. But these approaches merely suggested that Truman had something to hide. And in November 1950, Senator Millard Tydings of Maryland, the conservative Democrat who had chaired the investigation, went down in defeat before a Red-baiter who came close to outdoing McCarthy himself. Thereafter few Democrats wanted to sling stones at the Goliath of American politics. From February 1950 until the end of his tenure in the White House, President Truman had to endure his Wisconsin tormenter.

THE TRAVAIL OF KOREA

On June 25, 1950 communist forces from North Korea poured across the thirty-eighth parallel and attacked the prowestern government of South Korea. Acting quickly, Truman authorized American forces under General Douglas MacArthur to go to South Korea's aid. At first it seemed as if MacArthur's troops might be destroyed. But the Americans and South Koreans held on until September, when MacArthur engineered a brilliant amphibious counterattack north of the enemy's lines. His forces then drove across the thirty-eighth parallel and smashed northward until they came within reach of the North Korean border with China.

If MacArthur's counteroffensive had stopped near the parallel, or if it had moved less precipitously toward China, the war might have ended there and then, a glorious triumph for Truman and for the anticommunist cause. As it was, the Chinese threw masses of men into battle, and American soldiers fled back into South Korea. General Matthew Ridgway, who replaced MacArthur in April 1951, restored order, but the conflict dragged on until a truce was arranged in July 1953. It divided the country along lines similar to those in force before the 1950 invasion and sustained in power Syngman Rhee, the anticommunist ruler of South Korea. For the West, therefore, the war had succeeded in preventing communist gains; Truman's intervention had not been wasted. It also resulted in a huge escalation of defense spending from approximately $14 billion in 1949 to $44 billion in 1953. This figure, some 60 percent of the federal budget, sparked a boom in the economy lasting until 1954. But the conflict left 54,000 Americans dead and 103,000 wounded. It wholly diverted attention—and funds—from domestic reforms. It greatly strengthened the role of the military and of defense contractors in American society. And because Truman refused to escalate the war still faster, he played readily into the hands of McCarthyites. The war applied the *coup de grace* to the administration's standing with the electorate.

Such a protracted war naturally prompted sharp debate over the wisdom of Truman's actions. Some critics complained that American policies had helped provoke the war in the first place. Others questioned his decisions to involve the United States in the fighting and then to press on over the thirty-eighth parallel. Many others denounced him for refusing to broaden the war once the Chinese had jumped into it.

The complaint that America helped to provoke the war was favored by right-wing critics at the time. Truman, they argued, had practically invited a North Korean invasion by removing American occupation troops from South Korea in 1949 and by leaving Rhee's government almost defenseless against the well-drilled forces of the North. Dean Acheson, they emphasized, had outlined an American "defense perimeter" in Asia that appeared to exclude Korea. With such a "soft spot" exposed, the communists, supplied by the Soviet Union, naturally pounced on it in June, 1950.

Later left-wing critics, revisionists who renewed the debate over Korean policy in the 1960s, challenged Truman's policies from a different perspective. Rhee, they argued, was a dictatorial nationalist who had regularly vowed his intention to reunite Korea, by force of arms if necessary. His very presence antagonized the North. When he lost support in the May 1950 elections, revisionists suggested, he determined to provoke border incidents to reestablish his image and perhaps to force the United States to defend his regime. Other revisionists argued that America provoked an attack from the North by announcing plans in the spring of 1950 to negotiate a bilateral defense pact with Japan. To prevent such a development, revisionists surmised, North Korean leader Kim Il Sung attacked before the United States had the power to respond. Other revisionists went still further in chastising the Truman administration. Pointing to a position paper of the National Security Council (NSC-68), they showed that Truman's leading defense planners had agreed early in 1950 to seek enormous increases in American military might. How better to get the money out of Congress than by tempting or provoking the North Koreans to attack?

Because the relevant documents are unavailable to historians it is impossible to know why North Korea attacked in June 1950. It is therefore hazardous at best to evaluate the critiques of Truman. But some facts seem clear. Obviously, the United States was unwise in leaving Rhee's forces so weak and in implying that South Korea lay outside America's primary lines of defense. America could also have moved less threateningly toward a rapprochement with Japan. Conceivably, it could have assisted moderate factions to take over in South Korea. Such a policy—military preparedness allied to political and diplomatic moderation—might have preserved peace on the peninsula.

Still, Truman and Acheson had sound reasons for their prewar policies. The President's military advisers, including General MacArthur, had regularly called for the removal of American troops from South Korea, a place they considered costly to defend and of little strategic value. The military also needed all the strength they could find to bolster NATO. Moreover, arming Rhee properly seemed impossible—Congress would not have supplied the funds—and unwise, for Rhee might then have staged his own attack on the North. And though Truman might have worked to dispose of Rhee, whose

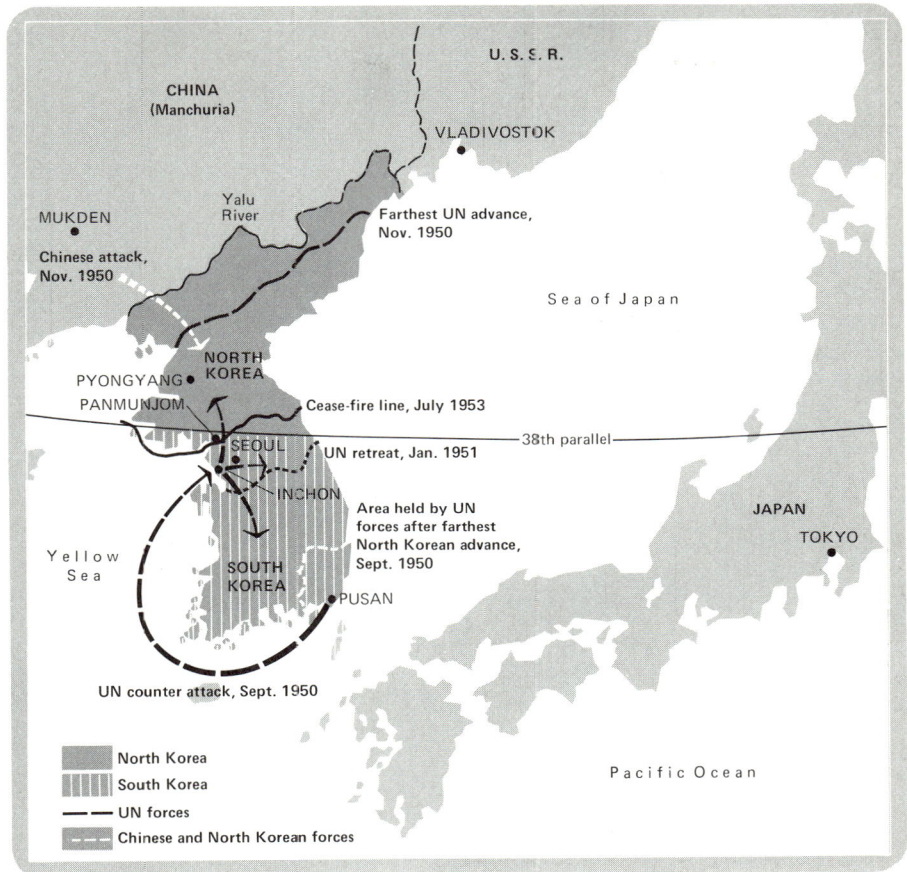

Korean War, 1950–1953

power was slipping in early 1950, North Korea acted first. For better or worse, America and Syngman Rhee were thrust together against a common foe.

The revisionist case distorts two other essential points. First, for whatever reasons, it was not South Korea but North Korea that mounted the attack, which was too well planned and coordinated to pass as a mere border incident. Second, though many American military leaders wanted to increase defense spending, there is no evidence to suggest that they yearned for a war in Korea, which they continued to dismiss as of little importance. Indeed, such a war would drain western defenses in Europe, which was Washington's major concern. The Korean War was a conflict that few people in America had expected and that fewer still were very happy to be involved in while it dragged on to 1951.

Truman's decision to resist the North Korean invasion prompted other criticisms. If Korea was hard to protect and of little military value, why bother to defend it? Key senators like Taft demanded to know why Truman did not consult Congress or ask for a formal declaration of war. Instead, Truman merely secured United Nations sanction (possible because the Soviets were boycotting the Security Council at the time), for common "police action" against the aggressor. Later, when the war deteriorated into an apparently endless stalemate, Truman's failure to consult Congress cost him dearly. Still later it offered an excuse for President Kennedy and Johnson to send American troops to Vietnam without congressional sanction.

In June 1950, Truman easily brushed aside complaints. The North Korean invasion, he declared, was part of a communist design to test America's will in the Cold War. The United States must fight to show that it would hold the line, that it would not repeat the disastrous appeasement policy of the 1930s. There must be no more Munichs. He added that he had to act quickly. If America waited for Congress to debate the issue, the North Koreans would overrun the peninsula.

Truman's arguments were a little self-serving, for no one could prove that the North Korean invasion was part of a broader communist design, or even that it had been encouraged by the Soviet Union. And while it was true that Truman had to act quickly, he could still have requested congressional approval at any time in the early weeks of the war. But the blatancy and the speed of the invasion made his arguments so hard to refute at the time that even critics like Taft grudgingly supported American intervention. In responding as he did Truman acted decisively, even courageously. Years later it is possible to fault his disregard of Congress, but harder to question the wisdom of the basic decision itself.

Truman's most controversial decision was authorizing MacArthur to push on toward the Yalu River, North Korea's northern border with China. His action seemed sensible at the time, for MacArthur had the enemy on the run. It also reflected the almost unanimous counsel of his top military and diplomatic advisers and of Allied leaders. There should not be South Koreans and North Koreans, British Foreign Secretary Ernest Bevin declared, only Koreans. The Chinese, Truman was reassured, were too tired to get involved in Korea. Moreover, Asian peoples were no match for America's technological superiority. "We are no longer fearful of their [Chinese] intervention," MacArthur told Truman at a special meeting on Wake Island in October. "The

United Nations soldiers retreating in Korea, January 1951. This was a low point for the allied forces in South Korea.

Chinese have 300,000 men in Manchuria. . . . Only 50,000 to 60,000 could be gotten across the Yalu River. They have no air force. Now that we have bases for our air force in Korea, if the Chinese tried to get down to Pyongyang [the North Korean capital near the thirty-eighth parallel] there would be the greatest slaughter.''

The astonishingly successful intervention of the Chinese in November 1950, of course, quickly proved the tragic foolishness of such advice. Truman's advisers, including not only MacArthur but also the Central Intelligence Agency, deserved to be condemned for predicting that the Chinese would stay out. But Truman himself might have paused before accepting such counsel, for the Chinese had implied through diplomatic channels that they would attack UN forces that pushed north of the thirty-eighth parallel. In ignoring such a possibility Truman and his advisers displayed exaggerated faith in western technology and contempt for Oriental military potential. As George Kennan pointed out at the time, Truman and his aides were also bemused by the insidious belief, another product of the modern age, that total victory is the purpose of war. In urging MacArthur to drive toward the Yalu, Truman went beyond containment to seek what later became known as a policy of liberation. Nothing could have been more disastrous.

The conflict with China accelerated the war's most dramatic clash of wills—between Truman and MacArthur. As the Chinese advanced, the general became progressively more restive and querulous. Truman, he complained, should escalate the war. The administration must blockade mainland China, "unleash" Chiang Kai-shek for raids in Korea or South China, and authorize air-sea attacks on Chinese "sanctuaries" in Manchuria. Without such steps, MacArthur insisted, America could never win the war.

Truman, however, shrank from embarking on such a course. He recognized that any attempt to blockade China's long coastline would tie up a substantial part of America's navy, which was needed elsewhere. A blockade might also lead to confrontation with other nations, including Russia. In any event, a blockade could do nothing to stop the flow of supplies that came overland from the Soviet Union.

With similar prudence, Truman rejected the idea of helping Chiang raid China. Contrary to MacArthur's assumption, such attacks would not have prompted native uprisings against the communist regime—Chiang remained too unpopular for that to happen. Rather, Nationalist incursions, to be at all effective, would have required an enormous American commitment. The United States might have become involved in a renewal of the Chinese civil war, an eventuality that MacArthur himself shied away from.

Truman was equally wise to refrain from bombing Chinese "sanctuaries." Strategic bombing during World War II had suggested that such attacks rarely worked wonders. In Korea, they would have done nothing to stop China's major asset, masses of foot soldiers who needed only the most meager rations to keep pressing toward the south. Employing bombers would also have frightened America's western allies, who needed no reminding that Russian territory touched the Yalu. Suppose the bombers caused damage to Soviet installations: what then? At the very least Russia would have been free to attack American "sanctuaries" in Japan. Stalin might even have taken advantage of America's commitment in Korea to push his way into western Europe. Either response might have promoted nuclear war. For all these reasons Truman resisted MacArthur's entreaties. As General Omar Bradley, the army

General Douglas MacArthur in Korea, 1950.

chief of staff, put it, they would have involved the nation in "the wrong war, at the wrong place, at the wrong time, and with the wrong enemy."

MacArthur, however, was an imperious, egotistic adversary who could barely conceal his contempt for the likes of people such as Truman. Having served in the Pacific for more than a decade, he failed to comprehend the administration's primary concern for Europe. He had equally little understanding of the sensitivities of the western allies, whom he considered unreliable. He was a passionate globalist who believed that the United States, all by itself, should protect the world against the tide of Marxism. "I believe we should defend every place from communism," he declared. "I believe we are able to. . . . I don't admit that we can't hold communism wherever it shows its head." For all these reasons he was among the most sincere of the Asia-firsters. "It seems strangely difficult for some to realize," he wrote House Minority Leader Martin in April 1951, "that here in Asia is where the Communist conspirators have elected to make their play for global conquest . . . that here we fight Europe's war with arms while the diplomats there still fight it with words; that if we lose the war to communism in Asia the fall of Europe is inevitable; win it and Europe would probably avoid war and yet preserve freedom." With characteristic flourish, MacArthur closed his letter by proclaiming, "there is no substitute for victory."

As MacArthur had intended, Martin made public the letter. A classic confrontation then ensued between civilian and military authority. Truman had already tired of MacArthur's insubordination. He had also doubted MacArthur's handling of the war. The general had overconfidently split America's forces in the fall of 1950, and the Chinese had driven speedily down the middle to the south. Now MacArthur had gone the limit, ignoring presidential orders to keep quiet and challenging the very essence of administration policy. Certain of the course he had to follow, Truman nonetheless requested the advice of his chiefs of staff, who agreed that MacArthur had to go. The President then relieved him from command. If he hoped to preserve civilian rule, he could hardly have done otherwise.

The news of MacArthur's dismissal prompted critics to heap abuse on Truman's head. The GOP National Committee proclaimed that the President had perpetuated a "super Munich." McCarthy grumbled, "the son of a bitch [Truman] ought to be impeached." MacArthur then began a triumphal return to the United States, where throngs of people crowded to sing his praises. To an emotional session of Congress he pulled out all the stops: "I still remember the refrain of one of the most popular barracks ballads of that day which proclaimed most proudly that 'Old soldiers never die; they just fade away.' And like the old soldier of that ballad, I now close my military career and just fade away—an old soldier who tried to do his duty as God gave him the light to see that duty. Good-bye."

Truman wisely did not attempt to counter such theatrics. But he did work to strengthen America's military posture in Asia and elsewhere. In 1951 America signed separate bilateral defense pacts with Japan and with the

Philippines. It agreed to the so-called ANZUS treaty, a mutual defense pact involving Australia and New Zealand. In part to secure French agreement to the inclusion of West Germany in NATO, it stepped up aid to French forces in Indo-China. By 1954 the aid had totaled $1.2 billion in a losing cause.

Truman also called upon loyalists in Congress to expose MacArthur's bombast. Led by Senator Richard Russell, they brought out the fact that all three chiefs of staff had rejected MacArthur's argument. They then exposed the inconsistency of the GOP partisans who were supporting escalation. Taft, for instance, was hardly a globalist like MacArthur, and in early 1951 he had led a "Great Debate" against Truman's plan to commit American troops to a NATO army in Europe. Taft had also criticized America's commitment in Korea, and after the Chinese intervention he had joined other partisans in suggesting that America cut its losses and get out. Yet when Truman dismissed MacArthur, Taft—and many Repulicans with similar beliefs—leaped to the general's defense. The GOP partisans had placed political expediency ahead of ideological consistency.

By the summer of 1951 Truman's patience began to bring modest results, and MacArthur disappeared to the back pages. But MacArthur's dismissal had served as a public acknowledgment that total victory was impossible, that "limited war" would continue to be the policy of the administration. And limited war, as one writer put it, was like a slight case of pregnancy. In their heads Americans might understand the necessity for restraint; in their hearts they wanted to win, as their country always had. Or they wanted to get out. Unless the administration could find an honorable way to end the fighting, it would suffer dearly at the polls in 1952.

Reversal in 1952

Early in 1952 Truman announced he would retire at the end of his term. He could hardly have done otherwise, for almost no one in his party wanted him to run again. Since 1950 he had suffered not only at the hands of McCarthyites and MacArthurites but also from corruption among some of his own friends and aides. Only 23 percent of the American people, a record low, signified their approval of his administration in late 1951.

With their albatross out of the way, the Democrats turned to Governor Adlai Stevenson of Illinois. Though a relative newcomer to electoral politics, Stevenson had already captured the affection of many reporters and intellectuals, who deeply admired his intelligence, his liberalism, and his patrician cultivation. Urban bosses liked his stand on labor and welfare issues and noted his apparent strength at the polls in Illinois. Upright, witty, articulate, Stevenson could be expected to carry on the New Deal–Fair Deal tradition and to defend Truman's internationalist policies. Though Stevenson was perhaps too intellectual for mass taste, he seemed a fresh contrast to the tired

Adlai Stevenson consulting with his friend and supporter Eleanor Roosevelt.

old regulars who had surrounded Truman. To the columnist Marcus Childs, the governor was "Lincolnian"; to David Lilienthal he was a tower of "wisdom and wit and strength"; to Max Lerner, a liberal writer, he was the "first figure of major stature to have emerged since Roosevelt."

Republicans, meanwhile, took no chances. Rejecting Taft, the controversial favorite of the Right, they selected General Eisenhower as their nominee. "Ike" was genial, nonpartisan, and widely admired as a war hero; he was expected to offend no one. As Truman's appointee to develop a NATO army, he was clearly a "Europe-firster," whom no one could accuse of being an isolationist or a McCarthyite. Only the nomination of Richard Nixon as Eisenhower's running mate—creating a ticket that one critic likened to an

It would be very very fine if one could command new and amusing language—witticisms to bring you a chuckle. Frankly, I have no intention of trying to do so. The subjects of which we are speaking these days, my friends, are not those that seem to me to be amusing. . . . Is it amusing that we have stumbled into a war in Korea; that we have already lost in casualties 117,000 of our Americans killed and wounded; is it amusing that the war seems to be no nearer to a real solution than ever; that we have no real plan for stopping it? Is it funny when evidence was discovered that there are Communists in government . . . ?

Eisenhower, stepping up his crusade against Korea and communism, slashes at Stevenson's attempts at humor.

The Eisenhowers and the Nixons receiving the GOP nomination, July 1952.

alliance between Ulysses S. Grant and Dick Tracy—suggested that the GOP had pursued an abrasively partisan line for the past four years.

As the campaign developed, Eisenhower edged closer to his party's right wing. At the so-called Surrender on Morningside Heights in New York City, he met Taft, who had been nursing his grievances in silence, and agreed to support a conservative domestic policy if elected. He endorsed (with some qualifications) the party's platform calling for the "liberation" of countries under communist control. With other partisan orators he stressed the anti-Truman slogan of K_1C_2—Korea, Communism, and Corruption. Nixon denounced Stevenson as "Adlai the appeaser," who "carries a PH.D. from Dean Acheson's cowardly college of communist containment." Leaving nothing to chance, Eisenhower tried to secure McCarthyite support by deleting a paragraph from a Wisconsin speech praising his old boss, General Marshall. He closed the campaign by promising to go to Korea if elected. Ike, it appeared, would get the country out of the "mess" that Truman had caused in Asia.

Stevenson countered Eisenhower's attacks with wit and energy. But as a Democrat he was inevitably associated with Truman's policies. No one, therefore, was surprised when he was overwhelmed in November. Though he got 27.3 million votes, 3.2 million more than Truman received in 1948, he still trailed Eisenhower, who attracted a record 33.9 million voters, 12 million more than Dewey's total four years earlier. Breaking deeply into the Democratic coalition, Eisenhower swept all the big urban states and carried four states in the ordinarily Democratic South. Republicans even won majorities in both houses of Congress, for the second time since 1930. The result not only ended twenty years of Democratic dominance; it appeared to be a virtual revolution overthrowing the electoral universe that Al Smith and Franklin D. Roosevelt had forged in the previous generation.

Democratic gains in congressional elections throughout the 1950s revealed that no such revolution had taken place. Republicans, weakened in the depression years, remained the minority party. But the election of 1952 suggested the enormously important effect that an attractive candidate could have, and the degree to which formerly partisan voters were prepared to split their tickets. It also showed that the South, which had begun to rebel against Truman in 1948, was heading toward the Republican column. These trends toward electoral independence and discontinuity were to expand in the 1960s. Above all, the election of 1952 left little doubt that voters wanted a change in the White House and that Trumanism was almost a dirty word. Like Hoover

Election, 1952

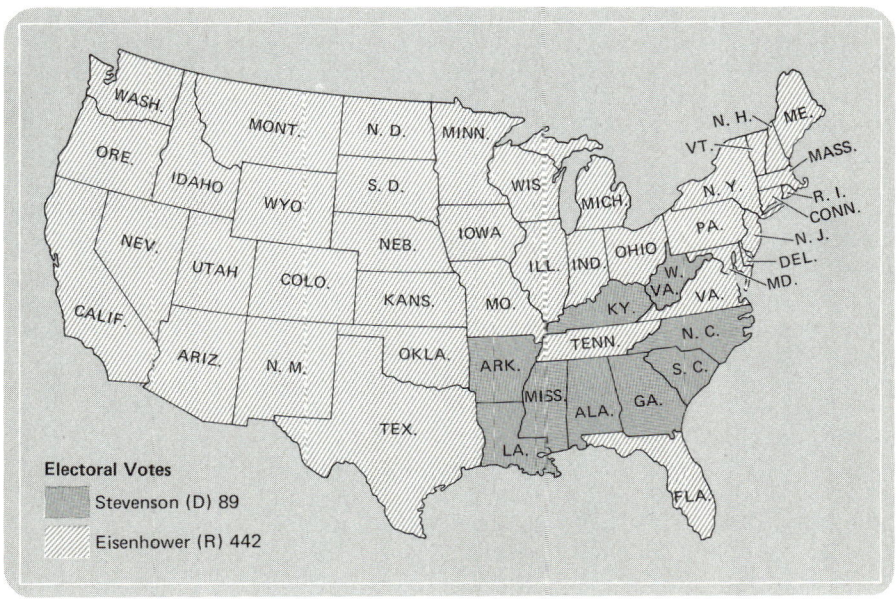

Electoral Votes
Stevenson (D) 89
Eisenhower (R) 442

in 1933, Johnson in 1969, and Nixon in 1974, Truman joined the group of modern American presidents who left office under clouds of disapproval.

Such a verdict, if that is what it was, was unfair, for Roosevelt's "Throttle-bottom" had proved a competent if uninspiring leader. Though partisan in dealing with Congress, he had managed to broaden the partial welfare state of the New Deal. Though inflexible and unsophisticated in diplomacy, he had occasionally proved enlightened, as in his support of foreign aid for Europe, and sometimes decisive as in his intervention in Korea. Given the domestic and international tensions of the time, to say nothing of the constraints imposed by the bureaucracy, by organized interest groups, and by the partisan atmosphere of domestic politics, he did a creditable job. As he left office in early 1953, it remained to be seen whether the GOP could do much better.

Suggestions for reading

Among the many accounts of foreign policy in the Truman years are Herbert Feis, *From Trust to Terror: The Onset of the Cold War, 1945–1950* (1970); Louis Halle, *The Cold War as History* (1967); and the revisionist interpretation by Walter LaFeber, *America, Russia, and the Cold War, 1945–1971** (1972). See also the books by Gaddis and Ambrose mentioned at the end of chapter 10. Revisionist accounts include Thomas Paterson, *Soviet-American Confrontation* (1974); Lloyd Gardner, *Architects of Illusion . . . 1941–1948* (1970); and Thomas Paterson, ed., *Cold War Critics** (1971). Important memoirs are George Kennan, *Memoirs, 1925–1950** (1967); and Dean Acheson, *Present at the Creation* (1969). Gaddis Smith, *Dean Acheson** (1972), is a useful biography. A revisionist account of the decision to drop the atomic bomb is Gar Alperovitz, *Atomic Diplomacy: Hiroshima and Potsdam** (1965). But see also Herbert Feis, *The Atomic Bomb and the End of World War II** (rev. ed., 1966), which refutes Alperovitz. A general study of Soviet-American relations is Adam Ulam, *The Rivals: America and Russia Since World War II** (1971).

Books on more specialized aspects of foreign policy include R. N. Gardner, *Sterling-Dollar Diplomacy* (1956); Tang Tsou, *America's Failure in China, 1941–1949** (1963); Herbert Feis, *The China Tangle* (1953); James Jones, *Fifteen Weeks** (1955), on the Truman Doctrine and the Marshall Plan; Robert Osgood, *NATO: Entangling Alliance* (1962); and Harry B. Price, *The Marshall Plan and Its Meaning** (1955). For the Korean War, consult David Rees, *Korea** (1964); and Ronald Caridi, *The Korean War and American Politics* (1968).

The most balanced book on the Truman administration is Alonzo Hamby, *Beyond the New Deal: Harry S. Truman and American Liberalism* (1973). Bert Cochran, *Harry S. Truman and the Crisis Presidency* (1973) is critical. Cabell Phillips, *The Truman Presidency** (1966) is laudatory. Barton Bernstein and Allen Matusow, eds., *Politics and Policies of the Truman Administration** (1970), is revisionist. Also, Richard Kirkendall, ed., *The Truman Period as a Research Field: A Reappraisal* (1974), offers conflicting interpretations. Richard Neustadt, *Presidential Power** (1960), includes case studies from the Truman administration. For political trends see V. O. Key, Jr., *Southern Politics* (1949); and the book by Samuel Lubell cited at the end of chapter 6. For the 1948 campaign consult Allen Yarnell, *Democrats and Progressives* (1974); Norman Markovitz, *Rise and Fall of the People's Century* (1973);

and Irwin Ross, *The Loneliest Campaign** (1968). James T. Patterson, *Mr. Republican: A Biography of Robert A. Taft** (1972) is a recent biography. Susan Hartmann, *Truman and the 80th Congress* (1971), competently covers its subject.

Books dealing with aspects of domestic policy are Edmund Flash, Jr., *Economic Advice and Presidential Leadership* (1965), on the Council of Economic Advisers; R. Alton Lee, *Truman and Taft-Hartley* (1967); Allen Matusow, *Farm Policies and Politics of the Truman Administration* (1967); Richard O. Davies, *Housing Reform During the Truman Administration** (1966); and A. E. Holmans, *United States Fiscal Policy, 1945–1959* (1961). For civil rights see William Berman, *The Politics of Civil Rights in the Truman Administration* (1970); and Donald McCoy and Richard Ruetten, *Quest and Response* (1973).

The subject of anticommunism has attracted many writers. Among the important books are David Shannon, *The Decline of American Communism* (1959); Earl Latham, *The Communist Conspiracy in Washington** (1966); Alan D. Harper, *The Politics of Loyalty, 1946–1952* (1969); Richard Rovere, *Senator Joe McCarthy** (1959), a brilliant study; and Robert Griffith, *The Politics of Fear** (1970), which focuses on the role of the Senate. Books highly critical of the Truman administration's anticommunism are Athan Theoharis, *Seeds of Repression: Harry S. Truman and the Origins of McCarthyism* (1971); and Richard Freeland, *The Truman Doctrine and the Origins of McCarthyism* (1971). Daniel Bell, ed., *Radical Right** (1963), includes essays stressing the role of social tensions in causing anticommunist hysteria. Michael Rogin, *The Intellectuals and McCarthy* (1967), criticizes the Bell volume and focuses on the impact of domestic politics.

12

The middle-class world of the 1950s

"We've grown unbelievably prosperous and we maunder along in a stupor of fat," the historian Eric Goldman wrote in 1960. "We live in a heavy, humorless, sanctimonious, stultifying atmosphere, singularly lacking in the self-mockery that is criticism. Probably the climate of the late 1950s was the dullest and dreariest in all our history." The journalist William Shannon agreed. The decade, he wrote, was one of "flabbiness and self-satisfaction and gross materialism. . . . The loudest sound in the land has been the oink and grunt of private hoggishness. . . . It has been the age of the slob."

Many liberals echoed Goldman and Shannon. The decade of the 1950s, these critics recognized, was a period of unprecedented prosperity. It was like the 1920s, they said: materialistic, self-satisfied, conformist, politically conservative, and apathetic.

The case against the 50s

Primary targets of such criticism were the suburban middle classes, which expanded dramatically in the postwar years. In 1940, 74.4 million of America's 132 million people (57 percent) had lived in cities, then defined by the census as places with 2500 or more people. By 1950, the Census Bureau recognized that this arbitrary definition excluded millions who lived in suburbs; so it broadened its definition of cities to include "densely settled urban fringes . . . around cities of 50,000 inhabitants or more." The number of urbanites then rose to 96.5 million in 1950, 124.7 million in 1960, and 149.3 million in 1970—73.5 percent of America's much-expanded population of 203 million. Meanwhile the number classified as "rural farm" dropped precipitously, from 30 million in 1940 to 23 million in 1950 to only 13.4 million in 1960.

These figures did not mean that central cities were growing. Quite the contrary, many of America's largest cities lost people between 1950 and 1960. The density of urban places during the same period declined from 5,408 inhabitants per square mile to 3,376. These one-time city people, plus millions more from the countryside, were flocking to the "settled urban fringes," which—thanks to the ubiquitous automobile—grew three times as rapidly as the overall population. By 1960 a "megalopolis" stretched much of the way between Boston and Washington. Cities, once thought of as concentric, self-contained areas, were now seen as linking up with one another in linear patterns sprawling along new roads and highways. Suburban areas around newer cities—Los Angeles, Dallas, Houston, Phoenix, San Diego—expanded fantastically. By 1970 some 80 million Americans lived in "suburbs." This was approximately 15 million more than lived in central cities, and more than the nation's entire population in 1900.

Naturally, the motives that inspired so many migrants varied widely. Millions fled the urban cores to escape countermigrations of blacks: in the 1950s alone America's twelve largest cities lost 2 million whites while gaining 1.8 million nonwhites. Millions more moved from the country to the city or from suburb to suburb in an apparently unceasing drive to better their social and economic status, to improve educational opportunities for their children, and—probably most important—to secure space and privacy. Some of these migrants were wealthy business and professional people who found open spaces many miles from downtown sections. Others were blue-collar workers of limited means—people who borrowed heavily to buy tiny houses or to rent flats in hastily constructed apartment houses. Such suburban areas, often heavily industrial, offered few of the amenities ordinarily associated with life outside the central city. The variety of suburbs, and of the motivations of the people who caused them to grow, almost defy description.

Generally, however, it is fair to identify most of the suburbanites as members of the white middle classes, which grew rapidly during the postwar era of bureaucratization, specialization, and technological change. As the number of farmers declined, and that of manual workers increased only slightly, the number of Americans classified as white-collar workers rose rapidly throughout the decades since 1940. By the mid-1950s such people outnumbered blue-collar laborers for the first time in American history. By 1970 they were close to 40 million strong, compared to 28.5 million blue-collar workers, 11 million service workers, and 3 million farm workers. Having

Surburban housing, often constructed of modular units, was built at a great rate during the 1950s.

escaped blue-collar status, many of these ''new'' white-collar families sought the space, the privacy, and the life-styles of the middle classes. In this way suburbanization and the process of becoming middle-class tended to develop together, as they already had in earlier decades, and to establish themselves as the most significant demographic movements of the 1950s.

These middle-class suburbs distressed many observers in the 1950s. Places like Levittown, Pennsylvania, one of many mass-produced communities catering to lower- and middle-income groups, received special criticism. So did more costly but aesthetically dull developments plastered on the once rural landscape. John Keats, author of the antisuburban book *The Crack in the Picture Window* (1961), dismissed them as "developments conceived in error, nurtured by greed, corroding everything they touch." To him as to

> Little boxes on the hillside
> Little boxes made of ticky-tacky
> Little boxes on the hillside.
> Little boxes all the same.
> There's a green one and a pink one
> And a blue one and a yellow one
> And they're all made out of ticky-tacky
> And they all look the same.

The folk singer Malvina Reynolds describes American postwar life.

other critics it seemed almost criminal that once picturesque countrysides should be bulldozed for houses or apartments, each with a TV antenna scarring a treeless sky. It seemed that a conspiracy of mercenary builders and ignorant architects was fastening a noose of vulgarity around the nation's cities.

Critics worried also about the human values nurtured by such humdrum surroundings. The "heroes" of Keats's book were John and Mary Drone—dull, purposeless materialists. Richard and Katherine Gordon, authors of *The Split-Level Trap* (1961), thought that the monotony of suburban existence promoted mental anguish and "Disturbia." And William H. Whyte, Jr.'s, widely discussed *Organization Man* (1956) bemoaned the fate that met the middle-class suburbanites of Park Forest, Illinois. Though Whyte considered Park Forest a pleasant, friendly place where newcomers were made to feel at home, he concluded that it was hell for people who valued privacy and nonconformity. The middle classes, Whyte implied, were losing themselves in a vast suburban sprawl (what others called "slurbs") of mediocrity and conformity.

The sociologist David Riesman made many of the same points in his book *The Lonely Crowd* (1950), which described the growth of conformist pressures not only in suburbia but in all areas of middle-class life. To Riesman, America had moved from an "inner-directed" culture in which people (through parental guidance) developed individualized goals to an "other-directed" society molded by peer-group pressures. Such a society, Riesman realized, could be more stable and even more tolerant than one composed of self-made men. But it helped create unventuresome little people like the boy who was asked, "Would you like to be able to fly?" and who answered, "I would like to be able to fly if everybody else did."

The alleged conformity of suburbia.

Drawing by Claude, © 1956 The New Yorker Magazine, Inc.

To writers like Dwight Macdonald the alleged deadness of contemporary life was especially clear in the arts. Unlike Great Britain or other western societies, Macdonald thought, America could not sustain a High Culture. Instead, it had purely commercial television and radio, comic books and cartoon strips that sold by the millions, and "masscult," a parody of High Culture that featured sentimental painters like Norman Rockwell and pseudo-theologians like Norman Vincent Peale. Worst of all, America was becoming swamped by "midcult," which Macdonald thought "watered down and vulgarized" the standards of High Culture. Examples of midcult were Hemingway's *Old Man and the Sea* (1952), Thornton Wilder's nostalgic *Our Town*, and selections by such purveyors of "culture" as the Book-of-the-Month Club. So long as readers preferred *The Saturday Evening Post* and *Readers Digest* to serious literature, America would remain a nation of cultural philistines.

Many of these critics focused on what they saw as the self-indulgence, purposelessness, and lack of discipline in American society during the 1950s. The United States, wrote the novelist John Updike, "is like an unloved child smothered in candy. God doesn't love us any more. He loves Russia. He loves Uganda. We're fat and full of pimples and always yearning for more candy. We've fallen from grace." The economist John Kenneth Galbraith, in his book *The Affluent Society* (1958), showed that Americans spent billions on consumer goods—TV sets, home freezers, household gadgets, above all, automobiles—while scrimping on necessary public services. Conservatives worried that the consumer society of the 1950s was inducing national flabbiness. "If you ask me," George Kennan wrote, " . . . whether a country that is in the state this country is in today: with no highly developed sense of national purpose, with the overwhelming accent of life on personal comfort and amusement, with a dearth of public services and a surfeit of privately sold gadgetry . . . if you ask me whether such a country has, over the long run, a good chance of competing with a purposeful, serious, and disciplined society such as that of the Soviet Union, I must say that the answer is 'No.'"

Observers of many persuasions shared Kennan's concern over the nation's spirit. Mort Sahl, the comedian, put it simply by mocking the confusion of American "turncoats" in Korea. "The turncoats were steadfast," he quipped. "They refused to give anything except their name, rank, and the exact position of their unit." Paul Goodman, a radical critic, complained that productive work was no longer important, that far too many people shuffled papers or tried to "beat the system." Young people, "growing up absurd," wanted to be movie stars instead of useful adults. And other critics, including Pitirim Sorokin, a distinguished Harvard sociologist, worried that Americans, lacking a sense of purpose, were wallowing in sex. He concluded: "Unless we develop an inner immunity against these libidinal forces, we are bound to be conquered by the continuous army of omnipresent sex stimuli."

Sorokin's worries were exaggerated. Though Alfred Kinsey, an Indiana University researcher, published tomes (*Sexual Behavior in the Human Male* [1948] and *Sexual Behavior in the Human Female* [1953]) that suggested large numbers of young people were indulging in premarital sex (and breaking outdated laws in the process), he scarcely supported the notion that sexual immorality was sweeping the nation. His researches also suggested that American sexual behavior had changed primarily in the 1910s and 1920s, not in the supposedly degenerate postwar years. Scott Donaldson, a balanced observer of suburban trends, added that young people "talked a great deal about sex, but it's all rather clinical, and outside of the marriage no one seems to do much about it." The very alarm displayed at the publication of Kinsey's "statistical filth" underlined the continued power of conventional ideas concerning sex, indeed of prudery, in the American consciousness.

The broadsides against philistinism were equally exaggerated. Scores of previous observers had lambasted America's material greed and cultural

. . . youngsters, instead of being sheltered and disciplined as they once were, are now exposed to the seamy side of sex in its rawest forms before they have the faintest concept of its total meaning in life. We have only to look about us to realize that, as a nation, we are preoccupied—almost obsessed—with the superficial aspects of sex, with sex as a form of amusement. This is not true sex, with the corollaries of love, marriage and childbearing. It is an almost hysterical bandying about of sex symbols, coming close to fetish worship. (Consider the present over-emphasis of the breast, the stressing of erotic qualities in perfume.)

Dr. Goodrich C. Schauffler, a gynecologist, joins others in the 1950s in bewailing the triumph of sex.

crudity. Like Macdonald, they tended to be elitists who would not accept the simple fact that people in most societies prefer personal comfort to High Culture. As one sensible writer pointed out, "the critic waves the prophet's long and accusing finger and warns: 'You may *think* you're happy, you smug and prosperous striver, but I tell you that the anxieties of status mobility are too much; they impoverish you psychologically, they alienate you from your family'; and so on. And the suburbanite looks at his new house, his new car, his new freezer, his lawn and patio, and to be sure, his good credit, and scratches his head, bewildered." Postwar Americans were not more materialistic than earlier generations—just incomparably richer. They were able to buy and to enjoy things that their parents could only dream about.

As careful critics recognized, it was also simplistic to paste labels on a society as diverse as the United States. What might apply to the corporate middle class (or some part of it) did not necessarily describe farmers, blacks, ethnics, blue-collar people, or many others in the enormously varied middle classes. What may have been true of some suburbanites was not in the least true of others—who resembled each other (if at all) primarily in their dependence on the automobile, their geographical mobility, and their lack of attachment to place. It was equally hazardous to contend that "other-directedness" was new or on the upswing. Indeed, peer group pressures in nineteenth-century American towns may have been more formidable than in the ever changing suburbs of the 1950s. Those who perceived only conformity also overlooked the continuing stress on personal achievement and—especially in the prosperous postwar years—the yearning for self-growth and psychological inner development. The very attention accorded such books as *Organization Man* suggested that many Americans, including the middle classes who were supposedly so mindless, were as anxious as their ancestors had been to surmount the homogenizing pressures of life.

A similar yearning for self-expression prompted some of the major trends in art forms during the decade. The "method" style of acting associated with young stars like James Dean and Marlon Brando attempted to approach "reality" through the emotions of the individuals on stage, not through rational speech or dialogue. Poets and dramatists reacted against the social realism of the 1930s and insisted on writing for themselves, not for causes. "A successful poem," the writer Leslie Fiedler explained, "is a complete and final act; if it leads outward to other action, it is just so far a failure." The director Alan Schneider later added, "we all have got to stop looking at all our plays as though they were socialist realism. . . . We can no longer go back to the well-made play because we haven't got a well-made world."

In the same way young painters like Jackson Pollock developed a wholly nonrepresentational style variously called Abstract Expressionism and Action Painting. Reflecting existentialist beliefs, they argued that a work of art must reflect the spontaneous, individual emotions of the creator. Art was a process of expression, not a static final product. Pollock, indeed, came to stand on his canvasses, flinging paint on them with apparently reckless abandon. "What was to go on the canvas," the critic Harold Rosenberg explained approvingly, "was not a picture but an event. . . . It is the artist's existence . . . he is living on the canvas. . . . What gives the canvas meaning is . . . the way the artist organized his emotional and intellectual energy as if he were in a living situation."

This desire to be one's self, to overcome organizational constraints, helped to explain the critical acclaim bestowed in the 1950s on novelists otherwise as diverse as J. D. Salinger, Saul Bellow, and John Updike. In *Catcher in the Rye* (1951) Salinger's "hero" is Holden Caulfield, a supersensitive adolescent bent on preserving innocence against "perverts" and "phonies" who wanted him to conform. Most of Bellow's protagonists, in books such as *Dangling Man* (1946), *Adventures of Augie March* (1949), and *Herzog* (1961), are bemused men who revolt against what Augie called the "shame of purpose-lessness." Like Huckleberry Finn (who also had "adventures"), they tried to be true to themselves. Updike's Rabbit Angstrom in *Rabbit Run* (1961) is a similarly confused young man who looks desperately—and unsuccessfully— for ways to bring back the excitement and meaning of his high school days. Characters like these were hardly tough like John Wayne or Gary Cooper,

> *The quest, I am beginning to think, whether it be for money, for notoriety, reputation, increase of pride, whether it leads us to thievery, slaughter, sacrifice, the quest is one and the same. All the striving is for one end. I do not entirely understand this impulse. But it seems to me that its final end is the desire for pure freedom. We are all drawn toward the same craters of the spirit—to know what we are and what we are for, to know our purpose, to seek grace. And, if the quest is the same, the differences in our personal histories, which hitherto meant so much to us, become of minor importance.*
>
> Saul Bellow's character Joseph in *Dangling Man* (1946) expresses a feeling later echoed by many of the most memorable characters in post war American fiction.

. . . we get a clear but exaggerated *picture of our American society. It has: slums of engineering—boondoggling production—chaotic congestion— tribes of middlemen—basic city functions squeezed out—garden cities for children—indifferent workmen—underprivileged on a dole—empty "belonging" without nature or culture—front politicians—no patriotism— an empty nationalism bound for a cataclysmically disastrous finish—wise opinion swamped—enterprise sabotaged by monopoly—prejudice rising— religion otiose—the popular culture debased—science specialized—sci- ence secret—the average man inept—youth idle and truant—youth sex- ually suffering and sexually obsessed—youth without goals—poor schools.*

Paul Goodman, in *Growing Up Absurd* (1957), expresses a radically unhappy view of American society.

masculine heroes of film. They had none of the rebellious individuality of James Dean. Rather, they were fearful, confused, buffeted about—passive victims of larger forces. But they did not surrender. They were existentialist antiheroes who at least survived.

These thrusts against conformity led in the late 1950s to a vogue among more radical students for books like C. Wright Mills's *Power Elite* (1956), Jack Kerouac's *On the Road* (1956), and Paul Goodman's *Growing up Absurd* (1957). The three men held differing social philosophies: Mills was a Marxist sociologist, Kerouac a "beat" novelist who celebrated free-wheeling noncon- formity, Goodman a philosophical anarchist who combined Veblen's passion for productive labor, Freud's stress on the need for physical love, and the urban planner Ebenezer Howard's vision of decentralized communities and garden cities. Yet all three men agreed that America—in Goodman's words a "rat race," in Mills's a "great salesroom, an enormous file, an incorporated brain, a new universe of management and manipulation"—stifled creative talent. For them, as for many less radical thinkers, large-scale organization was the enemy. Their appeal to young nonconformists suggested that the 1950s were less serene and complacent than they sometimes appeared.

CAUSES FOR ALARM

Still, there was no denying that many aspects of American life in the 1950s supported the critics of conformity and materialism. One of these was the growth of the huge, bureaucratic corporation. As Adolf Berle and Gardiner Means had pointed out in the early 1930s—and as James Burnham had stressed in his *Managerial Revolution* (1939)—"faceless" bureaucrats were dominating the ever growing corporations. These early writers had worried more about the power of such organizations than about the psyches of their employees. But by the 1950s it was clear that many corporations (to say nothing of government, the biggest bureaucracy of all) stressed "teamwork" and frowned on mavericks. Some, such as IBM, even outlined acceptable standards of dress and decorum. Alarmed, Mills perceived the coming of a "white collar" society in which people would be "estranged from community . . . in a context of distrust and manipulation, alienated from work and, in the personality market, from self, expropriated of individual rationality, and politically apathetic." Mills was wrong to assume that organizations could wholly transform people's minds. But he was perceptive in pointing to the growth of propagandists for "togetherness" and the "need to belong."

The call for togetherness also helped sustain a Cult of Domesticity in the 1950s. More than over before—or so it seemed—Americans yearned to enmesh themselves in the "tender trap" of marriage, parenthood, and the nuclear family. During the late 1940s and early 1950s people continued to marry young and to have children quickly. As a result the baby boom, which demographers had expected would decrease shortly after World War II, continued until the mid-1950s. The nation's population increased from 151 million to 180 million people between 1950 and 1960. This was the largest growth in any decade of American history (before or since). The rate of increase (19 percent) was the greatest since 1910, when heavy immigration had helped to swell the pace of growth.

Few people during the 1950s expressed much alarm about the ecological results of such expansion. The baby boom, they said, helped to sustain prosperity, especially in the construction industry, which was kept busy building approximately 1 million new homes per year throughout the 1950s. By 1960 more Americans owned their homes (with mortgages) than rented, for the first time in the twentieth century. The majority of such homes had the creature comforts that the media promoted as the joys of domesticity and parenthood.

The presumed blessings of domesticity helped to weaken feminism in the 1950s. Feminists, the Women's Bureau of the federal government had announced a few years earlier, were a "small but militant group of leisure class women [giving vent] to their resentment at not having been born men."

Adlai Stevenson added, "the assignment for you, as women and mothers, you can do in the living room with a baby in your lap or in the kitchen with a can opener in your hand. . . . there is much you can do about our crisis in the humble role of housewife. I could wish you no better vocation than that." Dr. Benjamin Spock, whose *Baby and Child Care* (1946) was a huge seller in the 1950s and 1960s, urged the government to pay mothers so they would not leave the home for employment.

Such defenders of domesticity overlooked continuing growth in female employment, a profound demographic development that helped sustain the movement for women's liberation a decade later. But movies and magazines undercut feminism. Hollywood glorified sweet types like Doris Day and Debby Reynolds or sex objects like Marilyn Monroe. Fashion designers popularized spike-heeled shoes, crinolines, and the "baby doll" look. The "ladies" magazines extolled the satisfactions of motherhood and home management. Women, like men in the apparently unventuresome postwar era, seemed to know and accept their status.

There was cause also to worry about the impact of the mass media, particularly television, which one critic labeled the "cheekiest, vulgarest, most disgraceful form of entertainment since bear-baiting, dog-fighting, and the seasonal Czarist Russian pogrom." Like others, he lamented the omnipresence of violence, the virtual absence of serious drama or music, above all the pandering to the commercial nature of the medium. Like the mass circulation magazines and newspapers, TV constantly flashed expensive luxury goods before the consumer. No one, of course, could prove that TV or the other media actually caused people to buy certain goods, much less to become conformists. Indeed, it was possible that the bombardment of images undercut the last vestiges of provincialism and broadened the experience, and the vision, of millions. But by 1960 it was also clear that TV, by invading practically every American home for several hours a day, was projecting a peculiarly middle-class world and stifling dissent. It was also ignoring (or stereotyping) the millions who belonged to minority groups. At best, the mass media were promoting the status quo.

Another sign of blandness in the 1950s was what some contemporaries labeled the "new piety." By 1960 this was reflected in a rise in the percentage of Americans (95%) who identified with a religious denomination. Lesser manifestations of this trend abounded: a new stamp issue proclaimed "In God We Trust"; "Under God" was added to the pledge of allegiance; the practice in Eisenhower's administration of opening meetings with a prayer. Subway posters proclaimed, "Go to church. You'll feel better. Bring your troubles to church and leave them there." Capitalizing on this search for faith, the evangelist Billy Graham "converted" millions during the postwar era, while Bishop Fulton J. Sheen and the Reverend Norman Vincent Peale reached out to the middle classes over the radio and in magazine columns. "Flush out all depressing, negative, and tired thoughts," Peale told his readers in *Look* magazine. "Start thinking faith, enthusiasm, and joy."

This kind of exhortation was nothing new in the American experience, where faith in faith had long enjoyed support. Peale's "power of positive thinking" was a modernized version of Christian Science. Nor was the search for piety hypocritical: the rapid growth of fundamentalist churches during the postwar era suggested that millions of Americans, including many migratory blacks and poor whites, earnestly sought comfort against the forces of urbanization and technological change. But the theologian Will Herberg was correct in stressing, in *Protestant Catholic Jew* (1956), that for most Americans religion had lost its theological meaning. Instead, the churches supported a "civic religion," which sustained the status quo and the "American Way of Life." Far from promoting a Great Awakening, the search for piety revealed a quest for social status and identity.

Like the churches, schools reflected this concern for helping people find their place in mass society. Such a note had been sounded as early as 1939 by Charles Prosser, a leading advocate of vocational education. "The important thing," Prosser said, "is not to teach students how to generalize but to supply them directly with the information they need for daily living." By the early 1950s this focus on "life adjustment" challenged many earlier pedagogical theories, including the stress on the Three R's, Dewey's idea that schools could promote social reform, or the progressive hope that teachers would stimulate the latent creativity of children. Instead, schools offered subjects like "How can I keep well?" "How can I look my best?" "How can I get along better with others?" and "How can hobbies contribute to my social growth?" The historian Richard Hofstadter complained that one New York community required a course in "Home and Family Living" for all children in grades seven through ten. The course featured such topics as "developing school spirit," "clicking with the crowd," "how to be liked," and "what can be done about acne?" Other reformers complained that college youth in the 1950s had become the "Silent Generation," interested in football, fraternities, and, upon graduation, in well-paid security with General Motors, Wall Street, and Madison Avenue. Campus radicalism was so hard to detect that Kenneth Keniston, an acute observer of American youth, complained as late as 1962, "I see little likelihood of American students ever playing a radical role, much less a revolutionary one, in our society."

Hofstadter and others exaggerated the staying power of "life adjustment" in the curriculum. Indeed, traditionalists (who complained that students weren't "learning" anything) successfully counterattacked in the late 1950s, especially after the Soviet Union beat the United States in the race to outer space. Diatribes against campus complacency were short-sighted, for American university students, sons and daughters of the more affluent classes, had rarely shown sustained interest in social reform. It is also clear that some critics of American education placed too much faith in the potential of schools to transcend environmental forces. Schools, after all, are rarely much different from society at large. But that was partly Hofstadter's point: schools, like churches, like corporations, seemed bent on preserving the existing order.

So, too, were many people who had been sharp critics of American life in the 1930s. These included such one-time foes of big business as Adolf Berle and David Lilienthal, both of whom changed their minds in the 1950s. Large corporations, they pointed out, were better able to preserve job security, to pay decent wages, to promote research and development. Labor leaders seemed equally tame in the 1950s. Though they grumbled loudly about Taft-Hartley, they eschewed the militant tactics of the late 1930s. With a few exceptions, such as auto workers' leader Walter Reuther, they neglected the problems of nonunion workers, of blacks, or of other minority groups. The reality of the 1950s for most union spokesmen was unprecedented affluence. In such an age it was foolish to promote class divisions, to talk about trust-busting, or to "spout Marxist clichés."

This moderation found approving interpreters among America's leading intellectuals of the 1950s. These included the historian Daniel Boorstin and the sociologist Daniel Bell. Both welcomed what they considered the stability and consensus of American society. In *The Genius of American Politics* (1953) Boorstin described the national experience as one in which compromise and practicality overcame ideologies and class conflicts. Bell, a prolific writer, gathered many of his essays into a volume entitled *The End of Ideology* (1960). America, he said, was a flexible, pluralistic nation in which many groups vied for position. It was a much more humane, stable society than the Soviet Union, which vividly exposed the dangers of absolutist ideology. These defenders of "consensus" underrated the degree of ethnic, racial, and class conflict in the American past, and they falsely assumed that ideology—or at least activism—was dead. "It's like an old man proclaiming the end of sex," one youthful rebel later sneered. "Because he doesn't feel it anymore, he thinks it has disappeared."

Bell was right, however, in arguing that leftist thinkers made little headway in the 1950s. Thanks to the Cold War, and especially to Korea, Communists and Socialists virtually disappeared. The Progressive party lost what little hope it had had for survival as a political force when Henry Wallace deserted it to back the Korean War. Liberal groups such as the Americans for Democratic Action continued to press for progressive domestic reforms, but they remained on the defensive against McCarthyites who branded intellectuals as "parlor pinks" or communists. As if to prove otherwise, the ADA insisted loudly that it, too, hated the Reds. The weakness of the Left in the 1950s revealed the pervasive impact of the Cold War, the intimidating force of McCarthyism, and the dominance of "middle American" values.

The primary support for such attitudes was the unparalleled affluence of the decade. In constant prices the GNP had already jumped from $205 billion in 1940 to $318 billion in 1950. During the 1950s it leaped again, to $440 billion in 1960. In per capita terms this meant an increase from $1,550 in 1940 to $2,100 in 1950 to $2,435 in 1960. It meant striking advances in life expectancy, education levels, and in disposable income. In the 1950s, consumer credit leaped from $8.4 billion to $45 billion. Workers, who had averaged forty-five

Economic growth, 1950–1960, compared to select years before and after this period

| | NATIONAL PRODUCT AND INCOME (In billions of current dollars) | | | | PER CAPITA DISPOSABLE INCOME (In current dollars) |
	GNP	PERCENT CHANGE FROM GNP OF PRECEDING YEAR (+ OR −)	NATIONAL INCOME	DISPOSABLE PERSONAL INCOME	
1929	103.1	n.d.	86.8	83.3	683
1933	55.6	− 4.2	40.3	45.5	362
1940	99.7	+10.2	81.1	75.7	573
1944	210.1	+ 9.7	182.6	146.3	1,057
1946	208.5	− 1.6	181.9	160.0	1,132
1950	284.8	+11.0	241.1	206.9	1,364
1951	328.4	+15.3	278.0	226.6	1,469
1952	345.5	+ 5.2	291.4	238.3	1,518
1953	364.6	+ 5.5	304.7	252.6	1,583
1954	364.8	+ 0.1	303.1	257.4	1,585
1955	398.0	+ 9.1	331.0	275.3	1,666
1956	419.2	+ 5.3	350.8	293.2	1,743
1957	441.1	+ 5.2	366.1	303.5	1,801
1958	447.3	+ 1.4	367.8	318.8	1,831
1959	483.7	+ 8.2	400.0	337.3	1,905
1960	503.7	+ 4.1	414.5	350.0	1,937
1970	977.1	+ 5.0	800.5	691.7	3,376
1973	1,294.9	+11.8	1,065.6	903.7	4,295

SOURCE: Adapted from Council of Economic Advisers, "Annual Report, January 1975" in *Economic Report of the President* (Washington, D.C., 1975), pp. 249, 267, 269

hours a week in the 1920s, enjoyed work weeks averaging less than forty hours by 1960, plus annual vacations of at least two weeks. The simplest way to describe the affluence of the 1950s is to note that the average American had twice as much real income to spend (and more time to spend it in) in the mid-1950s than in the supposedly boom times of the late 1920s.

Many forces produced this growth. Among them was the willingness of the private sector to risk funds for investment. Between 1946 and 1958, when a slump hit the economy, Americans pumped an average of $10 billion per year into new plant and equipment. Another was technological change including computers, which became important by the early 1960s. Labor-saving devices understandably alarmed many people, especially in agriculture and in such industries as textiles, where the labor force declined by more than 30 percent between 1945 and 1960. But technological advances also created jobs, especially for white-collar "service" workers. Such areas as electronics and plastics expanded phenomenally during the years between 1945 and 1960.

The public sector played an indispensable role in promoting this prosperity. Much of the economic growth of the period stemmed directly from governmental expenditures for World War II and Korea. Military spending, which approached $40 billion per year in the peacetime years of the 1950s, accounted for approximately 60 percent of federal budgets and 10 percent of the GNP. Overall public expenditures—federal, state, and local—had amounted to only 10 percent of the GNP in 1929; by the mid-1950s they accounted for more than 25 percent. Governments directly employed more than 8 million people by 1957, double the number in 1940. Government work, overwhelmingly white-collar, was the fastest growing area of the economy.

Books like Galbraith's *Affluent Society* accurately exposed many limits to this affluence: technological unemployment, depressed areas, slums, inadequate health care, decaying urban schools, racial injustice. The distribution of income remained inequitable, and poverty was much more widespread than people realized. Almost 13 million families earned less than $4000 per year before taxes in 1955. In the same year, the poorest fifth of American families earned 4.8 percent of the national income, while the top fifth earned 20.3 percent. Also, the rate of economic growth slowed down considerably late in the decade. The affluence of the 1950s did not reach as far or last as long as most people thought.

In history, however, what people think is often more important than reality. Sure that ever greater prosperity lay ahead, Americans remained blind to the signs of poverty and stagnation. Moreover, there was no denying the fact of economic growth or of the boundless supplies of gadgetry available (on credit) to the majority of people. The United States, the richest nation in world history, was wealthier than it had ever been and incomparably more prosperous than in the 1930s. In such a world it was not at all surprising that self-satisfaction and materialism seemed stronger than in many periods of the American past.

THE ASCENDANCY OF THE RIGHT

Those who hoped for social reform found this complacency ominous indeed. As progressives were forced to recognize, people were tired of the Korean War and of partisan controversy. They wanted to be left alone to enjoy their material rewards. Though Americans voted Democratic in congressional elections (even in 1956), they showed little taste for progressive legislation. Like the 1920s, the decade was the despair of reformers.

In such an atmosphere Senator McCarthy continued to thrive. Because the GOP controlled the Congress in 1953, he became chairman of his own investigating committee, which he used to step up his accusations of communist subversion in government. His top aide, Roy Cohn, and Cohn's friend, G. David Schine, toured American embassies in Europe, where they searched for leftist books in government libraries and made a laughing stock of the State Department. A few books were actually burned. McCarthy even cowed the new administration into permitting endless security checks on high-ranking employees, some of whom were forced to resign not because they were disloyal but because they were what the government now vaguely termed "security risks." Among these, amazingly enough, was J. Robert Oppenheimer, "father of the atomic bomb," whose security clearance was taken away in December, 1953, on the grounds that he opposed development of the H-bomb and had associated with left-wingers in the 1930s. A newsman who returned to Washington after an extended absence in 1954 was appalled. "I let myself into the State Department," he wrote, "and there encountered a few 'Acheson holdovers' cowering in their corners. They were aged and their voices were low. But oddly enough, some of the new Republican appointees whom I met seemed to have muffled voices too. . . . it was like Vienna all over again, where we had learned to beware of eavesdroppers."

McCarthy then turned his guns on the army, which had refused to give preferential treatment to Schine, a draftee. During the course of his investigation McCarthy discovered that a left-wing dentist, Dr. Irving Peress, had been permitted to resign from the service with the rank of major. Probing further, he demanded that army brass disclose the names of officers involved in the affair. When the army proved slow to cooperate, McCarthy exploded. "You are a disgrace to the uniform," he told Brigadier General Ralph Zwicker. "You're shielding communist conspirators. You're not fit to be an officer. You're ignorant." Attacks such as these made the hearings, which were televised in the spring of 1954, the most compelling entertainment of the year.

In making such accusations, McCarthy overreached himself. Seeing McCarthy on TV, many Americans began to realize what a barbarian he was. Conservative supporters of the military establishment stiffened. As his appeal ebbed, the Senate roused itself against his insults. (He had described Senator Robert Hendrickson of New Jersey as a "living miracle in that he is without question the only man who has lived so long with neither brains nor guts.") In December 1954 the Senate at last voted, sixty-seven to twenty-two, to "condemn" McCarthy for bringing the Congress into disrepute. McCarthy remained in the Senate, but he was burned out, a casualty of his exaggerations, his alcoholic tendency, and his tiresome repetitions. Three years later, at the age of forty-eight, he died.

McCarthy's downfall, however, did not deter the extreme right wing, which became ever more shrill as the decade progressed. It included members of such superpatriotic groups as the John Birch Society and the Christian Anti-Communist Crusade. One of the right-wing leaders, Fred Schwartz, announced that the communists planned to take over in 1973. "When they come for you, as they have for many others, on a dark night, in a dank cellar, they take a wide-bore revolver with a soft-nose bullet, and they place it at the nape of your neck." Robert Welch, founder of the John Birch Society, insisted that the Soviets were proceeding against America "on the soundest of strategy. It calls for paralyzing their enemy and their enemy's will to resist by internal subversion before ever striking a blow." Eisenhower, Welch concluded, was a "dedicated, conscious agent of the communist conspiracy."

This "Radical Right," as it was called, was much too extreme to be taken seriously by the voters. Unlike McCarthyism, which had a mass base, it appealed primarily to superpatriots and reactionaries who had been ranting against "big government" since 1933. Still, by 1961, a Gallup poll reported that the goals of the John Birch Society were approved by 7 million Americans. The far Right's hostility to big government also had the support of aggressive conservatives in Congress. Among these were Pat McCarran, an obsessively anticommunist Democratic senator from Nevada; conservative Democratic colleagues such as John McClellan of Arkansas and James Eastland of Mississippi; and reactionary solons like William Jenner of Indiana and Barry Goldwater of Arizona.

By mid-decade many of these men were focusing their attacks on the Supreme Court, which they said was "coddling" communists and other undesirables, including blacks. Led by Chief Justice Earl Warren, whom Eisenhower appointed to the court in 1953, the judges revealed their liberal orientation in 1954 by ruling unanimously (in *Brown* v. *Board of Education*) against school segregation. "Separate educational facilities," the Court said in reversing precedents dating from *Plessy* v. *Ferguson* (1896), "are inherently unequal . . . segregation is a denial of the equal protection of the laws." The Court in 1955 then called for school desegregation with "all deliberate speed." Outraged, Senator Eastland denounced the Court's "monstrous crime. . . . These antagonistic decisions are . . . bent upon the destruction of the American form of government and the mongrelization of the white race." Led by Eastland, nineteen southern senators and seventy-seven representatives signed a manifesto in 1956 that bound them to "use all lawful means to bring about a reversal of this decision which is contrary to the Court and to prevent the use of force in its implementation." Among southern senators only Lyndon Johnson of Texas and Estes Kefauver and Albert Gore of Tennessee refused to sign.

Having infuriated the South, the Court then asked for trouble with Red-haters and advocates of what President Nixon was later to celebrate as "law and order." In *Jencks* v. *U. S.* (1956) it ruled that a labor leader had been unfairly tried because he had not been permitted to see prosecutors' files. In *Service* v. *Dulles* (1957) it reinstated John Service, a State Department expert on China who had been dismissed in 1951 after six loyalty clearances. The decision forced the administration to clarify its procedures concerning so-called security risks in government. In *Mallory* v. *U. S.* (1957), it ruled that an accused rapist had been illegally charged because he had been held too long before being brought before a magistrate. Alleged criminals, the Court ruled, must be arraigned "without unnecessary delay." And in *Yates* v. *U. S.* (1956) the Court reversed the conviction of fourteen Communists jailed under the Smith Act of 1940. Mere advocacy of revolution, the Court stated, did not constitute grounds for convictions. The government must prove that defendants had "organized" revolution and that they had succeeded. The ruling caused the government to drop plans for further prosecutions of Communists.

These decisions began a judicial trend, much accelerated in the 1960s, toward greater federal guarantees for accused criminals and subversives. They showed that the Court had moved beyond the paralyzing anticommunism of the McCarthy era. The Bill of Rights, it seemed, meant what it said. But the decisions also prompted right-wingers to finance "Impeach Earl Warren" billboards along the nation's highways. A Cleveland paper intoned (after the *Jencks* decision) that the FBI might as well "close up shop, for the Court had opened their files to the criminal and thus afforded him a Roman holiday for rummaging through confidential materials as well as vital national secrets." Edward Corwin, professor of constitutional law at Princeton, wrote *The New York Times* to complain that the Court had gone on a "virtual binge" and "should have its aforesaid nose tweaked." Most alarming to friends of the Court, a bipartisan congressional coalition almost put through legislation in 1958 that would have stripped the Court of its appellate jurisdiction in cases dealing with loyalty programs, contempt of Congress, state sedition statutes, regulations of employment and oaths of allegiance in schools, and admission to state law practice. Only careful maneuvering by Majority Leader Lyndon Johnson managed the forty-nine to forty-one vote that prevented the law from passing the Senate.

A handful of liberal Democratic senators struggled against these right-wing pressures of the 1950s. They included Hubert Humphrey of Minnesota, a crusader for civil rights; Estes Kefauver of Tennessee, who battled for curbs on monopoly and false advertising; and Paul Douglas, an innovative reformer who developed in the 1950s much of the economic legislation of Kennedy's New Frontier and Johnson's Great Society. Still powerful in the national party, these liberals nominated a progressive ticket composed of Stevenson and Kefauver in 1956. (Senator John F. Kennedy, less experienced and less liberal than Kefauver, sought the vice-presidency and failed.) The prominence of such men suggested that liberalism was neither dead nor dying in the 1950s.

But it remained on the defensive. Bowing to the anticommunist hysteria, liberals like Humphrey and Douglas joined moderates like Kennedy in backing legislation in 1954 to outlaw the Communist party. In 1956 Democrats feared to mention national health insurance in their platform. Stevenson, attempting to placate the South, exclaimed during his campaign that the federal government must not send in money or troops to enforce desegregation. "I think that would be a great mistake," he said. "That is exactly what brought on the Civil War. It can't be done by troops, or bayonets. We must proceed gradually, not upsetting habits or traditions that are older than the Republic."

Stevenson lost more heavily to Eisenhower in 1956 than he had in 1952, even though his foe had suffered a heart attack in 1955. But if he had won, he would have had no chance of putting a liberal program through Congress.

There the power lay, as it had since the Democrats won majorities in 1954, with moderates led by Johnson in the Senate and by his Texan friend, Sam Rayburn, Speaker of the House. Shrewd and tireless, both men were cool to liberals like Humphrey or Douglas. They feared to provoke the right-wingers on both sides of the aisle. And like most Americans in the 1950s, they did not want to rock the boat. Even in 1959, when a band of young liberals entered Congress, and in 1961, when President Kennedy launched his New Frontier, these moderates remained in control. This "Four-Party Government," as political scientist James Macgregor Burns described the coexistence of the more conservative congressional wings of both parties with their more liberal national wings, remained a basic reality of American politics in the 1950s.

President Eisenhower

Dwight D. Eisenhower, who presided over most of the 1950s, was the nation's most admired war hero in 1945. Decent, democratic, decisive, he had seemed a nonauthoritarian officer as well as a just and likeable man. Truman had told him at Potsdam, "General, there is nothing that you may want that I won't try to help you get. That definitely and specifically includes the presidency in 1948."

By that time, of course, Truman had changed his mind. But politicians of both parties yearned to nominate their hero, both then and in 1952. Like the American people, they were taken by his presence, his air of command, by what the reporter Robert Donovan called his "leaping and effortless smile." People responded also to his moderation, his balanced judgment, and his apparent aloofness from the intrigue of politics. The new president, it appeared, was heaven-sent to deliver the nation from the acrimony of the early 1950s. Like a benign father bringing peace to a quarrelsome tribe, Eisenhower seemed untouchable at the polls.

Even liberals were prepared to accept him at first. Though to the right of Stevenson, he seemed to provide a sharp contrast to the conservatives in his party who had supported Taft. This image was more appearance than reality, for the new president considered Taft socialistic on such issues as public housing and aid to education. Nevertheless, Eisenhower was apparently willing to maintain the government's active role in the economy. "Never again," he said during the campaign, "shall we allow a depression in the United States." As soon as we "foresee the signs of any recession and depression . . . the full power of private industry, of municipal government, of state government, of the Federal Government will be mobilized to see that that does not happen." This "Modern Republicanism," as his liberal supporters in the eastern wing of the party liked to call it, suggested that the GOP had left Hooverism far behind.

In the late 1960s and 1970s historians of his administration began to appreciate still another of Eisenhower's virtues. This was his shrewdness. Far

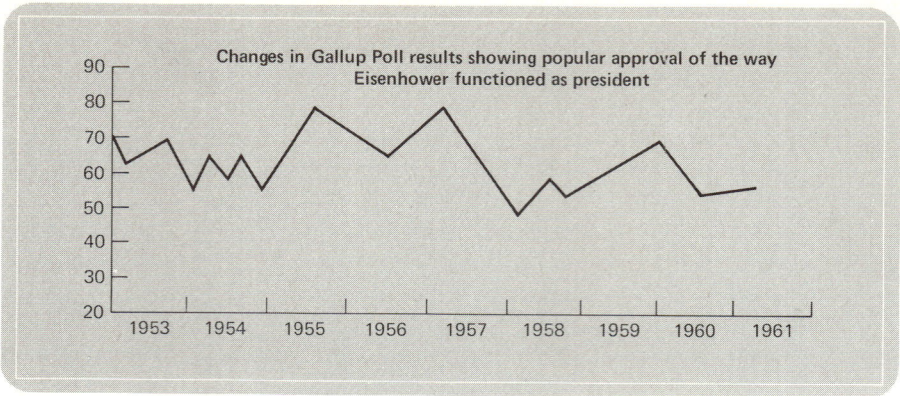

Changes in Gallup Poll results showing popular approval of the way Eisenhower functioned as president

SOURCE: Adapted from Irish and Frank, *U.S. Foreign Policy,* p. 104

The peak of Eisenhower's popularity was reached in mid-1955 and early 1957 when 79 percent of respondents approved of his handling of the presidency. He reached a low in early 1958 when only 49 percent approved.

from having been a placid father figure (a "counterrevolutionist entirely surrounded by men who know how to profit from it," the journalist Elmer Davis had complained in the 1950s), he seemed in retrospect to have been in purposeful control of his administration at all times. Even his convoluted syntax, which had been laughable at the time, seemed part of a deliberate plan. "Don't worry, Jim," he allegedly told his press secretary James Hagerty, who was nervous about an imminent session with reporters. "If that question comes up, I'll just confuse them." As the liberal writer Murray Kempton put it (with some exaggeration) in 1967, Ike "was the great tortoise upon whose back the world sat for eight years. We laughed at him; we talked wistfully about moving; and all the while we never even knew the cunning beneath the shell."

Even writers like Kempton, however, could not ignore qualities that prevented Eisenhower from making maximum use of his personal popularity. Among these was a passivity and lack of sophistication that astonished veteran observers in Washington. The best way to prevent selfishness in labor unions or management, he told the cabinet at one point, was to appeal to their sense of fair play. The way to deal with McCarthy was to ignore him. "I will not get into the gutter with that guy," he remarked, as if keeping himself pure

I haven't checked these figures, but eighty-seven years ago, I think it was, a number of individuals organized a governmental setup here in this country, I believe it covered eastern areas, with this idea that they were following up based on a sort of national independence arrangement and the program that every individual is just as good as every other individual.

One of many parodies in the 1950s of Eisenhower making Lincoln's Gettysburg address.

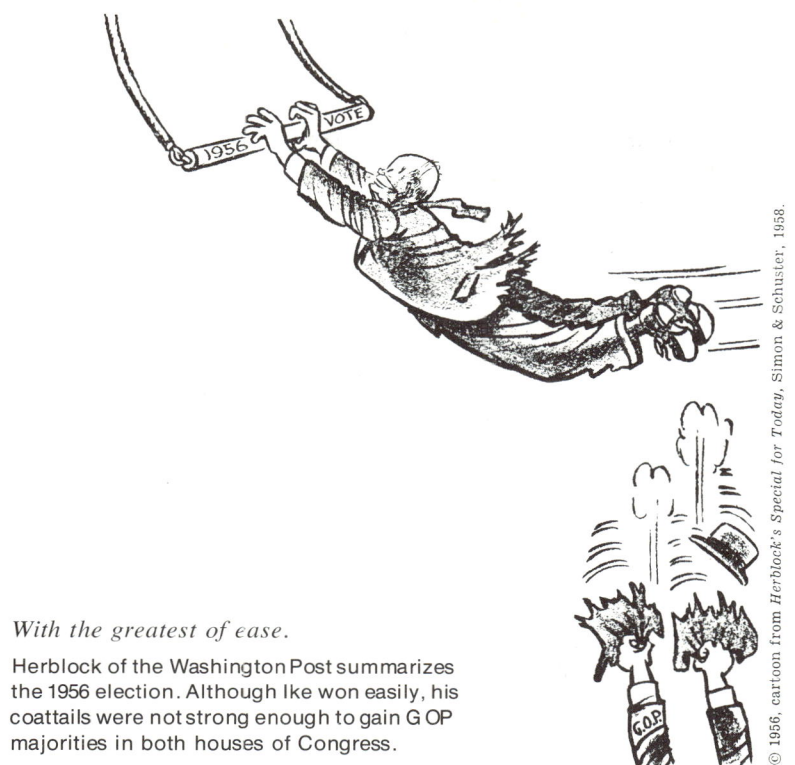

With the greatest of ease.

Herblock of the Washington Post summarizes the 1956 election. Although Ike won easily, his coattails were not strong enough to gain GOP majorities in both houses of Congress.

© 1956, cartoon from *Herblock's Special for Today,* Simon & Schuster, 1958.

would cleanse the country. Eisenhower also told political aides that he would not descend into making "idiotic promises or hints about elect-me-and-I-will-cut-your-taxes-by-such-and-such-a-date! If it takes that kind of foolishness to get elected, let them find someone else for the job." In fact, Eisenhower was neither so unsophisticated nor so nonpartisan as he sounded. Even his handling of McCarthy—as he may have suspected—had the virtue of letting his adversary find the rope to hang himself. His passive approach to important questions, however, was hardly purposeful leadership.

This approach rested on his view that the presidency must not become too expansive. "I am not one of those desk-pounding types," he explained, "that likes to stick out his jaw and look like he is bossing the show. I don't think it is the function of a President of the United States to punish anybody for voting as he likes." He told his cabinet appointees, "you have full authority. I expect you to stand on your own two feet. Whatever you decide goes. The White House will stay out of your hair." Because big government, like large corporations, had to rely on bureaucrats and managers, his approach had the virtue of freeing him from details. But the deliberate dispersal of power led also to inertia and procrastination. Eisenhower, in I. F. Stone's words, would be a "president in absentia, with a sort of political vacuum in the White House which other men will struggle among themselves to fill." Delegating authority meant also that he could not secure compliance with his own commands, for

Washington politicians had to feel the whip hand of the president before doing anything. "He'll sit there," Truman said of his successor, "and he'll say, 'Do this! Do that!' And nothing will happen. Poor Ike—it won't be a bit like the army."

Eisenhower's administration reflected his instinctive distaste for involving himself in the legislative process. He rarely applied pressure, and he often sounded ignorant even of important matters. After a Senate committee unanimously reported out to the floor a significant education bill in 1954, he blurted to newsmen, "I do not know the details of that particular legislation. . . . I'd suggest you go to [HEW] Secretary [Oveta Culp] Hobby to find out where we stand." At a press conference following introduction of his Justice Department's civil rights bill in 1957 he told reporters, "I was reading part of that bill this morning, and I—there were certain phrases I didn't completely understand. . . . I would want to talk to the Attorney General." No president since Coolidge had been more poorly informed about what was happening on the Hill.

His practice of paying little attention to details let aides like Sherman Adams, his chief assistant, and top cabinet officials handle many important decisions. Adams, a former governor of New Hampshire, was a "Modern Republican" who conceded the desirability of some activist policies. But he was also abrupt, flinty, as cold to self-important officials as New Hampshire stone in the winter. Until 1959, when ruffled politicians drove him from power by showing that he had used his influence for personal gain, he made more enemies for Eisenhower than friends. On presidential orders, he kept many important questions from receiving the top-level discussion and debate they ought to have had. If the "buck" stopped in the oval office under Truman, it floundered in the anterooms from 1953 to 1959.

Other important decisions were left in the hands of conservative businessmen more notable for their wealth than for their political experience. Democrats, indeed, cracked that Eisenhower's cabinet consisted of eight millionaires and a plumber (union leader Martin Durkin, who lasted less than a year as secretary of labor). Newsman James Reston added that "there is scarcely a member of the cabinet who can make a moving extemporaneous speech. It is humorless, obvious, unintellectual (almost anti-intellectual), and lacking in the one thing it has talked so much about—a crusading spirit."

Chief among these men, especially during the first term, were Secretary of Agriculture Ezra Taft Benson, Treasury boss George Humphrey, and Charles E. Wilson, who assumed command of the Defense Department. Benson, who served for the entire eight years of Eisenhower's presidency, was a devout Mormon who opened cabinet meetings with a prayer. He was an equally devout economic reactionary who vowed to get the government out of the business of supporting farm prices. In so doing, he hoped that marginal farmers would quit the land, overproduction would cease to be a problem, and federal aid would be unnecessary. This approach infuriated all farmers, marginal or otherwise, who demanded government assistance to 90 percent parity or more. The aroused Farm Bloc in Congress coalesced to defeat most of his efforts. For all Benson's persistence, overproduction escalated during the decade, and prices sagged. To keep pace, federal spending for agriculture rose from $1 billion in 1952 to $5.1 billion in 1961. Benson, like his predecessors, failed utterly to change the course of American farm policy.

George Humphrey was an old-fashioned fiscal conservative who considered it his job to reduce spending. "We have to cut one-third out of the budget," he said in 1953, "and you can't do that just by eliminating waste. This means, wherever necessary, using a meat axe." Later he added, "If you're going to live a good life, you've got to live within your income. A good wife can be a helluva good secretary of the treasury because that's all she needs to know." In 1957, when Eisenhower announced a mildly expansionary budget for the coming year, Humphrey bluntly called for restraint, saying that without it "we're gonna have a depression which will curl your hair." This contradiction created total confusion over the administration's economic program until 1958.

Wilson was equally anxious to cut back governmental expenditures. During the congressional elections of 1954 he went to Detroit, where thousands of unemployed were clamoring for aid, to celebrate individual initiative. "I've got a lot of sympathy for people where a sudden change catches them," he said, "but I've always liked bird dogs better than kennel-fed dogs myself. You know, one who'll get out and hunt for food rather than sit on his fanny and yell." As this remark suggests, Wilson had an affinity for gauche statements. One, in 1953, expressed his economic philosophy: "What was good for our country was good for General Motors, and vice versa." In short, the nation had no interests other than those of GM. Another avowed his belief in nuclear weaponry, chiefly because it cost less than large standing armies. "We cannot afford to fight limited wars," he said. "We can only afford to fight a big war, and if there is a war, that is the kind it will be." Appalled by such remarks, James Reston suggested that Wilson had invented the automatic transmission so he would have one foot free to put in his mouth.

Men like Wilson and Humphrey were not out of place in Eisenhower's administration. On the contrary, they reflected the President's fiscal conservatism. Ike once told the cabinet, Sherman Adams reported later, that "if he was able to do nothing as President except balance the budget he would feel that his time in the White House had been well spent." Eisenhower added, citing Lincoln, "in all that the people can do as well for themselves, the government ought not to interfere." He waited a month and a half before getting around to naming Arthur Burns, a conservative economist, as his top aide on economic policy, then told him, "I want you to be my adviser but I don't want to have to sit at a table and listen to a lot of talk." During his eight years as president, federal spending rose by only $8 billion, or 11 percent, while the population as a whole increased by approximately 18 percent.

This reluctance to pursue an expansionary fiscal policy cost him dearly by the late 1950s, when his attempts to limit spending helped to promote the deepest recession since the 1930s. Unemployment, which had remained at approximately 4 percent in the peacetime years of 1955 to 1957, suddenly jumped to 6.8 percent in 1958, a figure that involved close to 5 million people. Eisenhower responded by accelerating spending for highways, by relaxing monetary policies, and by liberalizing unemployment compensation. But he refused to consider heavy public spending for welfare or public housing, he vetoed bills to provide aid to depressed areas, and he rejected out of hand Douglas's call for a tax cut. The economy continued to flounder until 1961, so badly that it caused large drops in tax revenue—which in turn created huge budget deficits. Not surprisingly, Democrats insisted that only they could "get the country moving again." Eisenhower's conservative fiscal policy did more than anything else to harm his party in the election of 1960.

Random quotations from Eisenhower during the decade suggest his conservative views on other issues. On welfare: "If all Americans want is security, they can go to prison." On national health insurance: "I have been against compulsory insurance as a very definite step toward socialized medicine. I don't believe in it, and I want none of it myself." On federal aid to education: "I do not believe the Federal Government ought to be in the business of paying a local official. If we're going into that, we'll have to find out every councilman and every teacher and every other person that's a public official of any kind . . . and try to figure out what his right salary is." On the appointment of Warren as chief justice: "biggest damn fool mistake I ever made." On the TVA (privately): "I'd like to sell the whole thing, but I suppose we can't go that far." On the *Brown* v. *Board of Education* ruling (publicly): "I think it makes no difference whether or not I endorse it. What I say is the—the Constitution is as the Supreme Court interprets it; and I must conform to that and do my very best to see that it is carried out in this country;" and (privately): "I personally think the decision was wrong."

Occasionally, of course, Eisenhower proved flexible enough to accommodate pressure groups. Reactionaries like Goldwater, in fact, grumbled that he was promoting a "Dime Store New Deal." Despite Benson's appeals, Eisenhower signed the expensive farm bills of the decade. He assented to modest increases in welfare payments and in the minimum wage, and to small appropriations for public housing. In 1958 he approved the National Defense Education Act, which Congress hurried through in response to Russia's successful satellite, the Sputnik. The NDEA program provided federal aid for science and language training. In 1960 Eisenhower signed the Kerr-Mills Bill, which offered federal matching money to states that enacted their own health insurance plans for the elderly poor. And in perhaps the most important measure of his administration he readily signed a multibillion-dollar federal highway construction act in 1956. The measure passed because it satisfied all the important interest groups: state highway officials, who sought federal money; trade unions, who needed jobs for their members; farmers, who wanted better roads to market their goods; and city officials, who yearned for faster links with other urban centers. Unlike social welfare legislation, it commanded bipartisan majorities, for everyone thought well of the automobile. It passed Congress with ease.

Both Kerr-Mills and the highway act proved faulty. The Kerr-Mills approach ignored all except poor people over sixty-five. Worse, it resulted in widely differing standards for care. Many states provided little or no money, and their residents suffered accordingly. The impact of the highway law was also controversial. As expected, it provided a much-improved road network and jobs for thousands of workers. But planners thought nothing of running highways through scenic regions or of ripping up residential areas occupied by the voiceless urban poor. A consultant complained, "an aerial photo of any American city reveals devastation as obvious as that resulting from the London blitz. Saturation bombing is the only adequate comparison."

The quest for civil rights, much accelerated in the 1950s, was the most revealing test of Eisenhower's philosophy. After the Court's rulings in 1954-55 reformers thought optimistically that a new era of race relations was at hand. But the Deep South refused to change. Some areas ignored the decision; others bypassed it with "pupil placement" laws, which confirmed segregation in the schools. Jim Crow statutes continued to enforce racial discrimination in housing, transport, and public accommodations. And overtly racist organizations—Citizens Councils, White Americans, Incorporated, the Society for the Preservation of White Integrity—sprang up throughout the South. As early as 1955, when the Reverend Martin Luther King, Jr., attracted nationwide attention by leading a nonviolent boycott against segregation in buses in Montgomery, Alabama, it was clear that blacks were restless and angry and that a civil rights revolution was at hand.

The President was not wholly blind to these developments. In a series of executive actions he moved to improve conditions in the District of Columbia and in military camps. In 1957, when Governor Orval Faubus of Arkansas directly defied federal authority, he sent in troops to sustain token desegregation of a high school in Little Rock. He signed civil rights acts in 1957 and

1960, the first passed since Reconstruction. These laws established a federal commission on civil rights. They also gave the government added powers to promote equal voting rights in the South.

But Eisenhower honestly believed that only changing attitudes, not government, could alleviate racial tensions. Accordingly he did nothing to deal with the racial problems in the North. His refusal to applaud the Court's decisions also encouraged the southern resistance. Faubus, indeed, acted defiantly because he assumed that the White House would do nothing to stop him. In 1958 and 1959 the governor closed Little Rock's high school altogether rather than submit again to the law of the land. As reformers had warned, the Deep South easily circumvented the civil-rights acts of 1957 and 1960, which Eisenhower did nothing to promote. In his attitude toward civil rights the President revealed that he, like many contemporaries, failed to perceive the revolution in expectations that had been growing among blacks since World War II.

Popular complacency, to say nothing of the barriers posed by the Right and by Congress, would have prevented even the most charismatic of leaders from accomplishing very much during the 1950s. Eisenhower, therefore, was not to blame for the decade's rather barren legislative record. Moreover, he proved responsible in his use of presidential power. No postwar president was as respectful of the constitutional prerogatives of Congress. Particularly in his second term, however, he failed to respond to economic stagnation, to urban blight, and to racial confrontation. For this essential lack of vision—the product of his administrative style, his social philosophy, and perhaps his age (he was seventy in 1960, the oldest president in American history)—he failed in his responsibility to educate and to enlighten the people, whose support was necessary before momentum for change could develop. By contrast, both his predecessor, Harry Truman, and his successor, John F. Kennedy, at least tried to deal with the nation's social problems.

The Cold War continues, 1953–1961

Containment, the Republican platform announced in 1952, was "negative, futile, and immoral." It abandoned "countless human beings to a despotism and Godless terrorism." The United States, the party implied, must take steps to "liberate" these downtrodden masses from their oppressors.

The atmosphere in Moscow was hardly more promising for détente. When George Kennan arrived in May 1952 to take up his duties as ambassador, he found Soviet personnel at the embassy too terrified even to help him with his bags, much less talk with him. He discovered that five guards had been assigned to follow him, that he was prevented from talking privately with people, and that his residence was electronically bugged. When he complained of such treatment, he was declared *persona non grata* by the Soviet govern-

America's mood:
the public's view
of the most important problem
facing the country,
according to Gallup Poll results,
1953–1960

1953	Korean War
1954	Threat of war
1955	Working out a peace
1956	Threat of war
1957	Keeping out of war
1958	Economic conditions
1959	Keeping peace
1960	Relations with Russia

SOURCE: Irish and Frank, *U.S. Foreign Policy*, p. 107

ment. Not until the spring of 1953, when Charles ("Chip") Bohlen was finally confirmed as the new ambassador, did America get around to replacing him.

During Eisenhower's years in the White House several developments promised to soften this frigid state of affairs. Most important of these was the death of Stalin in March 1953 and his replacement by more conciliatory figures, including Nikita Khrushchev, who became the major power in Russia by 1956. Another was the Korean armistice in July 1953. Most important, though little realized at the time, both China and western Europe were developing into powers in their own right. By the 1960s the bipolar confrontation between Russia and America was giving way to a multiplication of power blocs.

Both nations acted sporadically to take advantage of these forces for coexistence. In 1953 Eisenhower startled hard-liners by calling for disarmament, and in 1955 he appealed for a condition of "open skies" over Russia and the United States, a proposal he hoped would lead to meaningful arms control. In 1955 Russia attended a summit conference at Geneva—the first between Soviet and American heads of state since the meeting at Potsdam ten years earlier. Though the conference settled nothing, it showed that the Russians were willing to mingle with American diplomats. In 1956, when Khrushchev denounced Stalin as a "distrustful man, sickly and suspicious," and recounted his "crimes" and "tortures" while head of state, it seemed certain that the Soviet Union was taking a more conciliatory course.

Despite this potential for mutual understanding, relations between Russia and the United States remained cold throughout the 1950s. The Soviet suppression of the Hungarian revolution in 1956, its continuing pressures on the Middle East, its threats to isolate West Berlin, and finally its apparent

© 1956, cartoon from *Herblock's Special for Today*, Simon & Schuster, 1958.

I'll be glad to restore peace in the Middle East too.

support of revolutionary activity in Cuba and other parts of Latin America, all antagonized the western powers. America's containment policy, which encircled Russia with naval and military bases and which included the use of high-level reconnaisance planes to spy on Soviet territory, kept the Russians uneasy and resentful. Persistent talk about liberating eastern Europe was more provocative still. As both sides developed hydrogen bombs and intercontinental missiles, the tension mounted.

Assigning blame for these tensions to individuals is neither easy nor especially helpful. Eisenhower and Khrushchev led societies whose fundamental differences prompted widespread feelings of insecurity and mutual distrust. Neither man had the freedom of action to end the Cold War. Indeed, as McCarthy's influence suggested, domestic obstacles to changing American attitudes were stronger than ever. The military, defense contractors, and the leading labor unions continued to promote a tough line. Influential politicians, including Republican Senate Leader William Knowland, constantly demanded that the administration act more firmly than it did. By contrast, advocates of détente were weak and scattered, and disarmament groups such as the Committee for a Sane Nuclear Policy (SANE) seemed almost subversive. In foreign affairs, as in domestic policy, Eisenhower had to operate under popular, institutional, and political constraints.

In contending with these forces, however, Eisenhower named as his secretary of state John Foster Dulles, one of America's most convinced anticommunists. The nephew of Robert Lansing, Wilson's secretary of state, and the grandson of John Foster, secretary of state under Benjamin Harrison, Dulles had been intimately involved in the making of foreign policy since 1907, when as a Princeton undergraduate he served as secretary to the Hague Peace Conference. In 1919 he had been at Versailles. Since then he had worked as an international lawyer based in New York City, as an adviser to Thomas Dewey and to the State Department under Truman, and as negotiator of the pact with Japan in 1951.

If Eisenhower seriously hoped for détente, he would have done well to choose someone else. For it was Dulles who drafted the "liberation" plank for the party in 1952. A stern Presbyterian, Dulles loathed "atheistic communism," and he took a moralistic approach to foreign policy. A skilled lawyer, he handled negotiations like a prosecutor in a criminal trial, not like a diplomat hoping for compromise. His rigid, humorless approach made him the butt of wits, who dubbed him "Dull, Duller, Dulles." It earned him the cordial dislike not only of the Soviets, but of many French and British statesmen of the period. He was hardly the man to promote international good will.

Consistent with his background, Dulles was ambitious for himself and his party. He was acutely aware of the fate that had befallen Acheson, his predecessor, at the hands of men like McCarthy. He resolved therefore to give the Right no cause for suspicion. This meant actively supporting self-styled security experts, who terminated the appointments of some 5000 State Department employees by August 1953, and by ignoring officials—no matter how expert—who might appear to be at all "soft" on communism. Among those who were not reassigned, and who therefore retired early, was Kennan, America's foremost expert on the Soviet Union. Sherman Adams, who tried to be objective, later conceded that Dulles's "point of view was often negative" and that he had induced a "strong aversion among foreign service career men to anything imaginative and original." Quite obviously, Dulles intended to captain a ship with a wholly submissive crew.

While purging the State Department, he also acted to commit the new administration to hard-line policies. In January he succeeded in getting Eisenhower to insert a section in his state of the union message calling in effect for the "unleashing" of Chiang Kai-shek. Such a policy appeared to be aimed at promoting the "liberation" of mainland China from communism. In March Dulles made no effort to work for détente following the death of Stalin. At the same time he let the Chinese Communists know, again with Eisenhower's blessing, that the United States might use nuclear weapons in Korea if they did not soon agree to an armistice. When China backed off in July, it appeared that his nuclear blackmail (undoubtedly assisted by a more moderate Soviet line following the death of Stalin) had helped to end the war.

By 1954, when he enjoyed Eisenhower's full confidence, it was clear that Dulles would rely on two related policies to sustain his anticommunist world view. One, which he spelled out in April, was already implicit in Secretary of Defense Wilson's policy of the "new look"—heavy dependence on nuclear weapons and strategic bombing. A potential aggressor, Dulles explained, "should know in advance that he can and will be made to suffer for his aggression more than he can possibly gain by it. This calls for a system in which local defensive strength is reinforced by more mobile deterrent power. . . . the main reliance must be on the power of the free community to retaliate with great force by mobile means at places of its own choice." In simpler language this policy of "massive retaliation" meant "more bang for the buck," an approach that Russia emulated in policies dubbed "more rubble for the ruble."

Dulles waited until January 1956 to define the related policy, which critics labeled "brinkmanship." Like massive retaliation, however, it was part of the Eisenhower–Dulles approach from the time it was first used against the Chinese concerning Korea. Its central assumption was that potentially unfriendly nations understood nothing but force, especially nuclear force. Therefore, the United States must be prepared to threaten war. "The ability to get to the verge without getting into the war," Dulles wrote, "is the necessary art. If you cannot master it, you inevitably get into war."

In applying these doctrines Dulles and Eisenhower paid particular attention to Asia. It was there that Republican stalwarts like Senator Knowland demanded firmness. It was there, too, that threats seemed worth making, for Asian communists lacked the nuclear might of the Soviet Union. The first test was in Indo-China, where rebels were gaining in their long war against French colonialism. Responding to French pleas, the Truman administration had already pumped millions of dollars into the area. But the forces of Ho Chi Minh, a Communist who led a broad-based nationalist coalition, trapped the French at Dien Bien Phu in May 1954 and threatened to drive them out of the country.

Many high-ranking members of the Eisenhower administration joined Dulles in recommending the use of American naval and air power—perhaps including atomic weapons—to assist the French. These included Admiral Arthur Radford, chairman of the joint chiefs of staff, and Vice-President Nixon. Eisenhower, too, believed that the loss of Indo-China to communism would be contagious. "You have a row of dominos set up," he observed, "and you knock over the first one, and what will happen to the last one is the certainty that it will go over very quickly. So you have a beginning of a disintegration that would have the most profound influences." Before acting, however, Eisenhower insisted that Dulles consult congressional leaders and the Allies. As he might have suspected, they rejected the idea of using American force against a popular revolutionary movement on the other side of the globe. Bowing to the inevitable after the ensuing fall of Dien Bien Phu, the United States accepted (but refused to sign) an accord worked out at Geneva. It created the Countries of Laos, Cambodia, and Vietnam, the last to be divided temporarily at the seventeenth parallel pending elections in 1956 that would determine the government of a unified nation.

To counter this loss to the West, Dulles embarked on what later critics would term "pactomania": formation of the South East Asia Treaty Organization later in 1954. Its signatories, the United States, Great Britain, France, Australia, New Zealand, the Philippines, Pakistan, and Thailand, contracted to consult in the event of a communist attack on one of them. A separate protocol covered Laos, Cambodia, and Vietnam. SEATO, however, did not include such important Asian nations as India, Indonesia, and Burma; it set up no military force like that which was being developed under NATO; and it required the members only to consult, not to fight. It became little more than a convenient excuse for American participation in Asian affairs.

The next test of administration policy in Asia involved China, where the Nationalists, who had fled to the island of Formosa, and the mainland Communists had been threatening each other since 1950. The administration continued the futile policy of nonrecognition of Communist China. In 1954 Dulles also negotiated a treaty that committed the United States to defend Formosa and the neighboring Pescadore Islands against attack from the mainland. The Communists responded by lobbing shells at Quemoy and Matsu, two Nationalist-held islands close to the mainland. Eisenhower then asked Congress for blanket authority to use force in the area as he, the commander in chief, saw fit. This was a shrewd maneuver, for it left him armed in advance—as Truman never had been in Korea—with congressional sanction. Nine years later President Johnson would employ a similar tactic following alleged attacks on American ships in the Tonkin Gulf. As the more avid Asia-firsters complained, however, Eisenhower's action stopped short of "unleashing" Chiang Kai-shek or of adopting massive retaliation against the Communists. Mao Tse-tung's forces bombed the islands sporadically throughout the 1950s and took the Tachens, a small group of islands north of Quemoy and Matsu, without any countermove from the United States. As in Indo-China, Eisenhower stopped short of getting America's military involved.

The failure to dislodge Mao Tse-tung in China revealed the inappropriateness of the "liberation" policy proclaimed in 1952 and reasserted thereafter by the right wing. Liberation proved equally futile in eastern Europe, where the Soviets tightened their control throughout the 1950s. When Poland and East Germany rebelled against Russian rule, America did nothing. In 1956, when Russian tanks quashed a revolution in Hungary, the Eisenhower administration again stood by helplessly. Liberation, like massive retaliation, was useful for domestic political consumption. But it was too extreme to receive widespread endorsement either at home or among America's allies. And in the absence of large ground forces, which Eisenhower was cutting back, it was too incredible to be believed by the communists.

Moving into Hungary would have geen particularly difficult, for two days before Soviet tanks rolled into Budapest, the western allies broke openly over policy in Egypt. Here, too, Dulles's moralistic style contributed to America's difficulties. In 1954, General Gamal Abdel Nasser, the nationalistic strong man who had taken over in Egypt, induced Great Britain, which controlled the Suez Canal, to remove its troops from the area by 1956. Nasser then turned to the United States, Britain, and the World Bank for a loan to build the High Aswan Dam to harness the Nile River. At first Dulles encouraged the project, which appeared settled at the end of 1955.

Nasser, however, made threatening statements to Israel, which had relied on America for its sustenance ever since Truman proffered it instant recognition in 1948. In May 1956 Nasser recognized Communist China. He also negotiated an arms deal with Czechoslovakia, one result of which was to permit the arrival in Egypt of hundreds of Soviet technicians. The prospect of communist infiltration was disturbing enough, but Nasser also mortgaged Egypt's cotton crop—the nation's primary source of revenue—to pay for the arms. How, Americans asked, was Egypt to repay the loan for Aswan? Southern senators in particular grumbled that the United States was promoting foreign competition against American cotton. Their complaints revealed the thrust of economic considerations in postwar foreign policy. All these developments caused the United States to procrastinate in authorizing the loan. Egypt, impatient, then let it be known it would turn to the Soviet Union. This form of blackmail infuriated Dulles. Without consulting experts in the State Department, the western allies, or World Bank officials, he simply announced that the loan was off. He hoped his action would call Russia's bluff and show have-not nations they could not push the United States around.

His decision merely infuriated Nasser, who immediately nationalized the Suez Canal and closed it to Israeli shipping. Tolls, Egypt said, would help pay for the dam. The Soviet Union then came through with the aid that Dulles had refused. And two months later, after communications between Dulles and the western allies had all but broken down, Israeli troops stormed into the Sinai Peninsula. Britain and France, in what was obviously a well-planned move, assisted Israel.

When Russia stood behind Egypt, it looked as if World War III was on the horizon. Even before the Soviets rattled their rockets, however, Eisenhower had determined not to aid the western allies, and America sponsored a United Nations resolution condemning Israel, Britain, and France, and proposing that UN forces be dispatched to stabilize the situation. Without American backing, the invaders had no choice but to pull out.

Eisenhower's action revealed his essential good judgment concerning military affairs. Fighting a war, even a limited one, to promote western colonialism in Egypt would have been unwise. But the confrontation exposed the rifts in the western alliance that Dulles's cavalier diplomacy had helped to develop. In the Arab world it enormously expanded the popularity of Nasser, who resented his treatment at the hands of the West. And it enabled Russia to claim that it had come to the aid of anticolonialism in the Middle East. With more patience, Dulles might have avoided the whole damaging episode.

The Suez crisis also exposed the Eisenhower administration's lack of understanding of the forces animating the Third World. To Dulles, as to most Americans at the time, nations like Egypt were important only in terms of the Cold War. "Neutralism," he said, "was immoral." America's task was to prop up prowestern regimes, whether dictatorial or not—not to work for social reforms. Governments that turned to the Left, as Egypt's did under Nasser, must be restrained or, like Iran's in 1953 or Guatemala's in 1954, overthrown with the aid of the CIA. Reflecting this attitude, the administration attempted to preserve its influence in the Middle East by proclaiming the so-called Eisenhower Doctrine, approved by Congress in 1957. This promised military aid to friendly governments, thus helping to promote arms sales in that already explosive region. It also authorized Eisenhower to dispatch troops to counter communist advances. Using this authority, the President helped preserve anticommunist factions in Jordan in April 1957. In the summer of 1958 he went still further, by sending marines into Lebanon to preserve a right-wing government that was unconstitutionally clinging to power. These actions sustained western influence in the area. But they did nothing to come to terms with the forces of nationalism and reform in the Middle East.

This is not to say that Eisenhower's neglect of the third world reversed previous American policy. The Truman administration had paid equally little attention to the impoverished masses of Latin America, Africa, and Asia. But in Truman's time the forces of nationalism were not quite so evident as they became by the mid-1950s. By that time Eisenhower's administration should have developed more sensitivity than it did. It was not surprising that Vice-President Nixon, visiting Venezuela in 1958, was stoned as his car drove through the streets of Caracas, or that Cuba's Fidel Castro, relying heavily on anti-American diatribes, overthrew the dictatorial regime of Fulgencio Batista in 1959. "Revolution," the president's brother Milton Eisenhower concluded in 1960, "is inevitable in Latin America. The people are angry. They are shackled to the past with bonds of ignorance, injustice, and poverty. And they no longer accept as universal or inevitable the oppressive prevailing order. . . ."

These events in Latin America symbolized the Eisenhower administration's troubled life in foreign affairs during the second term. In 1957 the Soviets electrified the world by being the first to fire a satellite into space. Americans, once secure and arrogant in their presumed scientific superiority, reacted with surprise and shock. In 1958 Dulles grew ill (he died of cancer in 1959), and Eisenhower assumed more direct control of policy, working harder than before for détente; in 1959 Khrushchev even paid a celebrated visit to the United States, and another summit conference was scheduled for Paris in May 1960. On the eve of the conference, however, the Soviets shot down an American U-2 reconnaisance plane that had been photographing Russian installations. Khrushchev placed the plane on display in Moscow and induced the pilot to tell all. In the process he tricked Eisenhower into several easily exposed lies and finally into an admission of America's illegal peacetime

Khrushchev, Eisenhower, Mrs. Khrushchev, and Soviet Foreign Minister Andrei Gromyko, during Khrushchev's visit to the United States, 1959.

espionage. In this atmosphere the summit conference broke up on the very first day, and the Soviets withdrew an invitation for Eisenhower to visit Moscow later in the year. For the remainder of Eisenhower's presidency Soviet-American relations were more frigid than ever.

Actually, the U-2 affair was not so shocking as Khrushchev made out. He well knew that America had been making such illegal flights for some time. Having hit the plane, he could have crowed about Russia's obviously improved technology, and played the incident down. Instead, he used it to force a break between Russia and the United States, and he carried on his uncompromising behavior into the early Kennedy years. Why he did so was not wholly clear, for Soviet decision-making remained all but impenetrable to western eyes. Perhaps he, too, was under pressure from hard-liners at home. In any event, he was hardly the fun-loving, quasi-democratic figure that some American observers tended to extol.

The most frightening aspect of the U-2 affair, therefore, was not that America was involved in espionage. Rather, it was that such a flight should have been authorized when it was—on the eve of the conference. It was not clear why such a risk was taken, though Eisenhower properly assumed full responsibility for doing so. But evidence suggests that top military and intelligence officials opposed the idea of détente with the Soviet Union and that they pressed the President to go ahead with the flights. If so, the U-2 affair was an especially clear example of the role played by the military-intelligence community in the hardening of the Cold War. It was not for nothing that Eisenhower himself warned of the influence of a military-industrial complex in his farewell speech to the country in 1961.

A summary judgment of the Eisenhower administration's foreign policy must begin by reiterating the constraints under which he had to operate: unreasoning anticommunism among the public, economic pressures against détente, the power of the military-industrial complex, and, not the least important, Russian provocations such as the suppression of the Hungarian revolt. Moreover, Eisenhower himself ordinarily showed balanced judgment—in Vietnam, over Quemoy and Matsu, over Suez. To his credit, he secured peace in Korea, and he kept the country from war for the next seven and a half years. Rhetoric aside, he continued, rather than reversed, the major policies of the Truman administration. As revisionists have rightly observed, he seems the least bellicose of America's postwar presidents.

But questions remain. What if he had consistently pursued détente in the aftermath of Stalin's death? Suppose he had never named Dulles secretary of state, or, having named him, had taken command himself, as he began to do in 1958? Suppose he had pursued the suggestions of people like Kennan that America seek "disengagement" in central Europe. And suppose further that he had appreciated the strivings of China and the Third World? If he had done these things, he might have left behind a calmer world when he stepped down in 1961. He might also have succeeded in educating the citizenry about the dangers of rocket-rattling in the nuclear age. If so, Americans (and perhaps the Soviets) might have behaved with more restraint in the years to come.

> In the councils of Government, we must guard against the acquisition of unwarranted influence, whether sought or unsought, by the military-industrial complex. The potential for the disastrous rise of misplaced power exists and will persist.
>
> We must never let the weight of this combination endanger our liberties or democratic processes. We should take nothing for granted. Only an alert and knowledgeable citizenry can compel the proper meshing of the huge industrial and military machinery of defense with our peaceful methods and goals, so that security and liberty may prosper together.
>
> Eisenhower warns against the military-industrial complex, 1961.

The end of the Eisenhower order

John F. Kennedy's victory over Richard Nixon in the presidential election of 1960 appeared a striking repudiation of the past. After all, Kennedy was only forty-three when he took office—the first president to be born in the twentieth century, and the second youngest (next to TR) in American history. He was the first Roman Catholic to be elected president: Americans, it seemed, had progressed far since repudiating Smith in 1928. Most important, he imparted an air of vigor and purpose to the country. By struggling for a progressive program of domestic policies, he would get the country moving again. He would help the nation cross a "New Frontier."

People who expected wonders from the new president, however, would have done well to record several aspects of the campaign. Kennedy was not the liberals' favorite—that had been either Humphrey or Stevenson, who still commanded widespread support in a third bid for the nomination. In selecting Lyndon Johnson as his running mate, Kennedy merely underlined the political caution he had displayed in four years as a representative and eight years as an uninfluential senator from Massachusetts. "I'm not a liberal at all," he told an interviewer. "I never joined the ADA [Americans for Democratic Action] or the American Veterans Committee. I'm not comfortable with those people." Reassuring conservatives, he added, "I believe in the balanced budget," except in a "*grave* national emergency or *serious* recession." Eleanor Roosevelt, speaking for many liberals who distrusted Kennedy, explained, "I would hesitate to place the difficult decisions that the next President will have to make with someone who understands what courage is [Kennedy had written short biographical essays entitled *Profiles in Courage* in 1956] and admires it, but has not quite the independence to have it."

People like Eleanor Roosevelt were especially critical of some of Kennedy's statements. In 1949 he had said that Truman had "lost" China. "Those responsible for the tragedy of China must be searched out and spotlighted," he proclaimed. " . . . What our young men had saved, our diplomats and presidents had frittered away." Pursuing this anticommunist line during the campaign in 1960, he berated the Eisenhower administration for its "softness" regarding Quemoy and Matsu, and he appealed shamelessly to Cold War passions. "The enemy," he told an audience in Salt Lake City, "is the communist system itself—implacable, insatiable, unceasing in its drive for world domination. For this is not a struggle for the supremacy of arms alone— it is also a struggle for supremacy between two conflicting ideologies: Freedom under God versus ruthless, godless tyranny."

During his unprecedented television debates with Nixon—debates that probably enhanced his appeal with millions of voters who did not know him as well as Nixon—Kennedy also adopted a bellicose stance regarding Cuba's Fidel Castro, who was pursuing an anti-American line. When Eisenhower clamped an embargo on Cuba, Kennedy complained that it was "too little too

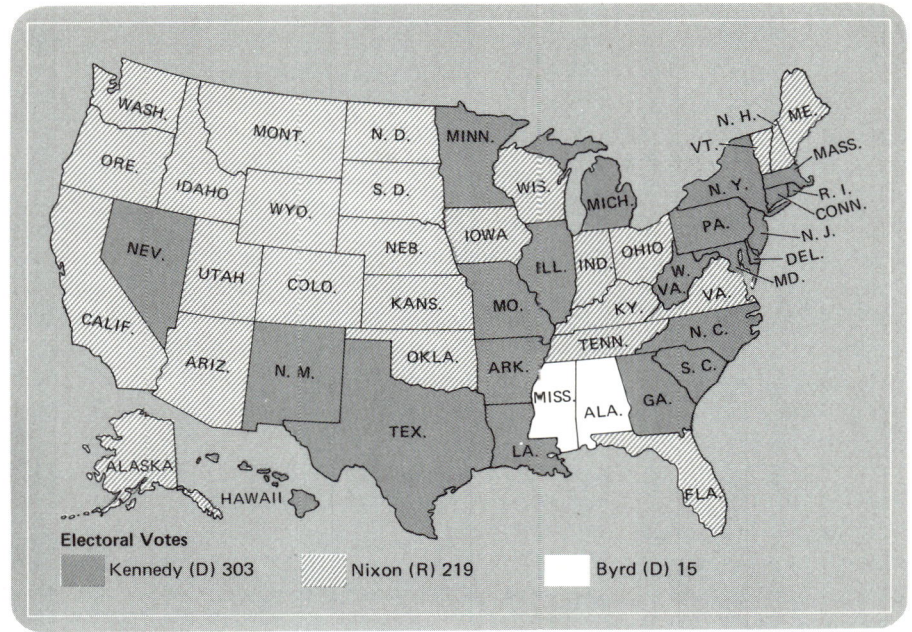

Electoral Votes

| Kennedy (D) 303 | Nixon (R) 219 | Byrd (D) 15 |

Election, 1960

late'' and that it followed an ''incredible history of blunder, inaction, retreat, and failure.'' The United States, he proclaimed, must ''strengthen the non-Batista exiles in the United States and in Cuba itself.'' This was an incendiary and demagogic statement, for he knew that anti-Castro exiles were even then being trained by the Eisenhower administration. In making it he exposed the passion for winning that critics perceived in the Kennedys. He showed that Cold War rhetoric was not the preserve of Nixon alone.

The campaign showed further that religious bigotry, though less overt than in 1928, remained very much alive. The election results revealed that Kennedy fared as well among Protestants as Stevenson had done in 1956. But in that year Stevenson had trailed badly among all groups. Compared to 1958, when Democrats made large gains in congressional races, Kennedy did poorly in Protestant sections, where the political scientist V. D. Key detected ''massive shifts'' away from the Democratic ticket. Overall, his Catholicism hurt him more than it helped.

The results of the election failed also to produce much of a mandate for anyone. Kennedy's total vote of 34.2 million exceeded Nixon's by only 118,000. It was a ''tremendous landslide,'' the young president observed wryly, ''that swept the Vice President and I [sic] into office by one-tenth of one per cent.'' Without very narrow victories in crucial states such as Pennsylvania, Missouri, and Illinois (where vote frauds in Democratic Cook

County may have made the difference), Kennedy would have lost the election. And his new Congress, while nominally Democratic, had twenty more Republicans in the House to bolster the conservative coalition.

It is hazardous to speculate on the major reasons for Kennedy's victory. Among them, however, was probably Nixon himself, who proved an energetic but unattractive candidate. Kennedy benefited also from Eisenhower's foreign policy setbacks, especially the U-2 affair. His constant focus on the nation's economic stagnation probably helped him most of all. He scored well—like many northern Democrats since the 1930s—in the populous black, ethnic, and industrial wards of urban America. He carried twenty-seven of the nation's forty-one largest cities, including all the biggest ones, where he rolled up a plurality of 2.7 million votes. This continuity in voting patterns reveals that Eisenhower's triumphs in 1952 and 1960 had been aberrations attributable to his unique personal appeal, and that Kennedy won because normally Democratic America reverted to form.

For these reasons the election suggests that voters in 1960 harkened as much to the past as to the future. The nation remained essentially Democratic, as it had since Franklin D. Roosevelt perfected the art of blaming Hoover for the world's problems. It remained divided, though less so than in the past, along religious lines. It responded, or so it seemed, as strongly as ever to appeals for fiscal conservatism, and to candidates of the political center. And it listened as attentively as before to inflammatory Cold War rhetoric. For all the talk about a New Frontier, it was fair to say in 1960, as it had been in 1952, that America, affluent and middle-class, still yearned as much for stability and consensus as for dramatic change.

Suggestions for reading

An important aid in understanding American life since 1945 is William Leuchtenburg, *A Troubled Feast** (1973). Books covering economic change in the 1940s and 1950s include John Brooks, *The Great Leap** (1966); H. P. Miller, *Rich Man Poor Man** (1964), a study of income distribution; Michael Harrington, *The Other America** (1962), a vivid account of poverty; David Potter, *People of Plenty** (1954), a far-ranging book concerning the effect of abundance on the American character; and E. L. Dole, *Conservatives in Power* (1960), which deals with government budgetary policy. Two books by John Kenneth Galbraith offer challenging interpretations of economic life: *American Capitalism** (1952) and *The Affluent Society** (1958).

Social trends are the subject of S. M. Lipset and Reinhart Bendix, *Social Mobility in Industrial Society* (1959); Peter M. Blau and Otis D. Duncan, *The American Occupational Structure* (1967); Robert C. Wood, *Suburbia** (1959); Scott Donaldson, *The Suburban Myth** (1969); William Dobriner, *Class in Suburbia** (1963); and William H. Whyte, *Organization Man** (1956). Like Whyte and Potter, David Riesman discusses the American national character in his widely read *Lonely Crowd** (1950). See also Thomas Hartshorne, *The Distorted Image: Changing Conceptions of American Character Since Turner* (1968); and Seymour Lipset and Leo Lowenthal, eds., *Culture and Social Character* (1961). Books covering aspects of thought in the 1950s also include Lawrence Lipton, *The Holy Barbarians* (1959), on the "beats"; Sam Hunter and John Jacobus, *American Art of the Twentieth Century* (1974); and Richard Kostelanetz, ed., *The New American Arts* (1967).

For religious trends see Will Herberg, *Protestant Catholic Jew** (2nd ed., 1960), a challenging sociological analysis; and Digby Baltzell, *The Protestant Establishment: Aristocracy and Caste in America** (1964). C. Wright Mills offers sharp critiques of American society in *White Collar** (1951), and *The Power Elite** (1956). Edward Banfield, *The Unheavenly City Revisited** (1974), gives a provocative critique of policies to aid the cities. So do Martin Anderson, *The Federal Bulldozer* (1967), and Herbert Gans, *The Urban Villagers** (1962), both of which show the unhappy results of urban renewal. For the role of the military see Edward B. Glick, *Soldiers, Scholars, and Society* (1971); and Samuel Huntington, *The Soldier and the State* (1957). A critique of the military-industrial complex is Seymour Melman, *Pentagon Capitalism* (1970).

Books on politics in the 1950s are Peter Lyon, *Eisenhower** (1974); Herbert Parmet, *Eisenhower and the Great Crusades* (1972); and especially James Sundquist, *Politics and Policy: The Eisenhower, Kennedy, and Johnson Years** (1968). Useful accounts by members of the Eisenhower administrations are Arthur Larson, *Eisenhower: The President Nobody Knew** (1968); Emmet John Hughes, *The Ordeal of Power* (1963), which is unflattering; and Sherman Adams, *First-Hand Report* (1961). I. F. Stone, *The Haunted Fifties** (1964), contains articles highly critical of the Eisenhower administration. Political trends are surveyed in Samuel Lubell, *The Revolt of the Moderates* (1956); and Heinz Eulau, *Class and Party in the Eisenhower Years* (1962). Special studies are Aaron Wildavsky, *Dixon-Yates* (1962), which covers electric power policy; and Alan K. McAdams, *Power and Politics in Labor Legislation* (1964). Biographies are Kenneth Davis, *Adlai Stevenson** (1957); and Joseph Gorman, *Kefauver: A Political Biography* (1971).

For the civil rights revolution see Anthony Lewis and *The New York Times, Portrait of a Decade: The Second American Revolution* (1964); and David Lewis, *King: A Critical Biography** (1970). Excellent on the status of blacks is Talcott Parsons and Kenneth Clark, eds., *The Negro American** (1966). J. W. Anderson, *Eisenhower, Brownell and the Congress* (1964), and Walter Murphy, *Congress and the Court* (1962), describe congressional opposition to decisions such as *Brown v. Board of Education*. Southern resistance is described in Numan Bartley, *The Rise of Massive Resistance* (1966); and Neil R. McMillen, *Citizens Council . . . 1954–1964* (1971). Other books dealing with the Supreme Court are G. Theodore Mitau, *Decade of Decision . . . 1954–1964** (1968); Alexander Bickel, *The Supreme Court and the Idea of Progress** (1970); John D. Weaver, *Warren* (1967); and Paul Murphy, *The Constitution in Crisis Times, 1918–1969** (1972).

Useful books on foreign policy include Seyon Brown, *Faces of Power: Constancy and Change in U. S. Foreign Policy from Truman to Johnson** (1968); Townsend Hoopes, *The Devil and John Foster Dulles* (1973); Richard Goold-Adams, *The Time of Power* (1962), also on Dulles; and the books on the Cold War cited at the end of the previous chapters. See also Norman Graebner, *The New Isolationism* (1956); Hugh Thomas, *The Suez Affair* (1966); David Wise and T. B. Ross, *The U-2 Affair* (1962); J. C. Campbell, *In Defense of the Middle East* (1960); Milton Eisenhower, *The Wine is Bitter* (1963), on Latin America; and Henry Kissinger, *The Necessity for Choice** (1961), on military policies. Two books dealing with the CIA are L. B. Kirkpatrick, *The Real CIA* (1968); and the less flattering account by David Wise and T. B. Ross, *The Invisible Government** (1964).

13

The 1960s:
from
altruism
to
disenchantment

Many idealists found the early 1960s the most exciting time in modern American history. Young civil rights activists were staging interracial sit-ins and freedom rides. The Reverend Martin Luther King, Jr., was dramatizing the crusade for racial justice. The folk singer Bob Dylan was composing memorable ballads for peace and justice. Chief Justice Earl Warren was leading the Supreme Court toward breakthrough decisions broadening the Bill of Rights. And John F. Kennedy, youthful, energetic, articulate, was in the White House. Despite his assassination in November 1963, many progressives kept the faith, and under Lyndon Johnson's leadership they enacted a remarkably wide-ranging body of reforms in 1964 and 1965. The 1960s, it seemed, would witness the triumph of social justice in America.

The new frontier

Kennedy's upbringing offered clues to anyone who wished to predict his behavior as president. His maternal grandfather had been a colorful mayor of Boston, his paternal grandfather a politically active saloonkeeper. Both had been upwardly mobile Irish Catholics anxious to gain acceptance in America. Kennedy's father, Joseph, made millions in a variety of speculative endeav-

John and Robert Kennedy discussing problems awaiting decision, 1960.

ors, contributed generously to the Democratic party, and was rewarded with the coveted ambassadorship to Great Britain. Fiercely competitive, Joseph instilled his own energy and ambition in his children. As president, Kennedy was to exalt activity and vigor almost as ends in themselves and to insist that the United States compete strenuously against its enemies. Though fatalistic in many ways—he thought of himself as an "idealist without illusions"—he clothed his doubts in an altruistic rhetoric that captured the mood of the time. "Ask not what your country can do for you," he proclaimed. "Ask what you can do for your country."

In seeking to implement his goals Kennedy deliberately rejected Eisenhower's low-key approach. He revealed—at least in his rhetoric—that he would use all the tools at his command and that opponents could expect retaliation from the White House. Kennedy replaced Eisenhower's businessmen with a corps of academicians, intellectuals, and dynamic younger executives, and he rejected the staff system. "Whereas Eisenhower wanted decisions brought to him for approval," one political scientist has written admiringly, "Kennedy wanted problems brought to him for decision."

Such an administrative style had obvious pitfalls. As the newsman Merriman Smith pointed out, some of the New Frontiersmen had "moments of short-sightedness, bias, prejudice, and needlessly argumentative verbosity."

The reporter Joseph Kraft added that Kennedy, like Truman, was rather too fond of action for action's sake. The President's "bang-bang" style, he complained, "favors people who know exactly what they want to do. It is tough on people who have dim misgivings—even if those misgivings happen to be very important." But most observers praised the new president's methods. Under Eisenhower, I. F. Stone wrote, "teamwork was conducted much in the manner of a football game—frequent huddles, great attention to coordinating everybody, and interminable periods spent catching breath between plays." Kennedy's approach, by contrast, resembled basketball. "Everybody is on the move all the time. . . . The President may throw the ball in any direction, and he expects it to be kept bouncing."

Reporters responded especially favorably to Kennedy's sense of humor. Told of Vatican complaints about his secular approach to politics, the President quipped, "now I understand why Herry the Eighth set up his own church." When people grumbled that his brother Robert was too young to be Attorney General, he joked that Bobby might as well get some experience before practicing law. Reporters also welcomed his articulateness and his accessibility, and people who saw him on television were immediately struck by his poise and good looks. In the TV age of the 1960s, when style and image frequently counted for as much as substance, Kennedy enjoyed great advantages.

These assets appeared to help in his dealings with a still conservative Congress. In early 1961 his followers in the House succeeded, by the narrow margin of 217 to 212, in liberalizing the obstructive Rules Committee. Later, Congress increased the federal minimum wage, set aside funds for manpower training and area redevelopment, and passed a trade expansion act that promised to lower traiffs throughout the industrialized noncommunist world.

Kennedy's popularity in office reached a peak in mid-1961 when 83 percent of respondents approved of his presidency. He reached a low of 57 percent shortly before his assassination in 1963.

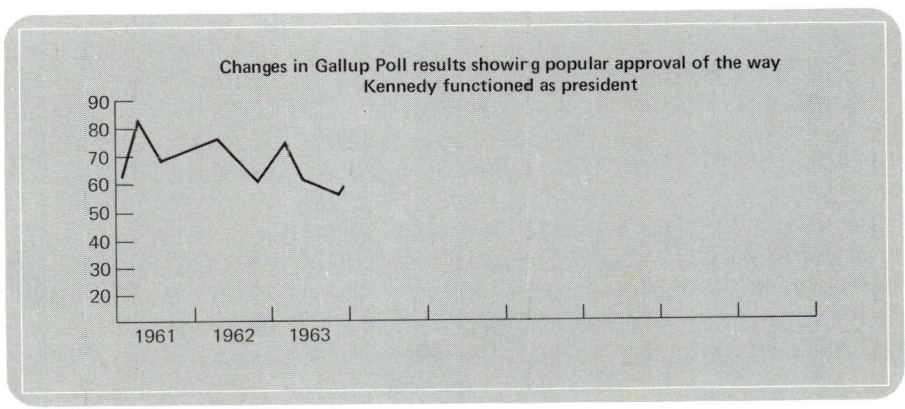

SOURCE: Adapted from Irish and Frank, *U.S. Foreign Policy*, p. 104

Before his death the House approved a multibillion-dollar tax cut, which the Senate passed early in 1964. This was a Keynesian measure that deliberately risked short-term budgetary deficits in the hope of promoting purchasing power. Kennedy's willingness to embrace this "New Economics" was the most striking manifestation of his gradual receptiveness to unorthodox ideas.

Kennedy also kept his promise to pull the country out of its economic slump. Increases in defense spending pumped new billions into the economy. So did his program to place a man on the moon: by 1969, when Neil Armstrong got there, the government had spent some $25 billion on space exploration. Primarily because of these expenditures, an upswing in the economy developed in 1961 and lasted until the early 1970s—the longest uninterrupted period of growth in modern American history. During this time some 15 million of 40 million American poor rose above the "poverty line" established statistically by the government, and median family income increased from $4000 to $8000, a jump in real dollars of more than 80 percent. Though these unprecedented advances did not significantly change the maldistribution of income, they were widely hailed. By developing faith in the government's ability to promote socioeconomic change, these impressive gains smoothed the way for Johnson's Great Society programs in 1964–65.

Though most liberals favored the tax cut, they observed that it was part of a generally cautious economic policy. During his tenure Kennedy made no serious effort to improve the distribution of income or to plug notoriously large loopholes in the tax laws. He worked harder for increases in defense spending than for social welfare. He encouraged Congress to enact tax breaks for big business. Even the tax cut, John Kenneth Galbraith grumbled, was "reactionary Keynesianism" that helped people spend more on unnecessary gadgetry. "I am not sure what the advantage is," he said, "in having a few more dollars to spend if the air is too dirty to breathe, the water too polluted to drink, the commuters are losing out on the struggle to get in and out of the cities, the streets are filthy, and the schools so bad that the young, perhaps wisely, stay away, and hoodlums roll citizens for some of the dollars that they save in taxes."

By late 1963 reformers were recognizing the limitations of other New Frontier laws. Efforts for tariff reduction, for instance, foundered amid disagreements among the western allies. The manpower training program could barely keep pace with technological change, and it made no attempt at all to attack hard-core poverty—a problem neglected until the end of Kennedy's presidency. Area redevelopment encountered opposition from business interests, which protested the granting of aid to potential competitors, and from labor leaders, who complained when money went to nonunion employers. In 1963, only two years after passage of the act, these pressure groups succeeded in killing a proposed increase in funds for the program.

Congress prevented many other measures from passing at all. These included medicare, aid to education, funds for mass transit, and creation of the Department of Urban Affairs. Some people thought that the lawmakers would have to be more responsive in 1964, an election year. But at the time of Kennedy's death the legislative logjam seemed as imposing as in the 1950s. *The New York Times* commented: "Rarely has there been such a pervasive attitude of discouragement around Capitol Hill and such a feeling of helplessness to deal with it. This has been one of the least productive sessions of Congress within the memory of most of its members."

Those who blamed Kennedy for this unproductive record were a little unfair. Like Truman before him, he lacked three advantages necessary for success on Capitol Hill: reliable progressive majorities, the support of pressure groups, and a popular mandate as expressed at the polls. Congressmen, accordingly, paid more attention to well-organized constituents than to presidential persuasion. "You can twist a fellow's arm once or even twice," a Kennedy aide explained. "But the next time he sees you coming he starts to run."

Kennedy's efforts for an aid to education bill revealed the power of these forces to sustain the status quo. As Kennedy well knew, opponents included many Republicans and Southern Democrats. Some of them objected to spending large sums of money for social programs; others feared that government aid would lead to federal dictation of curricula. In packing the House Rules Committee in early 1961, the President weakened these conservatives at their main bastion of defense. He also succeeded in dissuading Representative Adam Clayton Powell, a Harlem congressman, from attaching his antisegregation amendment to the bill. A similar provision, which denied aid to segregated schools, had forced almost all southerners, liberal or conservative, into opposing aid to education in the 1950s.

With these obstacles surmounted, Kennedy ran into yet another pressure group: the Catholic Church. As a Catholic, he felt he had to deny aid to parochial and private schools. Otherwise, angry Protestants would have accused him of religious favoritism. This decision, however, led prominent Catholic churchmen to oppose the bill. After much maneuvering, the measure sank under such pressure. Only later, in the more ecumenical spirit of the mid-1960s—and under a Protestant president who favored aid to parochial schools—did the bill command sufficient support to pass.

Kennedy's relations with influential spokesmen for big business provided another example of the way in which pressure groups could stymie presidential power. The President took office hoping to conciliate corporate leaders. "I'm not against business," he said, "I want to help them if I can." To prove his point he named Douglas Dillon, a prominent banker who had been under secretary of state in the Eisenhower administration, as secretary of the treasury, and Robert McNamara, head of the Ford Motor Company, as secretary of defense. But many business leaders remained uneasy, and when prices dipped on the stock market, they were quick to blame the White House. Annoyed, Kennedy commented, "I understand every day why Roosevelt, who started out such a mild fellow, ended up so ferociously antibusiness. It's hard as hell to be friendly with people who keep trying to cut your legs off."

His struggle with steel executives in 1962 merely intensified this hostility. This controversy began when Roger Blough, head of U. S. Steel, raised prices in defiance of an understanding previously reached with the White House. Other large steel companies followed Blough's example. Angry, Kennedy bared the weapons of the modern presidency. Antimonopolists in Congress, led by Kefauver, threatened an investigation. The Federal Trade Commission announced it would look into price agreements among large producers. McNamara implied that the Defense Department might deny contracts to corporations that refused to cooperate with Washington. The FBI appeared to be using its formidable powers to gather information against Blough's allies. Kennedy himself made it clear that he would have to review his policies favoring generous tax allowances to business. He observed, "my father always told me that all businessmen were sons of bitches, but I never believed it 'til now." Shortly after this display of strength Blough backed down slightly.

Kennedy's actions were not so potent as they appeared. Blough's retreat stemmed less from fear of the administration (though that mattered) than from the decision of Inland Steel, a dangerous competitor, to keep its prices at existing levels and therefore to bid for a larger share of the market. Inland's action showed that competitive pressures existed even in an industry as oligopolistic as steel. Simplistic talk about a monolithic "power elite" overlooked these fissures within the business community. But Inland's decision also revealed that leading business executives often possessed more power than Big Government or the presidency. Few confrontations offered a clearer example of the institutional obstacles facing elected officials.

As if these obstacles were not burden enough, Kennedy had personal liabilities that hurt his chances on the Hill. Some congressmen remembered him as a former colleague who had spent as much time socializing and promoting his personal ambition as he had fulfilling the duties of committee work. For these reasons he had never been an "insider" in Congress. Others sensed correctly that he was much more interested in foreign affairs than in domestic policy and that he found many congressmen long-winded and boring. As James Reston pointed out, Kennedy disliked "blarneying with pompous congressmen and simply would not take the time to do it." Still others were put off by the elitist tone of his administration. "All that Mozart string music and ballet dancing down there," one congressmen remarked, "and all that fox hunting and London clothes. He's too elegant for me." This populistic reaction to Kennedy's style showed that hostility to the Eastern Establishment—an ill-defined entity—remained a force in American politics. It suggested further that the very traits that assisted the president in his dealings with the media and with what the historian Eric Goldman called "Metro-America," the eastern urban elites, could become liabilities in managing Congress.

Kennedy also showed rather less forcefulness than he had led some progressives to expect. Always a pragmatic politician, he shied away from

America's mood:
the public's view of the most important
problem facing the country,
according to Gallup Poll results,
1961–1963

1961	Prices and inflation
1962	War, peace, and international tensions
1963	Racial problems

SOURCE: Irish and Frank, *U. S. Foreign Policy*, p. 107

promoting controversial programs. "There is no sense in raising hell and then not being successful," he said. This caution led him to rely on congressional magnates like Speaker of the House Sam Rayburn or senators Richard Russell of Georgia and Everett Dirksen of Illinois, the GOP leader. By avoiding confrontations, he hoped he might win the massive victory in 1964 that would give him the mandate he needed.

Progressives found Kennedy particularly cautious in the area of civil rights, where events were rapidly outdistancing the politicians. In February 1960 young people popularized direct action tactics by staging sit-ins at segregated lunch counters in the South. Two months later the Student Nonviolent Coordinating Committee (SNCC) joined the rapidly growing Congress on Racial Equality (CORE), King's Southern Christian Leadership Conference, and older organizations such as the NAACP in the battle for equal rights. By May 1961 CORE workers were staging integrated "freedom rides" into the South in order to desegregate transportation terminals—and getting beaten by angry mobs in the process. In 1962 James Meredith, a black man, tried to enroll in the University of Mississippi, only to be challenged by Governor Ross Barnett and by angry crowds. In a night of campus violence 2 people were killed and 375 injured, including 166 federal marshals. In April 1963, when King led nonviolent demonstrators in Birmingham, Alabama, police under Eugene "Bull" Conner repelled them with electric cattle prods, water hoses, and dogs. The melee, shown to shocked Americans on nationwide television, unleashed a wave of sympathy in the North for King's cause.

Many forces combined to encourage the adoption of these direct action tactics. Among them was the dramatic TV coverage that such methods attracted. More basic was the idealism and fearlessness of the young demonstrators, who were impatient with what they considered the calculations of the politicians and the legalism of groups such as the NAACP. The civil rights movement among young activists owed much to King, a spellbinding speaker whose deep Christian faith evoked ready responses among blacks in the South. Whites, too, found him "safe," for his doctrine of nonviolence suggested they need not fear race war.

The Birmingham, Alabama, police use dogs against civil rights demonstrators, 1963.

For blacks there was also a revolution of rising expectations. Since 1940 millions had either joined the armed forces or moved to the North. There they began to escape the poverty, isolation, and relative ignorance that had prevented collective actions in the past. There, too, they encountered a subtler brand of racism that exposed with even greater clarity the Jim Crow system of the South. In the 1950s these blacks had hoped, though briefly, that Supreme Court decisions like *Brown* v. *Board of Education* would bring on the revolution. By 1960, it was all too obvious that legal protection was not enough; only direct action could promote social justice.

Kennedy seemed to sympathize with the movement. During the 1960 campaign he had insisted that a presidential "stroke of the pen" could wipe out racial discrimination in federally supported housing. He had helped get Martin Luther King out of jail in Georgia—an act that solidified his vote among blacks in the North. Once in office, he appointed blacks to important offices—such as Robert Weaver as head of the Housing and Home Finance Agency, and Thurgood Marshall, a top NAACP lawyer, to a judgeship on the United States Circuit Court. When confronted by recalcitrant governors like Ross Barnett and George Wallace of Alabama, he used federal authority. The Justice Department, under his brother Robert, successfully attacked segregation in southern airports, and it brought more suits in support of voting rights than the Eisenhower regime had done since passage of the Civil Rights Act of 1957.

Martin Luther King, Jr., tells the throngs attending the march on Washington (1963),
"I have a dream . . . "

But the Kennedys remained too cautious to suit the activists. Forgetting the rhetoric of the 1960 campaign, the President waited until after the midterm elections of 1962—by which time hundreds of pens had been sent to him through the mail—to issue his order against discrimination in housing. The order, carefully limited and gently applied, had little impact. Bowing to men like James Eastland of Mississippi, chairman of the Senate Judiciary Committee, he appointed several segregationists to southern judgeships. And he disappointed activists by refusing to introduce a civil rights bill. "When I feel that there is a necessity for a congressional action, with a chance of getting that congressional action," he said in early 1961, "then I will recommend it to the Congress." For the next two years he adhered to this opportunistic course.

By mid-1963 the actions of segregationists like "Bull" Connor forced him to move more purposefully than he had before. Aroused to action, Kennedy called for passage of a civil rights law. When Congress dawdled, Kennedy acquiesced in a plan by activists for a march on Washington in August. To everyone's immense relief, the march, which attracted some 200,000 supporters, went off peacefully. King, the featured speaker, told the throngs (and millions more watching on TV) that he had a "dream, chiefly rooted in the American dream." "One day on the red hills of Georgia," he prophesied, "the sons of former slaves and the sons of former slave-owners will be able to sit at the table of brotherhood."

Even in these last months of his life, however, Kennedy failed to grasp the intensity behind the drive for racial justice. His proposed civil rights bill was moderate. It contained no provision for a commission on fair employment practices, and it limited the Justice Department's injunctive powers against racial discrimination to the area of schools. Its public accommodations section affected only those enterprises having a "substantial" impact on interstate commerce. Recognizing these loopholes, progressives in the House toughened the bill by adding the Fair Employment Practices Commission and by authorizing the Attorney General to intervene in any civil rights suit initiated by private parties. It was this tougher bill, not Kennedy's milder version, that the House passed in January 1964, two months after the assassination in Dallas.

It is all too easy, of course, to criticize Kennedy for his caution concerning civil rights and other domestic reforms. He had considerable obstacles to contend with, for Congress did not share the protesters' views. As late as March 1963—before the demonstration at Birmingham—almost everyone agreed that Congress would have ignored civil rights proposals. Even in 1964 the Senate seemed prepared to filibuster the bill to death. In moving cautiously Kennedy remained flexible enough to take advantage of the changing climate of opinion. Had he lived, he could justifiably have argued that his New Frontier rhetoric assisted in the passage of a range of reforms, including civil rights, by 1965.

Of course, he never got the chance to prove what he might have done in a second term. Moreover, it was not surprising that activists grew impatient. Kennedy, they said, was not so much altruistic as manipulative. He displayed more style than substance, more profile than courage. His rhetoric, other critics added, aroused exaggerated hopes and ultimately weakened the credibility of government. Though these criticisms were harsh, they revealed the disenchantment of many people late in 1963. Kennedy, James Reston concluded, had "touched the intellect of the country but not the heart."

NEW FRONTIERS ABROAD

Perhaps no twentieth-century president had been readier than Kennedy to engage the nation in world affairs. "Let every nation know," he proclaimed, ". . . that we shall pay any price, bear any burden, . . . support any friend, oppose any foe to assure the survival . . . of liberty." Confident about his expertise in the realm of foreign policy, he accelerated the centralization of policy-making in the White House, where McGeorge Bundy, a former Harvard dean, played an important role as national security adviser. Kennedy's secretary of state, Dean Rusk, was expected to have a lesser part. Bundy and Rusk, like Kennedy himself, tended to approach the world in the dualistic terms of the Cold War. "Our first great obstacle," Kennedy said, "is still our relations with the Soviet Union and China. We must never be lulled into believing that either power has yielded its ambitions for world domination."

Kennedy's globalism, his anticommunism, and his self-assured activism led him into one of the greatest blunders in the history of American foreign relations: the attempt in April 1961 to overthrow Fidel Castro in Cuba. The reasons for this decision seemed compelling enough beforehand. By 1961 Castro was welcoming Soviet aid and influence. Eisenhower's administration had been training anti-Castro exiles in Guatemala—something, it seemed, had to be done with them. The Central Intelligence Agency under Allen Dulles (John Foster's brother) warned that it was "now or never" in the struggle against Castro's growing power in Latin America. Procrastination, the CIA expostulated, would give Castro time to train pilots for the jet fighters Russia was supplying. Dulles and his top deputy, Richard Bissell, Jr., outlined a plan calling for American logistical support of an invasion by the exiles. Anti-Castro guerillas in Cuba, they implied, would rise in support of the invasion and topple the regime. When the Joint Chiefs of Staff supported the CIA's argument, the administration had every reason to anticipate success.

A few people expressed doubts about the wisdom of the plan. Among them were Senator J. William Fulbright, head of the Senate Foreign Relations Committee, and Marine Commandant David Shoup. Castro, Fulbright said, was a thorn in the flesh but not a dagger in the heart. American support of an invasion would destroy the remnants of good feeling for the "Yanquis" that existed among the people of Latin America. Shoup was more dramatic. He prepared an overlay map of Cuba and laid it on one of the United States. To the surprise of all, Cuba stretched some 800 miles, from New York to Chicago; clearly, it would not be conquered quickly. Shoup then placed a second overlay on the others. It was of a tiny island. What is that? he was asked. "That, gentlemen," he replied, "represents the island of Tarawa [where Shoup had won a Medal of Honor in World War II] and it took us . . . 18,000 marines to take it." The military lesson could not have been more obvious.

Kennedy's top people, however, were activists by temperament. Placing great faith in America's superior technological capacity, they assumed that a preinvasion air strike would wipe out Castro's defenses and assure the success of the landing. They also thought that an invasion would unleash popular discontent with the government. These characteristically American attitudes—exaggerated faith in technology, blindness to nationalism in the Third World—left Fulbright and Shoup without significant support. With remarkably little hesitation, the National Security Council approved the plan on April 4.

The invasion—at the Bay of Pigs on April 17—was an unrelieved disaster. The open movement beforehand of exiles both in Guatemala and Florida made it easy for Castro to anticipate the attack. Moreover, the air strike failed to destroy Castro's air force. With only six operational fighters he was able to knock out five of twelve planeloads of paratroopers, to strafe ground troops, and to disable a munitions ship loaded with exile soldiers. Richard Bissell and others then tried to persuade Kennedy to authorize the use of American planes as air cover. Kennedy refused, for he knew it was too late to salvage success. Castro then mopped up the remaining invaders. In trying to intervene, the New Frontiersmen revealed that they shared the Eisenhower administration's anticommunism—without possessing the General's military know-how or sense of restraint.

The New Frontiersmen showed better judgment on other foreign questions in 1961 and 1962. Greatly expanding initiatives begun under Eisenhower, the Kennedy administration promoted the Alliance for Progress in the Western Hemisphere. The Alliance promised to outlay some $20 billion by 1970 in American aid for social and economic programs. Other priorities, notably the war in Vietnam, later prevented the program from accomplishing much. But Kennedy's apparent hostility to right-wing elites in Latin America suggested that he sympathized with progressive forces. His support of the Peace Corps, which promoted educational, technological, and social change in the area (and in underdeveloped regions throughout the world), further enhanced his reputation abroad. By 1964 America's relations south of the border were temporarily warmer than they had been in 1960.

Elsewhere in the Third World Kennedy showed more restraint than he had in Cuba. In Laos, where communists, moderates, and right-wing forces struggled for control, he resisted the temptation to involve American manpower and supported instead a neutral coalition. After extended talks in Geneva, Averell Harriman, America's chief negotiator, worked out such an arrangement in 1962. The Pathet Lao, the native communist forces supported by Russia and North Vietnam, soon resumed the fighting, and Laos remained a war-torn land. But Kennedy had at least avoided direct American participation. His toleration of neutralism in the Third World, while limited, contrasted sharply with Dulles's hostility in the 1950s.

Kennedy also exhibited toughness with Khrushchev, who treated his young American adversary contemptuously at a brief meeting in Vienna in June 1961. America, the Soviet leader warned at the time, must agree to a German peace treaty by December. Otherwise, Russia would sign a separate agreement permitting East Germany to control access routes into West Berlin. Kennedy responded by reaffirming America's commitment to Berlin, by mobilizing reserve units, and by using the confrontation to get higher defense appropriations from Congress. He even endorsed, though only temporarily, erection of fallout shelters. Russia reacted by raising barriers (later to become the Berlin Wall) preventing the flow of East German refugees to the West. Suddenly, American and Russian tanks faced each other at the line between the zones. Fighting, perhaps leading to nuclear war, appeared at hand. But the military forces avoided incidents, Khrushchev let his deadline pass without further action, and tensions gradually subsided. Kennedy's management of the confrontation showed that he was tough and that he would employ brinkmanship to secure his ends.

The young president's handling of the Cuban missile crisis in 1962 revealed even more clearly his tendency to toughness and brinkmanship. The crisis

See how many are staying on our side.

One cartoonist's view
of the Berlin Wall, 1961.

began in October when U-2 planes discovered that the Soviets were emplacing offensive missiles on Cuban soil. Many angry American officials counseled for an air strike to prevent completion of the missile sites, and for a time it appeared that the President would authorize it. After tense discussions, however, this option was postponed. Such a strike, Robert Kennedy recalled, would have made his brother the Tojo of the 1960s. Instead, the administration proclaimed a "quarantine," or blockade, of the island. For two days Russian ships headed for the blockade, and the United States stood "eyeball to eyeball" with the Soviet Union. It was the most frightening confrontation of the Cold War. Khrushchev, however, proved wise enough to avoid naval engagements thousands of miles from Russian territory. On October 24 he ordered the ships to turn about, and on October 26 he promised to remove the missiles if the United States ended the blockade and renounced any intention of invading Cuba. The next day he changed his mind and sent a much more hostile message. Kennedy, however, shrewdly pretended that the second cable had never arrived. America acceded to Khrushchev's initial deal, and the crisis was over.

The President's defenders have emphasized his restraint during this confrontation. Kennedy, they point out, resisted pleas for an immediate air strike, then had the cunning to ignore the second Soviet note. Moreover, the President's admirers add, he showed wisdom as well as restraint. Permitting the installation of offensive missiles in Cuba, they insist, would have altered the balance of power by giving the enemy greater "first strike" potential. They argue also that JFK had to prove his toughness to Khrushchev, who had (presumably) found him indecisive at Vienna and during the Bay of Pigs fiasco. Kennedy, they conclude, had to act firmly or risk more provocative Soviet behavior concerning Berlin and western Europe.

These arguments are difficult to disprove—for Khrushchev's behavior seemed both antagonistic and erratic. But it is rather frightening to think of world leaders like Kennedy risking the destruction of Western civilization in order to establish *machismo*. It is equally frightening to learn—from later accounts—that Kennedy was very conscious at the time that toughness would assist his party in the imminent congressional elections. And it is questionable whether his brinkmanship was necessary. Though Khrushchev acted provocatively, his policy in Cuba would have made little difference in the existing military situation: offensive missiles were already well emplaced on Soviet soil. Indeed, in one sense Khrushchev was merely emulating the United States, which had missiles pointing at the Soviet Union from nearby Turkey.

Recognizing this parallel, Adlai Stevenson, who was Kennedy's ambassador at the UN, had recommended tentatively during the crisis that America avoid confrontation by suggesting an exchange. Russia would pull its missiles out of Cuba, and the United States would dismantle its bases in Turkey. Because the Turkish installations were not needed—Kennedy had previously ordered them removed, only to be disobeyed by the Pentagon—Stevenson's idea seemed a more measured response than a blockade. In any event, as Stevenson and others pointed out at the time, there was little to lose by trying to negotiate first. If Russia proved obdurate, there was still time for sterner stuff. But though the Russians were led to believe that the Turkish bases would be dismantled once the crisis was over, the administration's main—and public—response was the blockade. People like Stevenson, White House aides implied, lacked backbone.

Ironically the missile crisis had the unanticipated effect of sobering both sides in the Cold War. Shaken, both Kennedy and Khrushchev paid more attention to nuclear disarmament, and in the summer of 1963 Averell Harriman succeeded in negotiating a Russian-American ban on nuclear testing on land, on the seas, and in the atmosphere. The measure did not permit on-site inspection, nor did it prohibit underground testing, which continued virtually unchecked. Would-be nuclear powers like France and China refused to ratify it. But Kennedy properly called it "an important first step toward peace, a step toward reason, a step away from war." At his assassination in Dallas a few months later Russian-American relations were more relaxed than they had been since the end of World War II. For this improvement Kennedy's administration could take some of the credit. George Kennan was one of many who praised him accordingly. "I am full of admiration, both as an historian and as a person with diplomatic experience," he wrote before Kennedy's death, "for the manner in which you have addressed yourself to the problems of foreign policy. . . . I don't think we have seen a better standard of statesmanship in the present century."

Kennan, however, did not foresee the legacy of Kennedy's administration in two key areas of foreign policy: defense planning and Vietnam. In the former Kennedy was both opportunistic and demagogic. He came to office having argued on insufficient evidence that America was on the short end of a "missile gap." By February 1961 he knew otherwise. The United States, in fact, had an edge over the Soviets. Yet he acted immediately to improve America's airlift capacity, to speed up Polaris submarine development, and to "accelerate our entire missile program." Using the Berlin stalemate as an excuse, he asked for and received $6 billion in additional defense appropriations in the next six months alone. Russia's response, naturally enough, was to accelerate the production of its own weaponry.

Throughout his administration Kennedy harped on the necessity of balanced defenses—which meant readying America for guerilla warfare as well as nuclear conflict. It was with such wars in mind that he created, over Pentagon protests, the Green Berets, and that he flew himself to Fort Bragg to pick their special equipment. Given these actions, it was ironic that his admirers praised Secretary of Defense McNamara for restoring civilian control over military policy. McNamara's feat, a triumph of managerial expertise, could make a difference only if the "civilians" approached the Cold War differently from the "military." Under Kennedy they ordinarily did not. Far from curbing the potential of the military-industrial complex, the Kennedy administration left it well equipped to fight on land, at sea, or in the air— anywhere, it seemed, in the world.

That "anywhere" was Vietnam. Since the Geneva accord of 1954, which had promised elections on the question of unifying the country in 1956, conditions there had steadily deteriorated. The Eisenhower administration, recognizing that Ho Chi Minh would win such elections, conspired with South Vietnam to see to it that they were never held. Instead, America spent some $2 billion by 1960 to support South Vietnam's Ngo Dinh Diem, a vehemently anticommunist Catholic nationalist. Diem, however, lacked Ho Chi Minh's popular acceptance, and by 1957 his opponents in the south, derisively labeled the Vietcong (Vietnamese Communists), were starting to rebel. When Kennedy took office, civil war was raging, and the Diem regime, though dictatorial and repressive, could not control roads more than 100 yards from urban centers—and these only at night.

Kennedy was perceptive enough to recognize the excesses of Diem's regime, especially its repressive treatment of Buddhists. In September 1963 he stated, "I don't think that unless a greater effort is made to win popular support that the war can be won out there. In the final analysis it is their war. They are the ones who have to win it or lose it." When Diem balked at instituting reforms, Kennedy cut back economic aid. A month later, in

> *Vietnam represents the cornerstone of the Free World in Southeast Asia, the keystone to the arch, the finger in the dike. Burma, Thailand, India, Japan, the Philippines and, obviously, Laos and Cambodia are among those whose security would be threatened if the red tide of Communism overflowed into Vietnam. . . . Moreover, the independence of Free Vietnam is crucial to the free world in fields other than the military. Her economy is essential to the economy of all of Southeast Asia; and her political liberty is an inspiration to those seeking to obtain or maintain their liberty in all parts of Asia—and indeed the world. The fundamental tenets of this nation's foreign policy, in short, depend in considerable measure upon a strong and free Vietnamese nation.*
>
> Kennedy on Vietnam, 1956.

November, a military coup overthrew and killed Diem. Though Kennedy had not foreseen Diem's assassination, he knew in advance of the plot and made no attempt to prevent it. By letting the coup take place, the President showed that he did not want to associate America with ineffectively repressive regimes.

But Kennedy's growing disillusion with Diem never meant support for Ho Chi Minh. On the contrary, JFK regularly opposed the rebels in the south. "The Free World," he said, "must increasingly protect against and oppose communist subversive aggression as practiced today most acutely in Southeast Asia." His vice president, Lyndon Johnson, underscored America's commitment by going to Vietnam and publicly hailing Diem as the Winston Churchill of Southeast Asia. General Maxwell Taylor, a forceful advocate of larger American ground forces, and Walt W. Rostow, a top presidential adviser, insisted that Kennedy must step up aid to the Diem regime. By early 1963 McNamara and others were reporting confidently about favorable "kill ratios" and "actual body counts." By November America had some 17,000 military "advisers" in Vietnam, some of whom were engaging in combat and getting killed. This was more than eight times the number that had been stationed there at the end of Eisenhower's administration.

This escalation was not a prelude to an inevitable American involvement under President Johnson. Kennedy did not want to engage in a ground war in Southeast Asia. Had he lived, he might have acted with restraint. But the fact remains that Kennedy's stand on Vietnam, like his defense policy, was disingenuous. As president, it was his responsibility to educate the electorate about international complexities. His failure to do so, indeed his repetition of the dualistic clichés of the Cold War, revealed that he shared many of the assumptions of the Truman and Eisenhower years: communism was a united, world-wide conspiracy; America was the savior of the "free world"; technological superiority would overwhelm Asian opposition. Far from crossing "new frontiers" in foreign policy, he traveled over much old terrain.

The Johnson years, 1963–1968

Few presidents have received as much abuse as Lyndon Johnson, Kennedy's successor. By the late 1960s stories circulated about his towering ego, his crudity, his cruelty to members of his staff. Once he publicly addressed his press secretary, George Reedy, as a "stupid sonofabitch." He raged at another aide, Jack Valenti, "I thought I told you, Jack, to fix this fucking doorknob. . . . Where the goddam hell have you been?" The historian Eric Goldman, who served briefly as a consultant to the White House, repeated an alleged exchange between Johnson and a friend. Upset by criticism, the President supposedly asked, "why don't people like me?" The friend replied: "because, Mr. President, you are not a very likeable man."

Liberals especially distrusted Johnson. From 1948, when he squeaked into the Senate by eighty-seven votes, through the 1950s, when he worked with conservatives of the Eisenhower administration, they had found him uncooperative. They also observed his assiduous protection of southwestern oil and gas interests, his coolness to civil rights, and his close relations with hustlers like Bobby Baker, a top aide during his Senate years. In his fondness for wheeling and dealing, for long pointed collars and shiny suits, and for back-room stories, he seemed like a riverboat gambler, albeit with the drawl and the swagger of a Texas tycoon.

These unflattering portrayals overlooked other sides of Johnson. Though he alienated liberals, it was not because he was instinctively conservative but because he had to satisfy his Texas constituency. Indeed, he had begun his political career in the 1930s as an ardent New Deal congressman. Roosevelt himself had regarded him as future presidential material. Thereafter Johnson became an extraordinarily effective Senate majority leader from 1954 to 1960. As he grew more secure in his political base, he tentatively accepted many liberal programs, including the civil rights bill of 1957—which could not have become law without his patient negotiations on Capitol Hill.

I dreamed about 1960 myself the other night, and I told Stuart Symington [Democratic Senator from Missouri] and Lyndon Johnson about it in the cloakroom yesterday. I told them about how the Lord came into my bedroom, anointed my head and said, "John Kennedy, I hereby appoint you President of the U.S." Stuart Symington said, "That's strange, Jack, because I too had a similar dream last night in which the Lord anointed me and declared me, Stuart Symington, President of the United States and of Outer Space." Lyndon Johnson then said, "That's very interesting, gentlemen, because I too had a similar dream last night and I don't remember anointing either one of you."

Kennedy jokes about Johnson's egotism prior to the 1960 campaign.

Johnson's detractors also tended to ignore traits that made him one of the most dynamic chief executives in American history. One of these was his unflagging energy in working with Congress. Unlike Kennedy and Eisenhower, who disliked the hard negotiating involved in securing legislation, he undertook it himself. By 1968 this passion to be at the center of the action had worn him out. It deprived him of the assistance of men of ideas, who found him increasingly domineering. But it enabled him to know exactly how congressmen stood on issues and to move quickly in rewarding his friends and punishing his foes. No one since Roosevelt, his idol, had shown such careful attention to the details of legislation.

The President often resorted to what was known as the "Johnson Treatment," described by one senator as a "great overpowering thunderstorm that consumed you as it closed in on you." Johnson, the columnists Rowland Evans and Robert Novak explained, bore in on people he wished to convince, "his face a scant millimeter from his target, his eyes widening and narrowing, his eyebrows rising and falling. From his pockets poured clippings, memos, statistics, mimicry, humor, and the genius of analogy [which] made the Treatment an almost hypnotic experience and rendered the target stunned and helpless."

If the Treatment failed to work, Johnson was ready with other forms of pressure: seemingly endless phone calls, promises (or threats) concerning patronage, even simple appeals for justice. "You get the impression from reading all these [newspaper] stories that he's always twisting arms," one congressman noted, "but what he really twists is your heart. He says he's got to have your help, and tears are practically coming out of the telephone receiver."

In applying such methods Johnson had advantages denied Kennedy. Among these were friendships with many powerful figures on the Hill. Senators like Richard Russell of Georgia and Harry Byrd of Virginia had had little reason to help Kennedy; with Johnson, a crony of many years' standing, it was harder to be obstructive. Another advantage was his southern background, which made his support of civil rights all the more impressive. His Protestantism gave him an edge that Kennedy had lacked in handling the explosive question of aid to parochial schools. Above all, Johnson came to office at a time when Americans were shocked by Kennedy's assassination. As in 1933, they were yearning for purposeful leadership.

Johnson used these advantages brilliantly in late 1963 and 1964. On November 27, five days after the assassination, he made Kennedy's program his own by appearing before Congress and reminding it of the unfinished New Frontier, especially in the realm of civil rights. "No memorial oration or eulogy," he said, "could more eloquently honor President Kennedy's memory than the earliest possible passage of the civil rights bill for which he fought so long. . . . I urge you again, as I did in 1957 and again in 1960, to enact a civil rights law so that we can move forward to eliminate from this nation every trace of discrimination and oppression that is based upon race or color."

In 1964, Johnson persisted in similar appeals to carry out Kennedy's program—with breathtaking results. Congress approved the $13.5 billion tax cut Kennedy had called for in June 1963. It passed a controversial bill authorizing federal funds for mass transit. It quickly enacted an $800 million "war against poverty" program. And it passed the first effective civil rights bill since Reconstruction. The Civil Rights Act of 1964 created a Fair Employment Practices Committee, banned discrimination in public accommodations, gave the Attorney General injunctive powers in cases involving school segregation as well as voting rights, and authorized the government to withhold funds from public authorities practicing racial discrimination.

Given the national mood, these measures might have passed in any event. Still, Johnson made a difference. The poverty program, though originally conceived in the closing weeks of the Kennedy administration, owed its shape and scope to LBJ's efforts. The tax cut escaped the Senate Finance Committee only after he promised Senator Byrd, the committee chairman, that he would cut federal spending. The bill then passed the Senate, seventy-seven to twenty-one, with the consensus that he demanded. Johnson was most effective of all in shepherding the civil rights bill. Instead of settling for half a loaf, he encouraged House liberals to tack on tougher amendments to Kennedy's original bill. As moderates had warned, his action provoked a Senate filibuster. But Johnson held firm, and fence-sitting senators soon began to feel the pressure from home. After fifty-seven days the Senate invoked cloture for the first time in the history of civil rights legislation.

As if to ensure Johnson's continued success, the Republicans then nominated Senator Barry Goldwater of Arizona to oppose him in November. Right-wingers hailed the choice, for Goldwater was an avowed reactionary who opposed civil rights legislation and progressive federal taxation, and who called for bombing in Vietnam. At the GOP convention he antagonized moderates in his own party by courting support from the right-wing John Birch Society. "Extremism in defense of liberty is no vice," he proclaimed. His partisans proclaimed, "In Your Heart You Know He's Right," but opponents countered with "In Your Guts You Know He's Nuts."

In fact, Goldwater's nomination suggested a major trend of the future: the rise of ideology (especially of conservatism) in American politics. The successes of other right-wing politicians of the late 1960s and 1970s—Governor George Wallace of Alabama, Governor Ronald Reagan of California—revealed that many Americans were dissatisfied not only with liberalism but with the center as well. In 1964, however, Goldwater's ideology seemed particularly extreme. No major party candidate for the presidency had ever seemed farther from the mainstream of American political thought.

Johnson took full advantage of Goldwater's exposed position on the issues. The GOP stance on Vietnam, LBJ implied, was irresponsible. "We are not going South and we are not going North," he said on September 28. "We are going to continue to try to save their own freedom with their own men, with our leadership and our officer direction." On October 21 he added (in the same vein as FDR in 1940), "we are not going to send American boys nine or ten thousand miles away from home to do what Asian boys ought to be doing for themselves." On domestic questions he emphasized his liberal sympathies by naming Hubert Humphrey as his running mate, and he appealed to the center by reminding people of Goldwater's extremism. "Right here is the reason I'm going to win this thing so big," he told a friend. "You ask a voter who classifies himself as a liberal what he thinks I am and he says 'a liberal.' You ask a voter who calls himself a conservative what I am and he says 'a conservative.' You ask a voter who calls himself a middle-roader, and that is what he calls me. They all think I'm on their side."

To no one's surprise Johnson won overwhelmingly, by 43.1 million to 27.1 million. Goldwater carried only Arizona and five southern states. The GOP, once moribund in Dixie, now seemed wrecked everywhere else. Democrats also secured huge majorities of 68 to 32 in the Senate and 295 to 140 in the House. The enormous shifts in voting since 1960 showed that the electorate was becoming unpredictable and unstable in presidential elections.

Exhilarated, LBJ interpreted the election as a mandate for further domestic reform. "Hurry, boys, hurry," he told his aides. "Get that legislation up to the Hill and out. Eighteen months from now ol' Landslide Lyndon will be Lame-Duck Lyndon." Driven at a furious pace, the Democratic Congress responded with the most far-reaching legislation since 1935. Chief among its accomplishments were medicare and aid to elementary and secondary education. Medicare, funded by an increase in social security taxes, provided for health care to the aged. A corollary program, medicaid, offered free care to poor people of all ages who qualified for public assistance. The education act set aside an initial appropriation of $1 billion. Much supplemented in succeeding years, it gave the federal government an unprecedented role in educational policy.

Hardly pausing for breath, Congress approved many other reforms in 1965. It appropriated generously for manpower training, authorized $900 million to improve conditions in Appalachia, passed a housing act that

A supreme congressional politician, President Johnson was an incompetent and ineffective national politician. This should not have been too surprising. After all, he had had experience in only two national campaigns: one when he was the vice-presidential candidate, the other when he was running for President against a man Noam Chomsky [a radical antiwar intellectual] could have beaten. In his political instincts he was more a South American caudillo than a North American leader.... The President as a man impressed increasing numbers of Americans as high-handed, devious and disingenuous, the embodiment of a political system that wilfully deceived the people and denied them a voice in vital decisions.

Arthur Schlesinger, Jr., a liberal historian and Kennedy partisan, offers a widely held view of Johnson, 1969.

Selma, Alabama, 1965.
The Civil Rights Act of that year
prompted an intense
and often imaginative effort
to get blacks to register to vote.

included provisions for rent supplements, set aside $1.6 billion more for the war against poverty, and established the Economic Development Act for depressed areas with the potential for growth. It created the Department of Housing and Urban Development and the National Endowment for the Arts and the Humanities, authorized an additional $2.4 billion for education, including colleges and universities, and approved a new immigration law ending quotas based on pseudoscientific theories. When police in Selma, Alabama, roughed up blacks seeking to register to vote, new outrage exploded among civil rights advocates. Prodded by Johnson, Congress then approved the Civil Rights Act of 1965. This far-reaching piece of legislation authorized federal examiners to register voters, and it banned literacy tests. Along with passage of the twenty-fourth amendment (1964), which outlawed the poll tax in federal elections, it enabled thousands of formerly disfranchised people to register, to vote, and later to elect black officials in record numbers throughout the South. It was a fitting capstone to a congressional session of unparalleled productivity, and it made Johnson—once the whipping boy of liberals—the greatest champion of progressivism since FDR.

DISILLUSIONMENT WITH LIBERALISM

That very year, however, the euphoria began to disappear. Altruism turned to frustration, then to disenchantment. By 1966 Americans were tiring of listening to the "best and brightest"—the journalist David Halberstam's apt phrase describing the liberals, intellectuals, and "experts" who had ruled since 1961. Explaining this rapid change in mood tells much about the strengths and limitations of modern liberalism, about the stubbornness of the nation's problems, about the relative weakness of governmental institutions, and—in the last analysis—about the role of traditional attitudes.

This change of mood gradually affected Capitol Hill. Between 1966 and 1968 the lawmakers increased the minimum wage, created a Department of Transportation, and established a Model Cities program. In 1968 they approved another civil rights act—against discrimination in housing. But by then Congress was already cautious in authorizing funds for rent supplements, housing, and the war against poverty. For the next decade congressional advocates of reform remained as stymied as they had been from 1937 to 1963.

Johnson's programs, by falling far short of expectations, were partly to blame for these developments. Funds for Appalachia, many people observed, went primarily for short-run projects and to road-building, which gave out-of-state profiteers access to valuable raw materials. Aid to education failed to provide money for teachers' salaries or for renovation of urban schools, which continued to deteriorate. Medicare, too, left reformers dissatisfied, for it assisted only the elderly, was financed by regressive social security taxes, and failed to bring about reforms in the medical establishment.

The urban reforms of the Great Society (and of previous liberal administrations) caused particular disenchantment. Some programs, such as aid to mass transit and rent supplements, never received adequate appropriations. Public housing, started in 1937, suffered from many handicaps: insufficient funding, bureaucratic red tape, hostility from real estate interests, and fears by surrounding residents of "black invasions." By 1969 only 700,000 public housing units had been built, leaving some 4 million Americans in substandard dwellings. Urban renewal and rehabilitation (begun under Truman) was perhaps most controversial of all. In some cities these programs worked fairly well—much better, in fact, than critics were prepared to admit. Elsewhere, however, urban renewal resulted in "projects"—sterile, high-rise developments that deteriorated into zones of social pathology—or it destroyed viable communities (usually of blacks or other groups without political power) and replaced them with middle-income housing or commercial developments. "At a cost of more than three billion dollars," a liberal critic observed in 1965, "the Urban Renewal Agency has succeeded in materially reducing the supply of low-cost housing in American cities."

The urban poor complained especially loudly about federal welfare policies. Many government programs, such as aid to the blind, to the disabled, and to dependent children, continued to require state contributions—stipulations that resulted in wide variations and (especially in the poorer southern states) in wholly inadequate standards. Welfare recipients had to meet strict residency requirements (declared unconstitutional in 1969) and unnecessarily demeaning tests. Mothers who sought aid for dependent children had to prove that there was no man at home to provide support. This "absent father" rule

> *What will the projects look like? They will be spacious, parklike, and uncrowded. They will feature long green vistas. They will be stable and symmetrical and orderly. They will be clean, impressive, and monumental. They will have all the attributes of a well-kept, dignified cemetery.*
>
> Jane Jacobs, a critic of urban planners, describes modern public housing design.

may have helped to disrupt marriages. (It, too, was declared unconstitutional, in 1968.) All these provisions required an ever increasing bureaucracy of social workers. Though dedicated and humane, these workers offended militants who demanded an end to "snooping" and to governmental "paternalism" in general. Social workers, one young slum dweller protested, "are rat fink types. They act like they think we're not human. They think they've got all there is, and all they do is convert us to think and do what they think and do." Gilbert Steiner, a liberal expert on welfare programs, concluded in 1971 that the Kennedy–Johnson public assistance policies left a legacy of a "services approach that had failed, a work and training approach that could not get off the ground, an asserted interest in day care but no viable day care program, . . . and a steadily increasing number of AFDA [aid to families of dependent children] recipients."

Easily the most controversial of the Great Society programs was the much ballyhooed "war on poverty," which Johnson hailed as a "milestone in our 180-year search for a better life for our people." This broad-ranging program operated under a newly created Office of Economic Opportunity (OEO), which received close to $10 billion in federal money between 1965 and 1970. Among its programs were loans for farmers and rural coops, aid to migrant workers, work experience programs, and adult education. More significant were VISTA (volunteers in service to America), which was a "domestic peace corps" of young people who lived with and provided services to the poor; the Job Corps, residential centers offering counseling and job training for unskilled young people; and the Neighborhood Youth Corps, a program providing work and on-the-job training for students and dropouts. Most important of all were the community action agencies under the Community Action Program (CAP). These agencies, of which there were 1000 by the end of the decade, sought to develop neighborhood solutions to the problems of poverty. Some focused on educational programs such as Head Start for preschool children and Follow-Through for elementary school students. Others concentrated on legal services. Still others worked hard to develop family planning services or to provide day care centers for children. All the community action agencies were supposed to avoid "paternalism" by giving poor people "maximum feasible participation" in planning.

By the late 1960s, it appeared that the war on poverty was getting nowhere. Of all its efforts, only the Neighborhood Youth Corps and work experience programs were actually providing jobs to help the employable poor. Indeed, the war in Vietnam, by heating up the economy, did much more than did the OEO to create jobs. The unemployable poor—the aged, crippled, and, above all, nonsupported mothers and their dependent children—had to turn to the nation's creaking welfare "system." By 1969 the plight of such people (the number of mothers and dependent children on relief had risen from 3.5 million to 8 million since 1961) was so desperate that the Nixon administration proposed a program of family assistance payments setting a floor below which income would not be permitted to fall.

Many of the limitations of the war on poverty (and other programs) stemmed from lack of funds. Average expenditures per year by the OEO were approximately $1.7 billion. Even when added to the $5 billion per year for medicare and the $1 billion per year for poor school districts under the education act of 1965, this was a piddling sum (approximately $250 per poor person), which could not begin to take care of the 25 to 35 million Americans who were classified as poor in the mid- and late 1960s.

Even with proper funding, the war on poverty would have been burdened with its own dubious assumptions. Head Start, though praiseworthy in purpose, could not compensate for deprivations rooted in cultural and familial forces. Advocates of day-care centers wrongly assumed that there were large numbers of qualified people to run them, or that mothers would willingly deposit their children in them to accept menial employment. The Job Corps, it developed, was a very costly program that falsely assumed that the hard-core

An antipoverty worker tutors a child in Alabama.

poor could be trained to think and work like other people. By the late 1960s Job Corps centers were already beginning to be closed down.

The community action agencies were the most controversial of all the OEO programs. Though most of them were well run, a few fell into the hands of the wrong kinds of entrepreneurial leaders: in Syracuse, an extreme example, $7 million of the $8 million expended by mid-1967 went for salaries and administration—and only $1 million to the poor. Leaders in some communities soon adopted the fashionable revolutionary rhetoric and the racial separatism of the late-1960s (see chapter 14). Such leaders alarmed local politicans, who moved quickly to prevent federal money from flowing toward those rivals for power. In 1967 these politicians succeeded in getting Congress to require state approval of community action initiatives. Thus expired—in two years—the much-acclaimed stress on local administration and on "maximum feasible participation."

CAP suffered from other fundamental misconceptions. One of these was the assumption that poverty could be fought on a neighborhood basis. This view, useful in promoting participation by the poor, underestimated the mobility in and out of slums. The warriors against poverty also assumed—again with little evidence to guide them—that poor people could organize themselves. This was not always the case, for the "culture of poverty" in some (not all) areas tended to fragment, demoralize, and disorganize the poor. Elsewhere, racial and ethnic groups confronted one another. Contrary to the expectations of those who thought that community action could mobilize the poor against "power elites," the experience in many areas suggested that hard-core poverty was all but immune to attack by approaches such as CAP. In retrospect, it is reasonably clear that the poor would have benefited more from WPA-like public employment programs or from legislation guaranteeing a minimum annual income for all. Such programs would have done more to give poor people pride, economic security, and the ability to think of the future.

Some of these misconceptions stemmed from Johnson's passion for rapid accomplishment. He simply did not give Congress time to contemplate its actions. As the sociologist Nathan Glazer observed later, the war on poverty was enacted with "nothing like the powerful political pressure and long-sustained intellectual support that produced the great welfare measures of the New Deal." Donald Rumsfeld, head of the antipoverty effort under the Nixon administration, added that "few programs were ever so unformed at birth, and few were so completely and broadly defined, for good or ill, by the times in which they were implemented. Perhaps the story of Community Action must be told by a poet or a mystic rather than a politician or a historian."

Other critics complained that Johnson, like most New Deal liberals, relied too heavily on the presumed benefits of federal spending. Throw money at problems, he seemed to say, and they will go away. The journalist David Broder observed, "His primary purpose was to provide all the tangible benefits that Federal initiative could devise and Federal money could buy. There was no pause to consider how each of the new Federal programs meshed with all the others, or whether the function was one the national government could most appropriately undertake." To Broder and others Johnson's programs merely encouraged pressure groups (including welfare mothers) to demand ever greater sums from Uncle Sam. Johnson, critics concluded, was too much the bread-and-butter liberal who spent money as if there were no tomorrow.

To the extent that these critics perceived Johnson as a lavish spender they were unfair. As the war on poverty revealed, the money expended on domestic programs between 1965 and 1968 was modest. Much more was needed to attack social problems. Critics were closer to the mark, however, in suggesting that spending on welfare services—as opposed to providing public employment or a guaranteed minimum income—was no panacea. In this sense Johnson was indeed something of a paternalist—a politician trying to develop middle-class behavior and values in poor people whose primary needs were jobs and money.

Johnson's greatest error—and Kennedy's before him—was to promise so much. Kennedy had talked about getting the country moving again, about crossing new frontiers. Johnson went still further: there was to be a "war" on poverty, an end to racial injustice, a "Great Society." Such high-sounding rhetoric was inspiring, at least for a while. But it aroused unrealistic expectations, radical protest, middle-class backlash, the acrimony that settled over the nation by 1966 and the political conservatism that came about thereafter. It led others, including many young radicals, to blame Johnson for "running out of ideas" and to attack liberals in general. "Liberalism," one militant said, "drifts in smug self-satisfaction, preening itself with its pragmatic and value-free cleverness in social problem solving. . . . The time for radicalism has struck." As in the years after the New Deal reforms of 1933–35, much of the energy and idealism that might have been invested in improving the programs already passed was poured instead into alienated protests against the "establishment" reformers who had produced them.

It was unperceptive of such people to dismiss Johnson's programs or to denounce the liberal orthodoxies on which they drew. LBJ was much more than a simple opportunist, and his policies, especially in the realms of health and education, offered much to ordinary people. The civil rights acts of 1964 and 1965 were among the most far-reaching pieces of legislation passed in American history. In criticizing such reforms many radicals could do little more than demand more of the same, while Marxists called for changes that were simply unrealizeable within the framework of American values and institutions.

Still, by the late 1960s the disillusion with Johnsonism was not wholly groundless. LBJ's Vietnam policy (see chapter 14) was an unmitigated disaster that drained support—and funds—from domestic programs and divided the country. Moreover, like his idol FDR, Johnson stopped short of fundamental social change. He made no effort to reform the tax laws, to redistribute income, or to attack monopoly. He was slow to perceive the flaws in welfare and urban programs. Like other liberals, he tended to ignore evidence that the Welfare State did more, as the economist Kenneth Boulding put it, to redistrib-

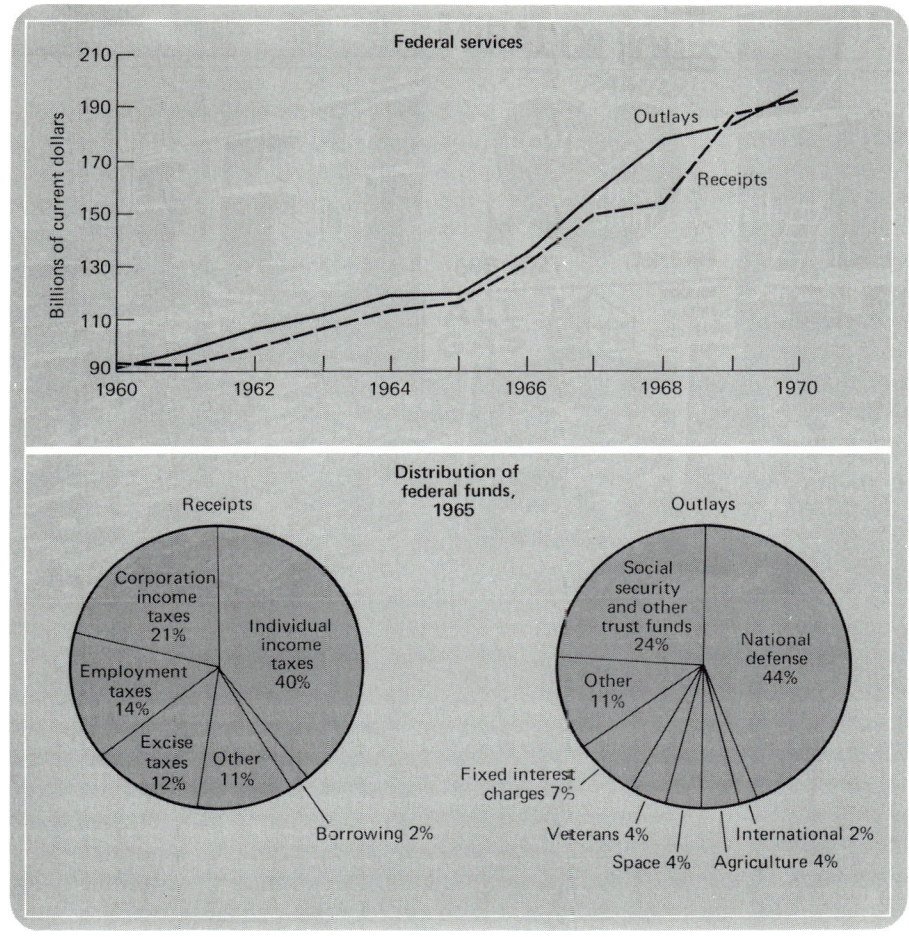

Federal services

(Line graph: Billions of current dollars vs. years 1960–1970, showing Outlays and Receipts)

Distribution of federal funds, 1965

Receipts
- Corporation income taxes 21%
- Individual income taxes 40%
- Employment taxes 14%
- Excise taxes 12%
- Other 11%
- Borrowing 2%

Outlays
- Social security and other trust funds 24%
- National defense 44%
- Other 11%
- Fixed interest charges 7%
- Veterans 4%
- Space 4%
- Agriculture 4%
- International 2%

SOURCE: U.S. Bureau of the Census, *Statistical Abstract of the United States: 1974,* 95th ed. (Washington, D.C., 1974), p. 220; distribution of funds projected by *Statistical Abstract of the United States: 1964,* p. 387

Growth of federal services, 1960–1970, and percent distribution of federal funds by function, 1965

ute income "toward the deserving middle class and the people who know how to get on the gravy train than it had for the poor."

Accordingly, many thoughtful observers began to question the state's ability to solve social problems. "There is mounting evidence," the writer Peter Drucker said, "that government is big rather than strong; that it is fat and flabby rather than powerful; that it costs a great deal and does not achieve much. . . . The citizen less and less believes in government and is increasingly disenchanted with it." James Sundquist, a liberal political scientist, added in 1968: "There are many signs that the capacity of the United States to make policies and establish programs in the domestic field has outrun its capacity, or its determination, to finance and administer them." With people such as these in doubt about welfare statism, it is not surprising that reformers were forced to the defensive after 1965.

PRACTICALLY INSUPERABLE PROBLEMS

Poverty in the Cities   Johnson's critics also underestimated the size of the problems to be confronted. These, by the mid-1960s, revealed a socially divided nation. Racial tensions in the United States dwarfed those in any other advanced western society. Poverty, as books like Michael Harrington's *The Other America* (1962) revealed, affected as much as one-fifth of America's population, or nearly 40 million people, in 1960. The United States was a highly mobile society—perhaps the most mobile in the western world. The northward migration of blacks since World War II was particularly rapid. Between 1950 and 1970 the black population in metropolitan areas rose by seven million. Moreover, these cities offered fewer blue-collar opportunities than had been available to immigrants at the turn of the century. Thus it was that central cities stagnated or became dumping grounds for unemployed (or unemployable) rural migrants. In New York City, where the migrations were particularly large, the welfare load increased from 530,000 in 1965 to 1.2 million in 1972. This meant that one person in every six was on welfare and that the cost to the city was $1 billion per year. (CAP, by contrast, contributed only $50 million.) Many of LBJ's critics, radical as well as conservative, were too impatient to recognize the magnitude of these social problems and the reluctance of middle-class Americans to support the redistribution of income necessary to fight them.

America's urban problems reinforced romanticism concerning the frontier and the small town and in so doing impeded thoughtful discussion of remedies. Eric Sevareid, the liberal television broadcaster, told how warmly he (and others) remembered his small-town childhood. "I . . . loved . . . its memory always," he said of the town in which he had grown up. "It was, simply, *home*—and all of it home, not just the house but all the town. That is why childhood in the small towns is different from childhood in the city. Everything is home." Cities, by contrast, were "evil." Reflecting this antiurban bias, TV programs like *Ben Casey, Naked City,* and *East Side West Side* and movies such as *On the Waterfront* and *Pawnbroker* focused on the seamy side of city life.

Cities were not only seamy, Americans thought, but enclaves for minorities—Puerto Ricans, Orientals, Mexican-Americans, and above all, blacks, 80 percent of whom lived in urban areas by 1970. The "core" areas where these minorities lived were generally dirty, overcrowded, and—whites assumed—nests of drug addiction and violent crime. Like all stereotypes, this one was exaggerated in some respects: statistics on crime and drug addiction, never uniformly kept, were unreliable. The statistics on crime were misleading, for the baby boom of previous decades vastly increased the number of teenagers, the age group most likely to get arrested. Whites also failed to recognize the positive side of the cities, which offered wider economic opportunities than did farming regions or small towns, which languished in the postwar era. Compared to the black rural areas in the South, poverty-stricken Puerto Rico, or rural Mexico, America's cities seemed heaven-sent. But whites were correct in perceiving the "blackness" of core areas in the larger cities of the East and Midwest, in recoiling in fear from the spread of hard drugs on the streets, and in recognizing that ghetto areas were dangerous, especially after dark. Hence, whites continued to flee to the suburbs, which had 76 million people by 1970 (cities had 64 million). Confronted with such widespread hostility to cities—and to the blacks with which they were intimately identified—Johnson and urban reformers had difficulty finding support.

Those who continued to press for urban programs in the late 1960s were divided about what to do. Some, like Lewis Mumford, complained of the density of cities; others, such as Jane Jacobs, author of *The Death and Life of Great American Cities* (1963), thought that heterogeneous, closely settled neighborhoods such as Greenwich Village in New York were the ultimate in civilized living. Some reformers continued to press for public housing, but others complained that slums were a reflection, not a cause, of social disorganization. "Once upon a time," one reformer mused sadly, "we thought that if we could only get our problem families out of those dreadful slums, then papa would stop taking dope, mama would stop chasing around, and junior would stop carrying a knife. Well, we've got them in a nice new apartment with modern kitchens and a recreation center. And they're the same bunch of bastards they always were."

Advocates of racial justice were equally divided by the end of the decade. Most white reformers continued to favor federal initiatives to promote desegregation in housing, schools, and employment. Destroy the legal basis for discrimination, they said, and tensions would abate. Some liberals, however, developed doubts about cherished beliefs. In 1965, Daniel Moynihan authored a study for the government, *The Negro Family*. It stressed the social disorganization of black families. Despite increases in black income, he argued, illegitimacy and female-headed households characterized a larger number of nonwhite families than in the 1950s. A year later James Coleman and others published a massive statistical study, *Equality of Opportunity,* concerning American schools. They found that neither the level of spending for education nor desegregation made as much difference in explaining educational achievement as did socioeconomic class. Many activists challenged these findings, especially the Moynihan report, which appeared to resurrect old stereotypes about fun-lovin', indolent "darkies" who drifted from woman to woman. Find economic opportunities for black men, they argued, and families would stabilize. To others, however, reports such as these were unhappy reminders that class and cultural forces as well as "white racism" would continue to plague attempts to promote racial harmony.

The Great Society reformers also had the formidable task of trying to maintain harmony within the West's most polyglot society. According to the 1960 census, America had more than 19 million nonwhites (a term that included Orientals and American Indians as well as blacks), 9.3 million foreign-born whites, and 23.8 million people of mixed or foreign-born parents. The white ethnics alone comprised nearly 20 percent of the nation's population in 1960 of 183 million. Most of them lived unobtrusively, hoping to become accepted. But many jealously guarded their cultural identities, marrying within their own groups, and viewing outsiders with suspicion. The ethnic machines, which some people thought had been eclipsed by Roosevelt's welfare programs, continued to thrive in cities like Chicago, where Mayor Richard Daley ruled over a coalition of ethnic and professional groups. Quite obviously, the melting pot had failed to boil away America's religious, cultural, and ethnic divisions. So long as these existed, it remained difficult to mobilize a reform coalition based on class or occupational lines.

Economic interest groups further divided the potential progressive coalition. In small and relatively homogeneous nations, such as England or Sweden, it was possible (though very difficult even there) to plan ahead. Not so in the United States, where unions, businessmen, farmers, and professional groups joined self-conscious blacks and ethnics in competing for governmental favor. Almost all had pipelines to Congress or to the bewilderingly large federal bureaucracy that had "modernized" the American political system since the 1930s. Neither Johnson nor other postwar American presidents really had the power to control these groups or the bureaucrats who assisted them. Indeed, it was to fight back against these forces that Kennedy and Johnson dramatically increased the White House staff and that Nixon, even more anxious for control, resorted to a range of illegal intelligence-gathering activities.

Large corporations were by far the most powerful of these groups. By mid-decade one-half of the productive assets of American manufacturing was controlled by 150 corporations; two-thirds was held by 500. General Motors, America's largest corporation, made $2 billion in profits after taxes in 1965, a sum greater than the revenue for forty-eight of the fifty states. Its sales exceeded the Gross National Product of all but nine nations in the world. Other big companies spread into far corners of the world during the 1960s. By 1970 American firms sold some $200 billion worth of goods abroad, three-fourths of which was made in American-owned overseas plants. United States private investment abroad (including portfolio investment in overseas securities) grew from $19 billion in 1950 to $49 billion in 1960, and to $101 billion in 1968. International Telephone and Telegraph, among the largest of these "multinational" corporations, had operations in ninety countries, 400,000 employees, and a president who earned $812,000 a year in salary. Like other such corporations, it possessed enormous potential influence over American foreign policies.

Corporate influence at home was still more obvious. The large firms not only employed millions of Americans, but served as important social and welfare institutions. Their investments in pension funds, which increased from $4 billion in 1940 to $100 billion in 1965, deeply affected the stock market and the level of general economic activity. The large corporations also continued to depend on, and to influence, government defense spending. Frequently unrestrained by competition, they remained free to increase prices, thus promoting inflation even in times of recession. As John Kenneth Galbraith argued in 1968, large corporations formed a potent "technostructure" that undermined the free market and made many of the nation's most fundamental decisions concerning production, wages, and technological change. J. P. Morgan would have been gratified.

If Johnson had been disposed to challenge the corporations—which he was not—he would have been unable to rely on their historic adversaries, the labor unions. Though union membership increased slightly in absolute numbers during the postwar years, the labor movement was hurt by the migration of many industries to the South, which was traditionally antiunion, and by the rapid expansion of the middle class, which limited the growth in blue-collar employment. Between 1955 and 1968 the percentage of unionized people in nonagricultural employment declined from 33 to 28 percent. Some of the stronger unions, such as the Teamsters (which had almost 2 million members by 1970), were plagued by corruption. The writer Norman Mailer concluded that such unions "sat closer to the Mafia than to Marx." Though Mailer exaggerated (as usual), he—and other critics—were right in noting the decline in labor militancy, which had been a cutting edge for reform in the 1930s. For every Walter Reuther, the socially conscious head of the United Automobile Workers, there were ten George Meanys, heirs to the Gompers tradition of placing the needs of union members before those of blacks or other poor people. Indeed, Meany, the durable head of the AFL, was often content to make deals with the large corporations: workers would get wage increases, and management an excuse to raise prices for consumers.

Such wage increases did not mean that industrial workers enjoyed lives of comfort, or even that they felt secure. On the contrary, they were among the first to be laid off during hard times, as in 1974–75. Their work on the assembly line seemed ever more tedious and alienating as definitions of the "good life" focused on the desirability of creative labor. Still, regularly employed industrial workers, like skilled craftsmen at the turn of the century, comprised the privileged elite of blue-collar labor. They enjoyed economic "clout" undreamed of in the 1930s. They used it to advance their own interests, not to promote the social welfare of others.

The Weakness of Government As reformers recognized only too well, governmental institutions reflected the power of these interest groups. Among these institutions was Congress, which regularly listened to influential constituents, not to reformers. "I have watched the Congress from either the inside or the outside, man and boy, for more than forty years," Johnson noted, "and I've never seen a Congress that didn't eventually take the measure of the president it was dealing with."

Other political institutions were almost as discouraging to reformers. The parties, for instance, depended upon an increasingly unstable and largely nonideological electorate. Instead of developing into forces for social change, they remained coalitions of quarrelsome interest groups. Similarly, state and local governments, while much expanded since the 1930s, lacked the financial resources (or the will) to enact significant reforms on their own, or even to contribute generously to federal-state welfare programs. America's federal system and decentralized parties made it essential that Johnson use every available presidential resource to enact *national* programs.

Federal bureaucracy, in some ways a modernizing influence, posed further hurdles to efficient social change. From 1947 to 1967 federal civilian employment increased some 30 percent—from 2 to 2.6 million. Most of this expansion occurred within the executive branch. Yet the growth was so uncoordinated that many liberals longed for the fresh, relatively simple days of Roosevelt's "alphabet soup," while others relied on approaches such as CAP, a deliberate attempt to set local pressures *against* the "dead hand" of bureaucracy. Still others, including Walter Heller, Johnson's liberal chairman of the Council of Economic Advisers, favored decentralization of administration through revenue-sharing with the states. (A Democratic Congress approved, and Nixon signed, revenue-sharing in the 1970s.) But Johnson, like his predecessors, often had to rely on the standard means of combatting bureaucracies: creating new ones as coordinators or rivals. The contrast between popular expectations and governmental performance, to say nothing of the cost of increased federal activity, prompted widespread doubts about the capacity of America's public institutions.

> *Legislators represent people, not trees or acres. Legislators are elected by voters, not farms or cities or economic interests. As long as ours is a representative form of government, and our legislatures are those instruments of government elected directly by and directly representative of the people, the right to elect legislators in a free and unimpaired fashion is a bedrock of our political system.*
>
> *Reynolds* v. *Sims* (1964), the Court's decision requiring reapportionment of state legislatures.

THE WARREN COURT: A CENTER OF CONTROVERSY

Johnson could not take much comfort from the most activist Supreme Court in American history. Liberal justices like Earl Warren, Hugo Black, William O. Douglas, and William J. Brennan, Jr., validated the sit-ins of the early 1960s and the civil rights acts of 1964 and 1965. In *Engel* v. *Vitale* (1962) and subsequent decisions they ruled against required prayers and Bible reading in public schools. In a series of cases starting with *Baker* v. *Carr* (1962) the Court struck at legislative malapportionment on both the state and national levels. Only population, it declared, could be the basis for representation. The Court then acted to broaden the rights of accused criminals. In *Gideon* v. *Wainwright* (1963) it declared that indigents charged with felonies in state courts had the right to free counsel; in *Escobedo* v. *Illinois* (1964) it stated that police must permit alleged offenders to consult with lawyers during interrogation; and in *Miranda* v. *Arizona* (1966) it required police to warn suspects that any statements they made could be used against them, and that they had the right to remain silent and to get free legal counsel. As if to antagonize traditionalists still further, the Court ruled against state laws banning the use of contraceptive devices, and it delivered a number of decisions against laws censoring allegedly pornographic material. All these cases marked significant departures from past judicial decisions.

These decisions infuriated conservatives. Southerners reacted as angrily as they had to *Brown* v. *Board of Education* in the 1950s. Traditionalists predicted (with some truth) that the apportionment decisions would involve the Court in what Justice Felix Frankfurter, a dissenter, called the "political thicket" of legislative districting. Catholics, fundamentalists, and others heatedly denounced the decisions concerning Bible reading in the schools, censorship, and contraception. Advocates of "law and order" complained that the Court was "coddling" criminals and hampering effective police work. In 1968 they pushed through the Crime Control and Safe Streets Act, which sanctioned so-called voluntary confessions in federal courts even if suspects were not informed of their rights. The act also authorized police to hold suspects for up to six hours before arraigning them, and to utilize wiretapping for a variety of purposes.

Most of these conservative complaints were considerably exaggerated.

What is wrong with this prayer? Only a Court composed of agnostics could find its defects . . . ; the Court has now officially stated its disbelief in God Almighty. This, to me, represents the most serious blow that has ever been struck at the Constitution of the United States. I know of nothing in my lifetime that could give more aid and comfort to Moscow than this bold, malicious, atheistic, and sacrilegious twist of this unpredictable group of uncontrolled despots.

Representative Mendell Rivers (Democrat, South Carolina) attacks the Supreme Court's decision concerning prayers in schools.

Far from opposing religion, the Court did not prevent children or teachers from praying or from reading the Bible, and it permitted states to supply textbooks to parochial schools. It continued to hold that church property was exempt from taxation. Its decisions concerning criminals merely gave indigents in state courts the rights that they already possessed in federal courts and that wealthier law-breakers such as the Mafiosi had long enjoyed. Subsequent studies suggested that these decisions had little impact on police behavior—only on morale. The apportionment decisions were unprecedented—Warren himself regarded them as the most significant judgments of his tenure. But by the 1960s they seemed long overdue. By then only the Court could have broken the political logjams that had permitted gross overrepresentation for rural areas. Warren also exaggerated the impact of these decisions, for while they gave more political power to the growing suburban areas, they did relatively little to strengthen minority groups. The nation's most deliberately malapportioned institution, the United States Senate, remained constitutionally sacrosanct.

What mattered, however, was what people thought the Court was doing. With crime disturbing America's cities it was convenient to blame the Court's decisions concerning police behavior. As blacks became more "uppity," segregationists considered it equally fair to chastise the judges for abetting civil rights, and especially for decisions striking down laws against intermarriage and against sexual relations between blacks and whites. By 1966 a Harris poll discovered that 65 percent of Americans opposed the tribunal's actions concerning criminals. Millions of people, it seemed, saw in the liberalism of men like Warren the same misguided mollycoddling that they suspected in the Great Society.

These criticisms were the more forceful because the Court was an appointive institution whose jurisdiction in sociopolitical issues was unclear. Indeed, it was hard to ignore Justice Frankfurter's complaint that the Court was concerning itself with nonjudicial matters. Problems such as malapportionment, he insisted, were for popularly elected presidents and legislators to cure. To such critics, the reluctance of democratic institutions—Congress, the presidency, the states—to settle these problems was proof of the relative weakness of representative goverment.

Affluence—bane of social change?

Affluence also helped explain the movement from altruism to disenchantment in the late 1960s. For a time the unprecedented economic growth of the period assisted the activists. The New Economic Policy, reformers were able to maintain, proved that purposeful government did make a difference. Moreover, prosperity freed thousands of Americans, especially college students, from preoccupation with earning their daily bread. The altruism of the early 1960s, like that of the progressive era (but unlike that of the New Deal) coincided with a decided upswing in the business cycle and with the movement of thousands of people into the middle classes.

But affluence was a mixed blessing. In affecting so many people it prompted exaggerated expectations. Poor people, blacks, ethnics, though

Economic growth, 1961–1970, compared to select years before and after this period

	NATIONAL PRODUCT AND INCOME (In billions of current dollars)				PER CAPITA DISPOSABLE INCOME (In current dollars)
	GNP	PERCENT CHANGE FROM GNP OF PRECEDING YEAR (+ OR −)	NATIONAL INCOME	DISPOSABLE PERSONAL INCOME	
1940	99.7	+10.2	18.1	75.7	573
1945	211.9	+ 0.9	181.5	150.2	1,074
1949	256.5	− 0.4	217.5	188.6	1,264
1961	520.1	+ 3.2	427.3	364.4	1,984
1962	560.3	+ 7.7	457.7	385.3	2,065
1963	590.5	+ 5.4	481.9	404.6	2,138
1964	632.4	+ 7.1	518.1	438.1	2,283
1965	684.9	+ 8.3	564.3	473.2	2,436
1966	749.9	+ 9.5	620.6	511.9	2,604
1967	793.9	+ 5.9	653.6	546.3	2,749
1968	864.2	+ 8.9	711.1	591.0	2,945
1969	930.3	+ 7.6	766.0	634.4	3,130
1970	977.1	+ 5.0	800.5	691.7	3,376
1971	1,054.9	+ 8.0	857.7	746.4	3,605
1972	1,158.0	+ 9.8	946.5	802.5	3,843

SOURCE: Adapted from *Economic Report of the President*, 1975, p. 249, 267, 269

better off then ever before, knew from TV and other modern communications how much they were missing. Indeed, the gap between black income (rising) and white income (rising faster) was widening, not narrowing. If people had given Johnson's programs a chance to percolate, this gap might have closed a little. But like the sit-down strikers in 1937, the disaffected refused to wait. Like Roosevelt, Johnson ultimately found himself caught in a wave of social protest that he could do little to channel in constructive directions.

Prosperity also dulled reformism of many adults in the middle and upper middle classes. Though some of these people remained energetic supporters of social change, many others focused on taking care of themselves. For such people, gains in real income meant the chance to buy big cars and stereo sets, to travel, or simply to buy a home and settle down. This privatism helps to explain why support for social change did not run deep. Simultaneously, egocentric materialism unleashed revulsion in a minority of young people, whose strident protests gradually produced backlash among their elders.

This is another way of saying that American attitudes toward the needy had really changed rather little since the 1930s. Although people continued to believe that the state ought to help those who could not help themselves, they also retained much of their historic distrust of Big Government. Thus, when militants attempted to secure social as well as legal equality, this "silent majority" balked. It was this instinctive retreat from social reform that complicated the problems Johnson faced in trying to reduce racism, poverty, and injustice.

For all these reasons Johnson had to strike quickly. If he had waited for lengthy studies or debate, he would have missed the first chance in thirty years to get significant domestic legislation on the statute books. His dilemma suggests the plausibility of the cyclical theory of American reform, which holds that bursts of legislation, long blocked by Congress, by unstable parties, by state and local governments, by the affluence of the politically influential middle classes, by historic fears of Big Government, suddenly cascade over the barriers, only to be followed by troughs of complacency. This theory is not helpful in predicting when or why such bursts occur. But it helps explain why they dissipate so quickly. It suggests that Johnson, for all his limitations, deserves credit for appealing to the mood of altruism while he could.

Suggestions for reading

William Leuchtenburg's *A Troubled Feast** (1973) is the best account of domestic developments in the United States during the 1960s and early 1970s. Other helpful books are William O'Neill's idiosyncratic *Coming Apart* (1971); and Ronald Berman, *America in the Sixties** (1968), an intellectual history. James Sundquist's *Politics and Policy** (1968) is the most thorough account of policy-making; and Seyom Brown's *Faces of Power** (1968) is the most useful survey of developments in foreign affairs.

Other books on politics include Arthur Schlesinger, Jr., *A Thousand Days** (1965), and Theodore Sorenson, *Kennedy* (1965). Both are pro-Kennedy accounts written by insiders. James M. Burns, *John Kennedy** (1960), is a remarkably objective campaign biography. The same author's *Deadlock of Democrccy** (1963) is an engaging interpretation of executive-congressional relations and presidential leadership from the late eighteenth century on. Books on electoral trends include Theodore White, *Making of a President, 1960** (1961), and *Making of a President, 1964* (1965); and Milton Cummings, ed., *The National Election of 1964** (1966). Studies using polling data and quantitative methods are V. O. Key, Jr., and Milton Cummings, *The Responsible Electorate . . . 1936–1960* (1968); and Angus Campbell et al., *The American Voter: An Abridgement** (1964). Other books dealing with aspects of the Kennedy administration are Lawrence Fuchs, *John Kennedy and American Catholicism* (1967); Grant McConnell, *Steel and the Presidency—1962** (1963); and Seymour Harris, *Economics of the Kennedy Years** (1964). Henry Fairlie, *The Kennedy Promise** (1973), is highly critical.

Lyndon Johnson's memoirs, *Vantage Point** (1971), are a self-serving account of his presidency. More critical is Robert Novak and Rowland Evans, *Lyndon B. Johnson: The Exercise of Power** (1966). So are two works by men who served in the Johnson administration: George Reedy, *The Twilight of the Presidency** (1970); and Eric Goldman, *Tragedy of Lyndon Johnson** (1955). The subject of welfare and antipoverty policy is well covered in Peter Marris and Martin Rein, *Dilemmas of Social Reform** (2nd ed., 1973); Sar Levitan, *The Great Society's Poor Law* (1969); and Gilbert Steiner, *State of Welfare* (1971). See also Richard Elman, *The Poorhouse State** (1966); Frances F. Piven and Richard A. Cloward, *Regulating the Poor: The Functions of Public Relief** (1972); and Ben Seligman, *Permanent Poverty** (1968). Jane Jacobs, *Death and Life of Great American Cities** (1961), is a provocative discussion of cities and urban policy, while Daniel Moynihan and Nathan Glazer, *Beyond the Melting Pot** (1963), reveals the ethnic dimensions of life in New York City. Joseph Goulden, *Meany* (1972), is helpful on the leader of the AFL. For civil rights in the early 1960s see Benjamin Muse, *The American Negro Revolution: From Nonviolence to Black Power, 1963–1967** (1968); Charles Silberman, *Crisis in Black and White** (1964), a very well written and provocative analysis; and Howard Zinn, *SNCC: New Abolitionists, 1964–65* (1964).

Books on foreign policy in the 1960s include Richard Walton, *Cold War and Counterrevolution** (1972), which is critical of Kennedy. Roger Hilsman, *To Move a Nation* (1967), is an interpretive account by a former member of the Kennedy administration. David Halberstam, *The Best and the Brightest* (1972), is a sustained critique of liberal foreign policy under Kennedy and Johnson. H. B. Johnson, *The Bay of Pigs* (1964), is helpful. For the missile crisis see Robert Kennedy, *13 Days* (1969); Elie Abel, *Missile Crisis** (1966); and especially Graham Allison, *Essence of Decision** (1971). Juan de Onis, *The Alliance that Lost its Way** (1970), laments the fate of the Alliance for Progress.

For Vietnam in the 1950s and early 1960s consult George M. Kahin and J. W. Lewis, *The United States and Vietnam** (1967); and Bernard Fall, *The Two Vietnams** (2nd rev. ed. 1967). Also helpful are Marvin Gettleman, ed., *Vietnam: History, Documents, and Opinions** (1970); and Neil Sheehan et. al., *The Pentagon Papers** (1971). Two books on military policies are William B. Bader, *The United States and the Spread of Nuclear Weapons* (1968); and A. C. Enthoven and K. W. Smith, *How Much is Enough? Shaping the Defense Program, 1951–1969* (1971). See also Richard Barnet and Ronald Müller, *Global Reach: The Power of the Multinational Corporations* (1974).

14

Turmoil

1965~1968

On March 31, 1968, a deeply lined, worn looking Lyndon Johnson appeared on television to announce his retirement from the presidency at the close of his tenure in January 1969. He said, "I shall not seek, and I will not accept, the nomination of my party for another term as president."

Though his announcement came as a surprise, it was greeted with relief by millions of Americans. By that time Gallup polls were reporting that only 36 percent of the people approved of his conduct of the presidency. Militants were so angry and threatening that Johnson hardly dared appear in public. Like Hoover before him, he had fallen victim to his own stubbornness and to unusually chaotic and turbulent times.

Among the many manifestations of this discord, which rent the country after 1965, three were outstanding. The first, the breakdown of the interracial civil rights movement, culminated in explosive social unrest, including race riots in the cities. The second, escalation of the fighting in Vietnam, led to massive antiwar activity. The third, the rise of radical protest movements and of the "counter culture," was in part the consequence of the other two and in part the cause of further divisions in society. Together these three forces produced domestic turmoil unprecedented in twentieth-century American history.

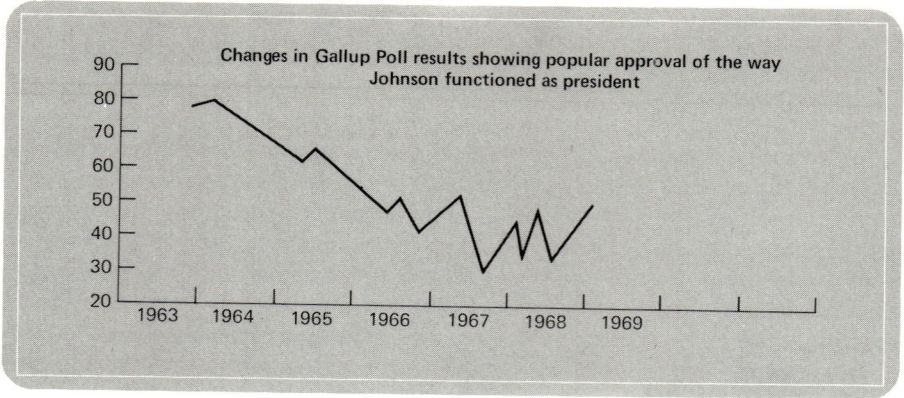

Changes in Gallup Poll results showing popular approval of the way Johnson functioned as president

SOURCE: Adapted from Irish and Frank, *U.S. Foreign Policy*, p. 104

Johnson reached the peak of his popularity shortly after he assumed the presidency in 1964 when 80 percent of respondents approved of the way he conducted his office and reached a low in mid-1967 when only 32 percent approved of his presidency.

From interracialism to black power

Since 1960, when the sit-ins first attracted national attention, the civil rights movement had been the vanguard of domestic reform. In providing a cause worthy of sacrifice it sustained the idealism that assists broader movements for change. As early as 1963, however, internal divisions were beginning to split the interracial coalition. By 1966 this disintegration produced widespread disruption and disillusion.

One source of discord was the militants' awareness of the limits of legal action in combating racial discrimination in the South. More black children attended segregated schools in the Deep South in 1964 than in 1954, the year of the supposedly epochal *Brown* decision. Jim Crow laws flourished throughout the region. Despite legal guarantees, blacks (and many poor whites) still were denied the vote. Though the civil rights acts of 1964 and 1965 eventually rectified some of these abuses, they came too late to pacify activists.

Militants in the North grew equally angry by 1965. Whites, they complained, discriminated against all blacks in the crucially important areas of education and housing, where de facto segregation was the rule. Urban renewal, activists added, usually meant "Negro removal." James Baldwin commented bitterly that housing projects "are hated almost as much as policemen, and that is saying a great deal. And they are hated for the same reason: both reveal, unbearably, the real attitude of the white world, no matter how many liberal speeches are made." Like many others, Baldwin recognized that the civil rights acts did nothing to assist social welfare or racial justice in the North, where almost 50 percent of America's blacks lived by 1960.

Even before 1965 growing discontent among Negro slum dwellers led to an increase in the strength of the Black Muslims. Led by their Messenger, Elijah

Muhammed, the Muslims combined faith in Islam with vehement separatism, anti-Semitism, and black racism. Like Marcus Garvey (and Booker T. Washington), they called for black self-help. Whites, they said, were agents of the devil; blacks must consider them enemies and refuse to mingle with or intermarry with them. Integrationists such as Martin Luther King, Elijah Muhammed argued, were tools of white society.

This black racism did not become a mass movement: perhaps no more than 20,000 people belonged to the Muslims during the mid-1960s. But it appealed to outcasts whom the interracial organizations failed to attract. It enlisted Cassius Clay (later Muhammed Ali), the heavyweight boxing champion of the world. It promoted the rise of Malcolm X, a charismatic leader who broke with Elijah Muhammed in 1963 to form the Organization for Afro-American Unity before he was assassinated by black gunmen in February 1965. At the time Malcolm had accomplished almost nothing. But his death made him a martyr. His appeal, like that of the Muslims, exposed the bitterness that was affecting many blacks even at the peak of interracial cooperation in the early 1960s.

By 1964 racial and sexual tensions began to divide civil rights workers in the South. The idealistic white activists endured great discomfort and real danger in trying to register blacks to vote. Two of them, Andrew Goodman and Michael Schwerner, were killed along with James Chaney, a black, in Mississippi in 1964. But many northern white girls were shocked by what they perceived as the sexual aggressiveness of their black co-workers. Others— relatively affluent, upward-mobile college students—were staggered by what they thought to be the ignorance and laziness of blacks in the rural South. "I really don't understand how they [blacks] can sit on the porch from six in the morning until nine in the evening without crossing their legs," one white wrote. Another added, "[Negroes] speak our same language but they look at things differently. Religion, Sex. It's sort of a different culture." Still other whites, accustomed to assuming positions of leadership in biracial movements, grew resentful as blacks sought to direct their own revolution.

Blacks detected these white attitudes. The white activists, they observed, returned to exclusive northern suburbs when the registration drives were over, leaving blacks to face the angry segregationists in the South. Blacks complained also about the mass media, which exalted the idealism of the whites while taking the blacks for granted. And many black militants developed misconceptions of their own. Some of these misconceptions concerned sex. "I think all those white girls down here sat up North dreaming about being raped by some big black Negro," a southern black said, "and came down here to see what it was like." The problem of leadership was more divisive. Only black people, the militants argued, could understand the black experience. Whites, accordingly, had no business trying to direct the movement. Attitudes such as these proved that ethnocentrism was not the exclusive preserve of the white race. They helped prevent successful interracial drives for civil rights in the South after 1965.

Newark, N.J., site of a major race riot in 1967. Above, damaged area of the riot. Below, armed police cars patrol the city.

Certain fundamental matters are clear. Of these, the most fundamental is the racial attitude and behavior of white Americans toward black Americans. Race prejudice has shaped our history decisively in the past; it now threatens to do so again. White racism is essentially responsible for the explosive mixture which has been accumulating in our cities since the end of World War II.

President Johnson's commission on the urban riots concludes its account of the causes of urban disorder in the 1960s.

Militant young blacks came vehemently to distrust "paternalistic" white liberals as much as segregationists. President Kennedy, they believed, coopted the movement by preventing militants from taking a prominent role in the march on Washington in 1963. SNCC leaders from Mississippi complained—with only partial justice—that liberals had blocked their Freedom Democratic party delegation to the 1964 Democratic Convention. Integration and nonviolence, these blacks believed, were goals for "Uncle Toms." "Do I really want to be integrated into a burning house?" Baldwin asked. Whites, he added, would give in only under the threat of force—"the fire next time."

Baldwin was prophetic. One consequence of this bitterness was racial violence in northern cities. This began on a relatively small scale in Harlem and in Rochester in 1964. In August 1965, five days after Johnson signed the civil rights law, black rioting broke out anew in the Watts district of Los Angeles. It caused the death of thirty-five people and property damage estimated at more than $30 million. In 1966 minor disturbances occurred in Chicago and other places, and in 1967 the greatest explosions of all took place in Newark, where 26 died and more than 1000 were injured, and in Detroit, the worst conflagration since the Chicago race riot of 1919. At Detroit 43 died, and 2000 were hurt. Much of the city's black belt was burned or destroyed. In 1967 alone 83 people were killed in 164 disorders (8 of them major), causing more than $100 million in property damage.

To many observers, envy of white prosperity and consumer culture seemed to motivate the rioters. "The rebellion," one rioter conceded, " . . . was all caused by the commercials. I mean you saw all those things you'd never be able to get. . . . Men's clothing, furniture, appliances, color TV. All that crummy TV glamor just hanging out there." Other people blamed the disturbances on destitute migrants—"riffraff" cast adrift in strange cities. Others wishfully thought the rioters were engaged in fun and games, rather like students tearing up Ft. Lauderdale during spring vacation. Firm police action, it was believed, would restore order. Still others suggested that class conflict lay at the root of the trouble. Most of the troublemakers, they argued, were poor blacks, sometimes joined by poor whites. The violence, they added, was not directed against people, but at ghetto property.

Many of these explanations contained some truth, for motives varied. But

White and non-white family income, 1950–1970
(Percent distribution of families, by race of head of family)

WHITE FAMILIES	UNDER $2,000	$2,000–$5,999	$6,000–$9,999	OVER $10,000
	(In current dollars)			
1950	22.2	62.6	11.6	3.5
1955	15.3	54.1	23.8	6.8
1960	11.0	41.3	32.5	15.3
1965	7.7	30.1	35.3	27.1
1970	3.8	18.7	25.9	51.6
NON-WHITE FAMILIES				
1950	53.4	43.2	3.2	0.3
1955	39.7	51.7	7.9	0.6
1960	31.7	47.9	15.4	4.9
1965	20.7	49.7	20.5	9.0
1970	11.1	35.0	25.6	28.2

SOURCE: Adapted from *Statistical Abstract of the United States*, 1974, p. 382

if the reports of study commissions were accurate, the rioters included few "riffraff"—these were too disorganized and marginal to play much of a part. Rather, the majority of rioters were upward-mobile blacks who felt most deeply what President Johnson's commission called "white racism." Though these blacks had gained economically, they sensed that they had far to go to close the widening gap that separated them from the white middle classes, and that whites would never let them move out of the ghetto. Thus it was that some of the worst riots, as in Watts and Detroit, occurred where blacks were relatively well-off and relatively well treated—where expectations had been whetted the most. By 1965 these blacks were impatient, and they did not know where to turn. If violence be rational, theirs was.

Another cause—and consequence—of the riots was the developing cry for "black power." This phrase, which frightened whites throughout the late

The media claims that I teach hate. Hate, like love, is a feeling. How can you teach a feeling? If Black people hate white people it's not because of me, it's because of what white people do to Black people. If hate can be taught, ain't no better teacher than white people themselves. I hate oppression. I am anti anybody who is anti-Black. Now if that includes most white people in America, it ain't my fault. That's just the way the bones break. I don't care whether or not white people hate me. It's not essential that a man love you to live. But "the man" has to respect you.

H. Rap Brown of SNCC offers his view of race relations.

1960s, first gained currency in June 1966, when James Meredith was shot and wounded while making a demonstration walk from Memphis, Tennessee, to Jackson, Mississippi. King and others then moved in to complete the march. But Stokely Carmichael, the head of SNCC, rejected King's faith in white liberals and in nonviolence. "We have got to get us some black power," he said. "We have to organize ourselves to speak for each other. That's black power. We have to move to control the economics and politics of our community."

Other black militants made Carmichael sound like a moderate. H. Rap Brown, who took over as head of SNCC in 1967, explained that "John Brown was the only white man I could respect and he is dead. The Black Movement has no use for white liberals. We need revolutionaries. Revolutions need revolutionaries." Julius Lester, a SNCC field secretary, published a book entitled *Look Out Whitey! Black Power's Gon' Get Your Mama!* "Now it is over," he said, "the days of singing freedom songs and the days of combatting bullets and billy clubs with love. We Shall Overcome (and we have overcome our blindness) sounds old, outdated, and can enter the pantheon of the greats along with the IWW songs and the union songs. As one SNCC veteran put it after the Mississippi march, 'Man, the people are too busy getting ready to fight to bother with singing any more.'" Huey Newton, a leader of the Black Panthers, founded in 1966, added that blacks must arm themselves in defense against the police and the military. "We make the statement," he said, "quoting from Chairman Mao, that Political Power comes through the Barrel of a Gun."

In the cultural realm "black power" did much to develop pride among black people. Carmichael said, "The only thing we own in this country is the

James Meredith, shot during his one-man walk through Mississippi. Outrages such as this accelerated the movement toward black power.

color of our skins. . . . We have to stop being ashamed of being black. A broad nose, a thick lip, and nappy hair is us, and we are going to call that beautiful whether they like it or not.'' This ''Black Is Beautiful'' theme (which Langston Hughes and others had promoted in vain forty years earlier) cut down the sale of bleaches, hair straighteners, and other cosmetics that blacks had bought for decades in attempts to hide their racial characteristics. It affected advertising, films, art, and poetry. It led to courses in black history, to renewed appreciation for African culture, and to growing confidence among black people generally. As James Brown's popular song proclaimed, ''Say It Loud—I'm Black and I'm Proud.''

By using the rhetoric of violence, however, extremists like H. Rap Brown cut deep divisions into the civil rights movement. Roy Wilkins of the NAACP, whose legal defense fund had been indispensable to civil rights activists—and who was far from being an ''Uncle Tom''—said that such rhetoric was the ''father of hatred and the mother of violence.'' A. Philip Randolph, who had led the all-black march on Washington in 1941, considered the new version of black power a ''menace to peace and prosperity.'' King complained that ''returning violence for violence multiplies violence, adding deeper darkness to a night already devoid of stars. Darkness cannot drive out darkness; only light can do that.''

Hoping to prevent white ''backlash,'' these nonviolent leaders stressed that blacks could attain power through economic organization and voter solidarity. They insisted also that Carmichael, Brown, and other extremists represented only a very small minority of blacks. The moderates in the movement made other telling points against the separatist argument. First, it was ideologically puerile—romantic paramilitarism carried away by its own rhetoric. Second, it was unrealistic. Blacks, comprising only 11 percent of the population, would be destroyed if they relied on violence. Hatred and violence, King said, ''intensify the fears of the white majority, and leave them less ashamed of their prejudices toward Negroes.''

King, however, could not wish away either the urban riots or the extremist rhetoric of the militant minority, both of which antagonized whites. As early as June 1966, 85 percent of whites thought blacks were too demanding, compared to only 34 percent in 1964. House Republican leader Gerald Ford asked, ''how long are we going to abdicate law and order—the backbone of our civilization—in favor of a soft social theory that the man who heaves a brick through your window or tosses a fire bomb into your car is simply the misunderstood and underprivileged product of a broken home?'' Johnson himself grew peevish, especially when Rap Brown branded him a ''white honky cracker.'' After appointing a commission to study the riots, he rejected its call in 1968 for far-reaching federal reforms. ''They always print that we don't do enough,'' he snapped. ''They don't print what we do.''

Reactions like these did not mean that a ''white backlash'' was overrunning the country or that the civil rights movement had failed. Polls in the more peaceful years after the riots revealed that most Americans approved of the gains that had been made. The civil rights laws remained on the books, blacks registered and voted in unprecedented numbers. schools and universities were desegregated, even in the Deep South. By 1970 southern blacks enjoyed as much legal protection as blacks in the North, where de facto segregation had long prevailed. But black spokesmen began pressing for more social and economic equality, including the end of discrimination in housing, and busing to achieve racial balance in the schools. At this point many whites balked, and the struggle for racial justice entered a period of stalemate. The altruism that had characterized the civil rights movement in the early 1960s seemed eons past by 1968.

Vietnam, 1964–1968

Three days after Kennedy's assassination President Johnson conferred with Henry Cabot Lodge, Jr., America's ambassador to South Vietnam. Lodge confirmed what people already sensed: the assassination of Diem earlier in the month had increased political instability in South Vietnam, while doing nothing to facilitate the military struggle against the National Liberation Front, the predominantly communist political arm of the Vietcong rebels in the south. Another president, recognizing that South Vietnam was engaged in a civil war, might have refrained from increasing America's commitment of 17,000 men. But not Johnson, who persisted in blaming North Vietnam and China for the fighting in the south. As if echoing Winston Churchill, who had told FDR in World War II, "I did not become the King's first minister in order to preside over the liquidation of the Empire," Johnson told Lodge, "I am not going to be the president who saw Vietnam go the way China went."

In 1964 Johnson did his best to conceal this determined attitude from the electorate. Troop levels were increased, but only to 21,000. During the election campaign he ridiculed the notion that he would escalate the number of American soldiers in Vietnam. After the Vietcong attacked American facilities at Bien Hoa in October, he declared, "We are not going to drop bombs."

Even before the 1964 election, however, signs appeared of the Johnson deceptions that lay ahead. Early in August he announced that North Vietnamese torpedo boats had attacked American destroyers in the Tonkin Gulf thirty miles off North Vietnam. He suppressed the truth: that the American warships had been assisting South Vietnamese commando raids; that the destroyers had been in combat zones close to shore; and that the alleged assaults, on dark nights in rough seas, may have been imagined by nervous American officers. The supposed attacks, in any event, caused no damage. Feigning outrage, Johnson ordered American planes to smash North Vietnamese torpedo bases and oil installations—targets picked carefully two months earlier. He also asked Congress to authorize him to take " all necessary measures to repel any armed attack against the forces of the United States and to prevent

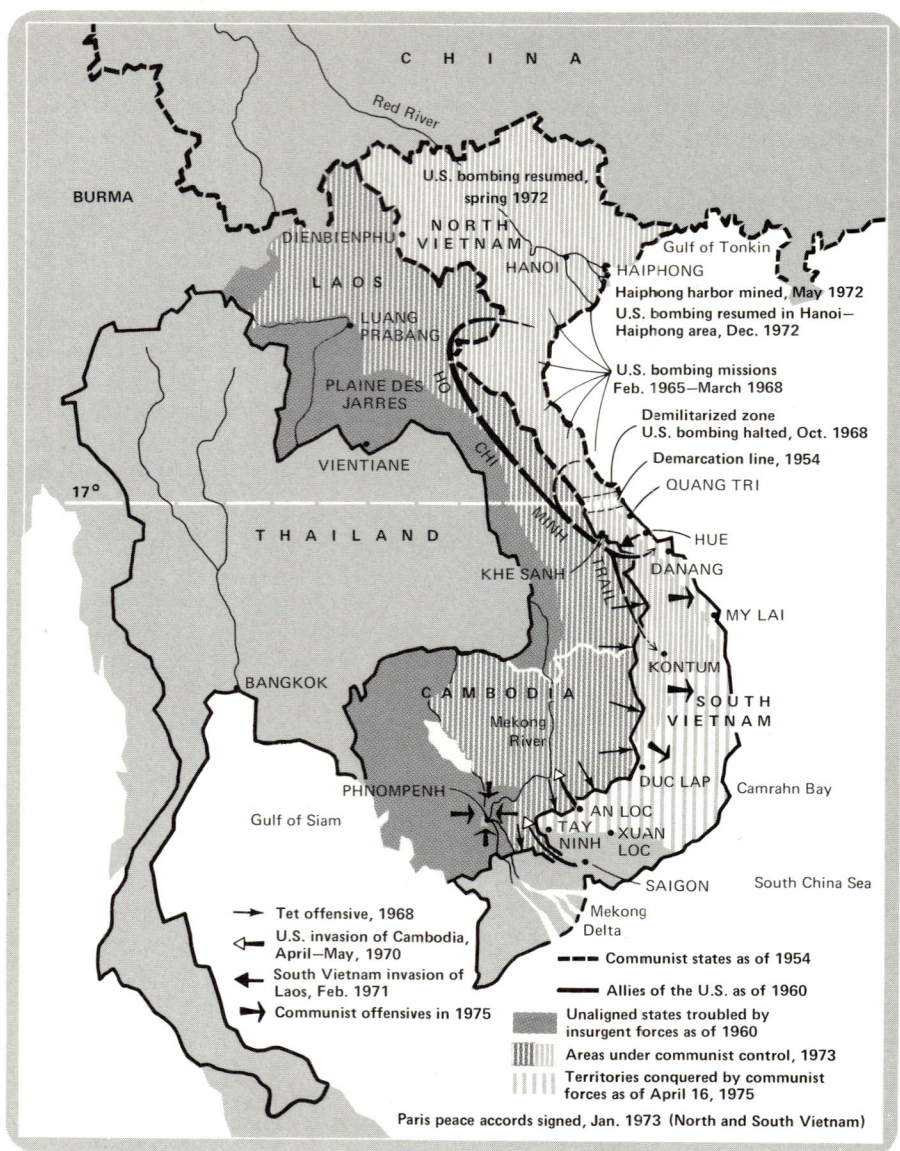

Map labels:

CHINA

Red River

BURMA

U.S. bombing resumed, spring 1972

DIENBIENPHU

NORTH VIETNAM

Gulf of Tonkin

LAOS

HANOI

HAIPHONG

Haiphong harbor mined, May 1972

LUANG PRABANG

U.S. bombing resumed in Hanoi—Haiphong area, Dec. 1972

PLAINE DES JARRES

U.S. bombing missions Feb. 1965–March 1968

VIENTIANE

Demilitarized zone
U.S. bombing halted, Oct. 1968

Demarcation line, 1954

QUANG TRI

17°

HUE

THAILAND

DANANG

KHE SANH

MY LAI

KONTUM

BANGKOK

CAMBODIA

SOUTH VIETNAM

Mekong River

DUC LAP

Camrahn Bay

PHNOMPENH

AN LOC

Gulf of Siam

TAY NINH

XUAN LOC

SAIGON

South China Sea

Mekong Delta

→ Tet offensive, 1968
◁ U.S. invasion of Cambodia, April–May, 1970
← South Vietnam invasion of Laos, Feb. 1971
➡ Communist offensives in 1975

- - - Communist states as of 1954
——— Allies of the U.S. as of 1960
Unaligned states troubled by insurgent forces as of 1960
Areas under communist control, 1973
Territories conquered by communist forces as of April 16, 1975
Paris peace accords signed, Jan. 1973 (North and South Vietnam)

Vietnam war and fall of Indochina, 1954–1975

further aggression." An alarmed Congress acceded, unanimously in the House and eight-eight to two in the Senate. Like Truman after the North Korean invasion, Johnson never troubled to ask for a declaration of war. The Tonkin Gulf resolution gave him enough latitude to increase the American presence there over the next four years.

The escalation itself occurred early in 1965 after the Vietcong rebels killed 7 Americans and wounded 109 at Pleiku. Within twelve hours of getting the news, American planes retaliated by dropping bombs in the north. Three days later Johnson authorized regular bombing, again on targets chosen in 1964. In April, after Vietcong attacks had almost succeeded in blowing up the American embassy in Saigon, he stepped up the dispatch of ground troops. By early 1966 the United States had nearly 200,000 soldiers in South Vietnam.

When critics complained of American escalation, Johnson reminded them of his efforts for peace. In April 1965 he promised both sides long-term economic aid. On December 24, 1965, he called a bombing halt, which lasted until January 31, 1966. He made Averell Harriman an ambassador-at-large and sent him on well-publicized missions in search of peace. In October 1966 Johnson went to Manila to pledge that the United States would pull out of Vietnam within six months of the end of the shooting. Later in the year secret negotiations to end the war started in Poland.

It is unlikely that Johnson really expected these overtures to succeed. Instead, he remained fixed in his central goal: to keep South Vietnam within the noncommunist orbit. Because its pro-American puppet governments had little popular support, this policy required further escalation, which destroyed chances for accommodation. By mid-1966 America had 265,000 troops in South Vietnam; by the end of 1967 it had more than 500,000. The war cost an estimated $100 billion per year by 1968—the amount spent yearly on *all* federal expenditures as recently as 1964. Bernard Fall, the best-informed writer on Vietnam at the time, estimated that it cost the United States between $300,000 and $500,000 per enemy death as of early 1966.

Johnson relied heavily on massive bombing of North Vietnam. The attacks sought to destroy military installations, oil reserves, and railway lines and to slow down the flow of supplies from the north to the Vietcong. However, the raids were counterproductive. North Vietnam, which had given little aid to the Vietcong before 1965, responded to the attacks by stepping up its delivery of goods. The raids also smashed urban areas and killed countless North Vietnamese civilians. Frequently American bombers used napalm, an incendiary substance that set human flesh aflame.

In the south, American military action was equally barbaric and destructive. "Pacification" programs to secure the countryside entailed burning of villages, forcible uprooting of civilians, and desecration of ancestral burial grounds. "Search and destroy" missions—again using napalm—killed thousands of villagers. Overwhelming American firepower defoliated forests, destroyed rice crops, and shattered the economy. Some American troops perpetrated atrocities, such as the one in the village of My Lai in 1968, which resulted in the killing of 347 civilian men, women, and children. During Johnson's presidency the war caused the deaths of some 28,000 Americans, perhaps 100,000 South Vietnamese, and untold numbers of young Vietcong rebels. Civilian deaths approached a million.

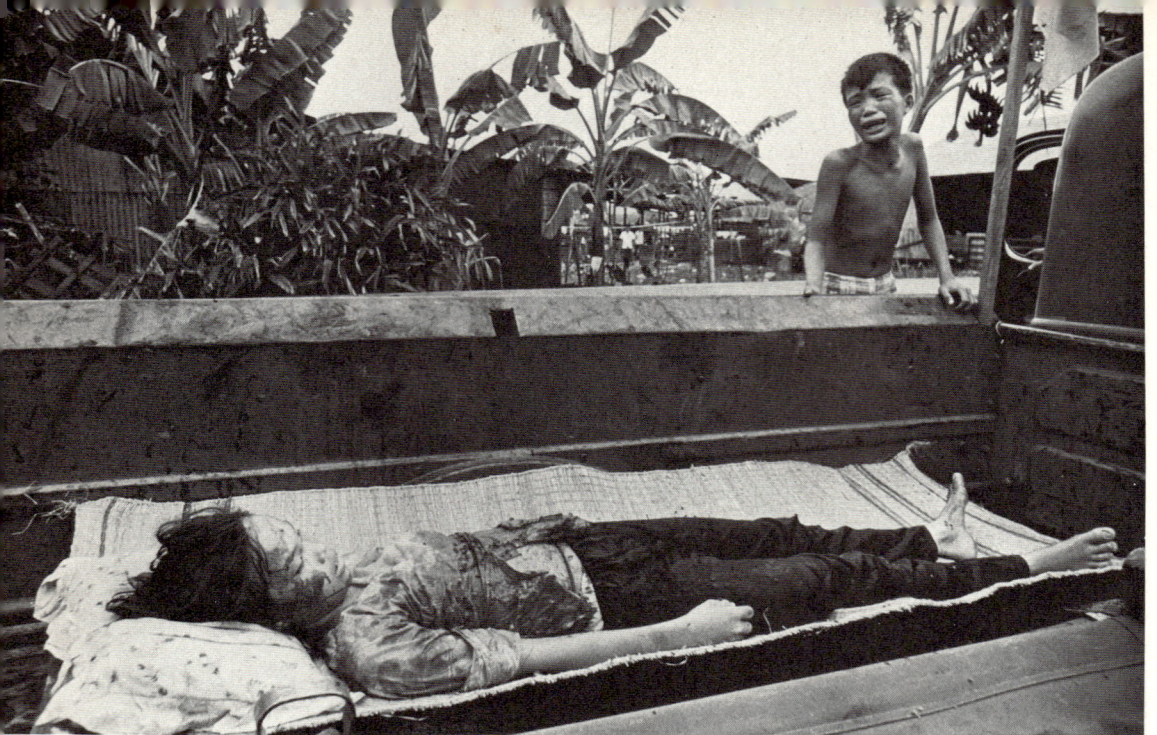

A scene from Vietnam.

Long before Johnson left office opponents of the war inveighed against these policies. Like the more progressive isolationists in 1917 and 1940, they complained that the war was undermining support for reform at home. They protested the immorality of bombing civilians, the abuse of presidential power, and the impact of the war on America's relations with the rest of the world. Other critics, such as Walter Lippmann and the political scientist Hans Morganthau, pointed out that the United States had no economic or strategic interests in Vietnam worth such a commitment.

Johnson remained deaf to such arguments. Indeed, he brusquely dismissed dissidents within his administration. "Kennedy," one observer explained, "didn't mind disagreement. It didn't bother him. But disagreement really bothers this president. He is going to do what you dislike anyway; so let's not upset him by having an argument in front of him." Discussions with Johnson, his press secretary George Reedy recalled, were "really monologues in which one man is getting reflections of what he sends out." In such an atmosphere it was not surprising that few top-ranking officials dared dispute with him, or that those who did, like McNamara in 1967–68, left office. As late as March 16, 1968, six weeks after the devastating "Tet" offensive by the Vietcong, which brought pleas for deescalation from Deputy Secretary of Defense Paul Nitze, the new secretary of defense, Clark Clifford, and even from former Secretary of State Dean Acheson, a staunch anticommunist, Johnson held to his position. "Let's get one thing clear," he said. "I am not going to stop the bombing. I have heard every argument on the subject, and I am not interested in further discussion.'' Though he finally softened his stance two weeks later—announcing the end of bombing in the north (save near the demarcation line) and reporting that America was beginning peace talks in Paris—these were not concessions to his advisers but changes in tactics. The NLF demanded that America withdraw, and the talks in Paris went nowhere.

Johnson's stubbornness derived from many misconceptions. Among them was his characteristically American view of communism as a united, worldwide conspiracy. This attitude led him to ignore opportunities for Soviet-American détente, which had appeared real after Leonid Brezhnev and Aleksai Kosygin replaced the more erratic Khrushchev in October 1964. In Latin America it caused him to neglect the Alliance for Progress and, in 1965, to send marines to challenge left-wing forces in the Dominican Republic. In Southeast Asia it prompted him to ignore the simple fact that the conflict in South Vietnam was a civil war. Communist China, he said, was responsible for the ''aggression'' of Ho Chi Minh from the north. Resurrecting the SEATO pact of 1954 (which neither required nor authorized American military intervention), he insisted that the United States was doing in Vietnam what Truman had done in Korea.

By focusing on China, Johnson vastly underestimated the tenacity of the South Vietnamese rebels. Theirs was a war of revolution, not only against puppets like Diem but against decades of western imperialism. This revolutionary nationalism helped to explain why superior American fire power, to say nothing of 500,000 men, failed utterly to control the countryside. Short of dropping nuclear bombs on the entire Indo-Chinese peninsula, there was no military ''solution'' to the ideological conflict in Vietnam.

Johnson also placed exaggerated faith in money and technology. When the North Vietnamese ignored his offer of economic aid in 1965, he was uncomprehending. ''I don't understand it,'' he said. ''George Meany [head of the AFL] would've grabbed at a deal like that.'' Encouraged by the statistics of Secretary of Defense McNamara, he persisted in believing that American air superiority would eventually destroy the enemy. But the bombing failed to stem the flow of supplies from the north. Vietnam, an agricultural country where supply routes wound through dense cover, was one of the last places in the world where strategic bombing could have been effective.

Ironically, the appalling cost of these misconceptions prompted doubts in America about long-held liberal dogmas. Among these was the view that progressive government required a strong presidency. In domestic policy, this remained an article of liberal faith. In foreign affairs, however, it seemed that isolationists like Charles Beard and Robert Taft had been wise in demanding an important role for Congress. This distrust of the presidency did not prevent Johnson's successor from exceeding his constitutional authority. But suspicion of the White House did add immeasurably to the discord that tore the nation apart after 1965.

Another partial casualty of the war was globalism—the view that the United States must preserve ''freedom'' everywhere. The war in Vietnam ultimately proved that this was not possible. America was not omnipotent; it had to think about priorities. Most of those who turned against globalism were not isolationists—they supported the United Nations, NATO, and aid to Israel. But they called successfully for cuts in foreign aid, they demanded a reduced presence in Asia, and they looked for ways to defuse the Cold War. They pointed especially to the split between the Soviet Union and China. This break, already deep in the 1960s, led both communist nations to look for détente with the United States. Thanks in part to the rethinking of foreign policy engendered by Vietnam, even hard-liners like Richard Nixon were later induced to respond.

THE ANTIWAR MOVEMENT

Second thoughts such as these were but small consolation to Americans who by 1968 were suffering under the travails of the longest war in the nation's history. Besides devastating Vietnam, it shattered the reform coalition in the United States and ultimately promoted the most alarming inflation since 1946. As much as any other development of the decade, the war eclipsed the idealism and hopefulness of the Kennedy era and precipitated the unrest that gripped the country between 1965 and 1968.

America's mood:
the public's view of the most important
problem facing the country,
according to Gallup Poll results,
1964–1968

1964	Integration
1965	Vietnam
1966	Vietnam
1967	Vietnam
1968	Vietnam

SOURCE: Irish and Frank, *U. S. Foreign Policy*, p. 107

Leading this unrest was the most militant antiwar movement in American history. This crusade began slowly, primarily because Johnson delayed major escalation until 1965. The United States, most people agreed, could easily clean up the "mess" in Asia. But by late 1965 students were already starting to stage mass demonstrations, to conduct "bleed-ins" seeking blood for the Vietcong, to burn their draft cards, and to chant, "hey hey, LBJ, how many kids did you kill today?" A stop-the-bombing march in Washington in November 1965 attracted 20,000 protestors, including Norman Thomas, the veteran socialist leader, James Farmer, the head of CORE, Dr. Benjamin Spock,

*I have to speak
to some college students
about Vietnam—
could you rig up a tank
with a loudspeaker?*

By 1968 Johnson hardly dared appear in public.

author of the best-selling *Common Sense Book of Baby and Child Care,* the cartoonist Jules Feiffer, and the novelist Saul Bellow.

Many developments helped to swell the antiwar movement after 1965. One, of course, was the terrific American escalation, which became too obvious to hide by 1966. Another was the shocking coverage—in news photographs and on television—of American patrols burning Vietnamese villages, of refugees fleeing the smoke of battle, of horribly burned and wounded women and children, of mutilated American soldiers. These scenes of bloodletting, plus the mounting casualty figures, made it increasingly difficult for Americans to believe the White House and the Pentagon. The "credibility gap" added desperation and fury to the protests.

Young people, especially college students, provided much of the energy behind the antiwar movement. Many of these activists were veterans of the civil rights struggle, where they had learned the tactics of nonviolent mass protest. White civil rights workers, cut off from their cause after 1965 by advocates of black power, channeled their idealism to the cause of peace. Most agreed with Martin Luther King, Jr., who proclaimed that the United States was "the greatest purveyor of violence in the world."

Other young people had more personal reasons for joining the struggle against war: they did not want to fight in Vietnam. As draft calls mounted (from 5000 per month in 1965 to 50,000 per month in 1967), graduate students—who had previously secured exemptions—began to be inducted. Alarmed, they moved from quiet disagreement with the war to participation in "teach-ins" on campus to mass protests. Their frightened parents often supported them. By 1967 the antiwar crusade had become a broad-based movement including pacifists, leftists, civil rights activists, draft-age students, and substantial numbers of otherwise apolitical middle-class parents. By 1968, after the Tet offensive, these poeple were angry enough to demonstrate against the Pentagon, to challenge LBJ himself in the political arena, and to turn college campuses into cockpits of turmoil.

The youth rebellion

The growth of education in the postwar period was staggering. In 1940 the average level achieved by Americans was grade eight. At that time one out of six people of college age attended colleges or universities; one in twelve graduated. By the late 1960s the average grade level was twelve; 50 percent of college age youth went on to college; and more than 20 percent graduated. The nation's colleges and universities reflected the major themes of twentieth-century American history: affluence, professionalization, and the rise of the middle class.

Until the early 1960s most people welcomed these advances. The campuses were peaceful, and students appeared to worry more about fraternities and football than about social issues. In the Kennedy years, however, students became a little more politicized. Some joined New Leftist groups like the Students for a Democratic Society. Others led civil rights demonstrations, served in the Peace Corps, or labored in the war against poverty. These altruists were not a majority of students, let alone of young people generally. Indeed, only 12 percent of students identified themselves as part of the "New Left" even at the peak of activity in 1970. But the protestors attended some of the nation's largest and most prestigious universities. They were articulate. Their role in civil rights demonstrations at Birmingham and Selma suggested that they could make a difference in the world.

By the end of the decade, many of these campuses displayed the same turmoil that affected society at large. Beginning with a demonstration for free speech at Berkeley in 1964, youthful protest became steadily more radical. In 1968, agitators at Columbia seized the president's office and forced the university to shut down. Elsewhere, militants littered campus offices, stormed buildings, shouted down visiting speakers, staged strikes, and battled police ("pigs") called in to restore order. In all, 221 major demonstrations took place on the campuses between January and June 1968. Until 1971, when the campuses quieted down, America's universities seemed to be centers of revolution.

Police remove a demonstrator from the campus at Columbia University, May 1968. A total of 81 men and 50 women were arrested.

Among the forces prompting such unrest were the social divisions outside the university. Like the radicals in the 1930s, activists protested against racism, concentration of wealth, and the "power elite." Like many old conservatives, they complained about bureaucratic government, "snooping" by federal agencies, the draft, and "globalism." Like radical students elsewhere—for unrest gripped universities throughout the world at the time—they tended to question all authority. Their enemies were not the universities but racism, social inequality, and the military-industrial complex promoting war in Vietnam.

Other students concentrated their assaults on the universities. In this way they differed from the youthful radicals of the 1930s, who had tried to protect the campus from external pressures. Places like Berkeley, the new rebels complained, had become enormous bureaucratic institutions—"multiuniversities" that treated students like IBM cards. Urban universities like Harvard and Columbia, students protested, gobbled up surrounding areas once occupied by poor people. As the Vietnam war escalated, militants also protested against venerable campus institutions such as ROTC. Others busied themselves with exposing the connections between multiuniversities, scientific research, and the CIA. For all these students, universities were the most visible and most vulnerable manifestations of the repressive Establishment.

Idealistic students complained especially that universities were degree mills where young people had to do what they were told so that they could enter the Establishment at the age of twenty-two. Meanwhile, universities succeeded in keeping their captives out of the job market, which was to say out of the "real world." Using the arguments of anthropologists and psychiatrists, the protestors claimed that higher education prolonged adolescence and made students restless and impatient. Other critics, like Paul Goodman, went further and opposed compulsory education in general. "We have been swept on a flood-tide of public policy and popular sentiment," he argued, "into an expansion of schooling and an aggrandizement of school-people that is grossly wasteful of youth and effort and does positive damage to the young."

The restlessness that Goodman perceived helped explain why so many otherwise nonradical students lent their support to (or at least acquiesced in) the demands of antiestablishment minorities. It also helped to account for the lack of consistent ideology among the youthful militants. Unlike the radicals of the 1930s, many of whom were moved by Marx, the New Left of the 1960s (except for a handful of romantics who adored China's Mao or Cuba's Ché Guevara) eschewed programmatic approaches to revolution. Rather, they focused on tactics. Inspired by the civil rights demonstrations, and then by the attention given to advocates of black power, they moved quickly into confrontation strategies against the Vietnam war and the "power elite."

It later became almost fashionable to deride these militants. The campus unrest of the late 1960s, people began to argue, was orchestrated by a small minority, most of whom were sons and daughters of radicals in the 1930s. The militants, critics added, were affluent, self-indulgent hypocrites who were quick to join the Establishment after graduation; antiwar protestors wanted to escape the draft. Conservatives also reassured themselves with the notion that demographic imperatives prompted the campus unrest. High birth rates in the 1940s and early 1950s, they contended, created a uniquely large percentage of college age people by the late 1960s. No such revolt of youth, these analysts concluded, was likely to recur.

Though there was some truth in these observations, conservatives had to admit that the young people scored a few victories. Students forced temporary administrative and curricular reforms in many universities. Off campus they were the backbone of the civil rights and antiwar movements. Many of the protestors made permanent commitments to social change by fighting against environmental pollution, by enlisting in Common Cause, or by backing Ralph

Nader and other foes of commercial and governmental exploitation. Many worked for antiwar political candidates in 1968 and 1972. The student movement, like the struggle for black power, was neither wholly negative nor wholly wasted.

It was a fact, however, that many student victories were pyrrhic by 1968. Indeed, youthful excesses appalled many reformers as well as conservatives. Slogans such as "Don't Trust Anyone Over Thirty," to say nothing of well-publicized campaigns like the "Filthy Speech" movement at Berkeley, were hardly calculated to appeal to the majority of Americans. Neither were insults to "pigs" and other symbols of authority. Excesses such as these created backlash, divided the movement, and sapped its effectiveness.

The counter culture

If young people had contented themselves with unsettling the universities, they might have seemed relatively harmless. But many embraced what became known in the late 1960s as the counter culture. The overlapping of the two movements, radical protest and rebellion against the life styles and values of the 1950s, gave unprecedented visibility to the youth movement of the 1960s.

The surface manifestations of the counter culture in themselves alienated traditionalists. Increasing numbers of young men (and some adults) let their hair grow long, donned love beads, and dressed in faded jeans, work shirts, and sandals. Young women, slouching about without bras or shoes, talked of sexual freedom. Many of these people took marijuana or other more dangerous drugs, and they lived as "hippies" in rural communes or in seedy urban areas like San Francisco's Haight-Ashbury district. The very sight of such apparently unkempt people was offensive to many more staid Americans.

Traditionalists also grew alarmed at the taste in popular music that appeared to addict many young people by the late 1960s. Earlier in the decade idealistic youth had flocked to hear folk musicians like Bob Dylan, Malvina Reynolds, and Joan Baez sing gentle lyrics of social protest. Reynolds asked (in complaining about radioactivity), "What Have They Done to the Rain?" Pete Seeger chimed in, "Where have all the Flowers Gone?" Though lyrics such as these were socially-conscious, they were otherwise harmless enough. One radical complained that Baez talked only about "clouds, flowers, butterflies . . . and the like." Arlo Guthrie, a leading folk singer, conceded that "you don't accomplish very much singing protest songs to people who agree with you. Everybody just has a good time thinking they're right."

By the mid-1960s, many folk singers were turning away from themes of social protest. Why this was so remains somewhat unclear, but the immense popularity of rock groups like the Beatles, who carried only a vague and tardy social message, undoubtedly led many ambitious singers to concentrate on

The joys of communal living.

achieving a louder sound and more insistent beat. Moreover, the war in Vietnam induced growing anger and despair. As early as 1964 Dylan wrote, "i know no answer and no truth for absolutely no soul alive i will listen to no one who tells me morals there are no morals an' i dream a lot."

Within the next three years folk music of social protest gave way to rock, and then to still louder "acid rock." John Lennon, one of the Beatles, scored a hit with "Lucy in the Sky with Diamonds," and Dylan himself wrote "Mr. Tambourine Man." Both frankly embraced the use of drugs. Another singer explained, "You take the drugs, you turn up the music real loud, you dance around, you build up a fantasy." By the late 1960s the most popular entertainers included groups like the Doors and the Rolling Stones. Jim Morrison of the Doors relied primarily on sexuality for his effect. Twice arrested for indecent exposure, he was supposed to be able to hold an erection throughout a two-hour performance. Mick Jagger, leader of the Rolling Stones, unleashed not only sexual instincts but violence. In 1969 at Altamont in California he called on the Hell's Angels, a gang of motorcyclists, to keep order at one of the Stones' concerts. When the crowd grew unruly, the Angels stomped a black man to death on the stage.

Advocates of the counter culture neither sought nor welcomed such violence. By the end of the decade, however, they flocked happily to extravaganzas such as the "Woodstock" concert at Bethel, New York, in 1969. This attracted some 400,000 people. Some of them came to hear Baez, Jimi Hendrix, and others. But for three days the majority seemed content to lie about in the mud, to share marijuana, and even to fornicate in the open. "Everyone swam nude in the lake," a journalist wrote. "Balling was easier than getting breakfast, and the 'pigs' just smiled and passed out the oats."

There was much more to the counter culture than love-beads and rock concerts. True believers posed sharp challenges to existing values. For them there was a "generation gap." Like Dustin Hoffman, "hero" of the hit movie, *The Graduate* (1969), they rejected what they considered the hypocrisy of people over thirty. Their idols, to the extent to which they had any, were sensitive types like Salinger's Holden Caulfield, rough diamonds like Humphrey Bogart (whose movies enjoyed popular revivals in the 1960s), or even outlaws like Bonnie and Clyde, whose rejection of the "straight" world was romanticized in a movie in 1969. Paul Simon's song *Sound of Silence* symbolized the gigantic gap that prevented understanding between young people and their parents.

The "revolution," these youths believed, was cultural and generational. Young people must transcend the old culture and advance to new thresholds of freedom. To Charles Reich, whose *Greening of America* (1969) celebrated the new culture, this meant rejecting the materialism and competitiveness of previous epochs and embracing "Consciousness III." There people would live in a world of love, beauty, and peace. The counter culture, another writer suggested, meant a "vision of a new American identity—a collective identity that will be blacker, more feminine, more oriental, more emotional, more intuitive, more exuberant—and, just possibly, better than the old one."

Central to the ideas of these true believers was the conviction that older people were repressed. Adults, caught in what Paul Goodman called the "rat-race," were afraid to let themselves go. Herbert Marcuse, whose books appeared to support the counter culture, argued that affluence was abolishing poverty in society. Eros, the symbol of affluence and the end of scarcity, would ultimately conquer aggression. The avant garde must transcend repression to live by an "aesthetic ethos." As the historian John P. Diggins pointed out, beliefs such as these aligned the counter culturalists more closely with the "lyrical left" that had challenged middle-class values prior to World War I than with the "old" Marxist left of the 1930s. Like Randolph Bourne, the New Leftists believed that "imagination is revolution." They added that drugs helped to explode repressions. The key was "not politics but psychedelics."

Surmounting repression meant rejecting taboos about sex. If Eros was to conquer, people must feel free to indulge in premarital sex, to challenge nuclear families, even to practice homosexuality or lesbianism. Such attitudes were complemented by the widespread use of the Pill by the end of the decade. By 1970 traditionalists were appalled at the spread of "X-rated" movies, of "gay liberation," and even of "swingers" magazines featuring photos of naked people advertising their wares. One such magazine had a circulation of 50,000 by 1972. As never before, sexuality was becoming a virtue, and pornography a consumer durable.

If sex was one avenue to transcendence, rejection of science was another. Theodore Roszak, a leading proponent of the counter culture, argued that American society resembled a "world's fair in its final days, when things start to sag and disintegrate behind the futuristic façade." To overcome this technological debauch people needed to reject scientism, computerism, reason generally. Roszak's prose (like Marcuse's) left many things unclear. Was emotion, not intellect, to rule the world? But he was clear in yearning for a more decentralized, less industrialized, less competitive cosmos. It was to discover such an Eden that the true believers moved to rural communes and scratched at the soil with hand-made tools.

In this way the foes of the old culture joined others in the 1960s who swelled the age-old chorus against materialism. "American civilization," Norman Mailer cried, "had moved from the existential sanction of the frontier to the abstract ubiquitous sanction of the dollar bill." Another writer added "people no longer have opinions: they have refrigerators. . . . The only way to catch a spirit of the times is to write a handbook on home appliances." Like Andy Warhol, a "pop" artist who lavished his talents on painting such commercial symbols as Campbell's soup cans and Marilyn Monroe, these critics thought that consumerism was the essence of American culture.

To replace material values Roszak and others called for a return to spiritualism. By this they did not mean orthodox religious faiths. Rather, like Henry Thoreau and the transcendentalists, they wanted human beings to achieve enlightenment through communion with nature. People, Roszak said, must develop a "new culture in which the nonintellective capacities of personality" will predominate. This faith in intuition underlay the growing popularity in the 1960s of mysticism, astrology, and Oriental philosophy. Human beings, these people believed, must seek harmony with, not victory over, the natural world.

Such faith in nature led to a movement for ecology, which gripped thousands of Americans who otherwise had little use for the counter culture. Among these were scientists who raised frightening visions. Barry Commoner, a Washington University biologist, argued that nuclear explosions, automobiles, detergents, and pesticides polluted the environment and increased the percentage of carbon dioxide in the atmosphere. Soon, he warned, temperatures would increase, the polar ice caps would melt, and water would inundate the world's great seaports. Paul Ehrlich, author of *Population Bomb,* crusaded for birth control, the ultimate guarantee of environmental protection. Mothers' milk contained so much DDT, he said, that it would be banned if sold on the market. He added, "we must realize that unless we are extremely lucky everybody will disappear in a cloud of blue steam in twenty years."

Many scientists challenged such forecasts of doom. While conceding the misery caused by population growth in underdeveloped nations, they observed that the American birth rate was declining in the 1960s to the lowest level, except for the 1930s, in American history. Others insisted that pesticides such as DDT were necessary to grow food for the world's hungry masses. Alarmists like Commoner, they thought, failed to grasp Theodore Roosevelt's central point—that resources must be used wisely for orderly growth.

Still, there was no denying the central thrust of many of the ecologists: that modern American society was incredibly wasteful and destructive. Even the much-reduced birth rate resulted in the addition of 24 million people to America's population in the 1960s. This was the second largest increase (next to the 1950s) in the nation's history. Awareness of demands on resources led many people to recycle glass and paper, to join consumer movements, and to push the Pill. Others challenged the desirability of growth itself, thereby rejecting Kennedy's "new economics." The counter culturists could hardly take full credit for awakening these activists to the nation's wastefulness— conservation, after all, was not new to the 1960s. But their passion for the harmonious life helped the movement for ecology to spread. It was their most lasting legacy.

By the end of the decade it became increasingly clear that sharp differences divided the youth movement. While many members of the counter culture held vaguely New Left views on social issues, they were essentially nonpolitical. Their primary grievance was with adult culture, not with capitalism. New Leftists and black power advocates, accordingly, accused the "flower children" of trying to cop out of society, instead of fighting it. The crusade for sexual liberation, C. Wright Mills grumbled, was a "gonad theory of revolution." These differences, resembling nineteenth-century divisions between transcendentalists and abolitionists, split the young radicals in manifold ways and left them considerably less potent than alarmists perceived.

Extremists further undercut the appeal of the youthful counter culturists— just as they hurt the New Left. Among these were Jerry Rubin and Abbie Hoffman, self-styled leaders of the Yippies. They were long haired, unkempt looking, savagely expressive. "When in doubt, BURN," Rubin counseled in 1967. "Fire is the revolutionary's god. . . . Burn the flag. Burn churches. Burn. Burn. Burn." People should "farm in the morning, make music in the afternoon, and fuck wherever and whenever they want to." Rubin and Hoffman were essentially antipolitical. Like two callous Holden Caulfields, they were indulging themselves, not organizing a revolution. Yet their rhetoric—overcovered by the media—disgusted men and women of peace. It was easy for the public to lump together the hippies and the New Leftists and to perceive a united movement against the established ways of life.

People like Rubin especially appalled some of America's older leftists, who complained that the counter culture was anti-intellectual, self-indulgent, and elitist. One critic observed that Rubin and others mistook "vividness, intensity, and urgency for cultural sensitivity and responsible morality." Paul Goodman, commenting on his experiences with members of the counter culture, said, "they did not believe there was such a thing as the simple truth. To be required to learn something was a trap by which the young were put down and coopted. Then I knew that I could not get through to them. I had imagined that the worldwide student protest had to do with changing political and moral institutions, to which I was sympathetic, but I now saw that we had to do with a religious crisis of the magnitude of the Reformation in the fifteen hundreds, when not only all institutions but all learning had been corrupted by the whore of Babylon."

Calm observers of the counter culture later perceived these excesses. They also recognized that the huge majority of Americans still cherished the work ethic, nuclear families, and censorship of pornography. John Wayne and Vince Lombardi, the Spartan coach of the Green Bay Packers, remained more appealing than Dustin Hoffman. Indeed, it became steadily more obvious that there was a larger gap between blue-collar young people and the college elitists than there was between the generations.

In 1968, however, few people could be sure that the youth movements would lose momentum by the early 1970s. And many who sympathized with the goals of the militants—such as the end of the Vietnam war—shuddered at some of their methods. With the media playing up extremists like Rubin and Hoffman, with long-haired demonstrators battling police outside the Pentagon, with campuses in turmoil, with hippies advocating free and open sex, with blacks tearing up the ghettos, it seemed that traditional values and institutions were endangered. By 1968 "backlash" among "middle Americans," a vague term embracing blue-collar workers, conservatives, and others who were angry and frightened by domestic turmoil, was growing throughout the country.

Black Power, Red Power, Women's Power

The rise of protest movements and of the counter culture alerted other aggrieved Americans to the potential of group solidarity. By the end of the decade these too had become highly vocal and increasingly demanding. Their outbursts added to the turmoil of the times.

Among these were many ethnic leaders. Though the more acculturated groups—Irish-Americans, Italian-Americans—tended to work within the existing "system," others shared the rage that animated blacks. Leaders of the Puerto Ricans, who were treated as badly as blacks, staged strikes and demonstrations. American Indians, hidden away on arid reservations, conducted sit-ins to demand revision of old "treaties" with the government. Cesar Chavez, the charismatic leader of the National Farm Workers, championed the cause of "Chicanos" in California. With the aid of eastern sympathizers, who helped boycott nonunion produce, he secured modest concessions from the landowners.

Chavez, an organizer in the old CIO tradition, did not endorse separatism. Other disgruntled leaders did. Some Indians raised the flag of "red power." Radical Chicanos called for "brown power," or *La Raza,* a culture divorced from white American society. Like the advocates of black power, they represented minorities within their movements. But their militance forced the moderates to take tougher stands, and their tactics of direct action created confrontations with civil authorities. Their abrasiveness was an unpleasant reminder of the ethnocultural divisions in American society and of the obstacles that had prevented proscribed groups from developing more than the rudiments of a middle class.

"Power" ideologies also helped to promote a revival of feminism, which had been quiescent since the 1920s. As Betty Friedan pointed out in *The Feminine Mystique* (1963), an influential demand for equal rights, the intervening decades had actually witnessed setbacks for the feminist cause. Smaller percentages of women were in colleges in 1960 than in the 1920s. Women formed steadily lower percentages of the professionally employed (which included teachers) and of holders of M.A. and Ph.D. degrees. As late as the mid-1960s, 90 percent of school board members were men, although the school board was considered a woman's "place." Studies revealed that poverty and unemployment among women, especially among black women, were widespread in the 1960s and that the gap separating men's and women's wages was widening. Friedan and others protested particularly against the plethora of state laws discriminating against women. These prohibited women from serving on juries, from making contracts, and even from holding property. And women who wanted to enter politics were regularly rebuffed. Shirley Chisholm, a black congresswoman from New York, recalled that her sex was a larger obstacle than her color. "I was constantly bombarded by both men and women," she said, "that I should return to teaching, a woman's vocation, and leave politics up to men."

Long-developing demographic and economic trends helped feminists like Friedan to be heard. Thanks in part to the Pill, which permitted women to plan their lives with some assurance, and in part to the huge expansion of clerical opportunities, the growth in female employment accelerated. By 1965 more than 25 million women were regularly employed. Of married women with young children almost 40 percent held jobs by 1968—a startling increase of nearly 15 percent since the mid-1950s. The majority of these women worked because they needed the money, not because they wished to liberate themselves from the home. But the existence of such an army of female wage-earners virtually assured a decent reception to arguments for equal justice in work.

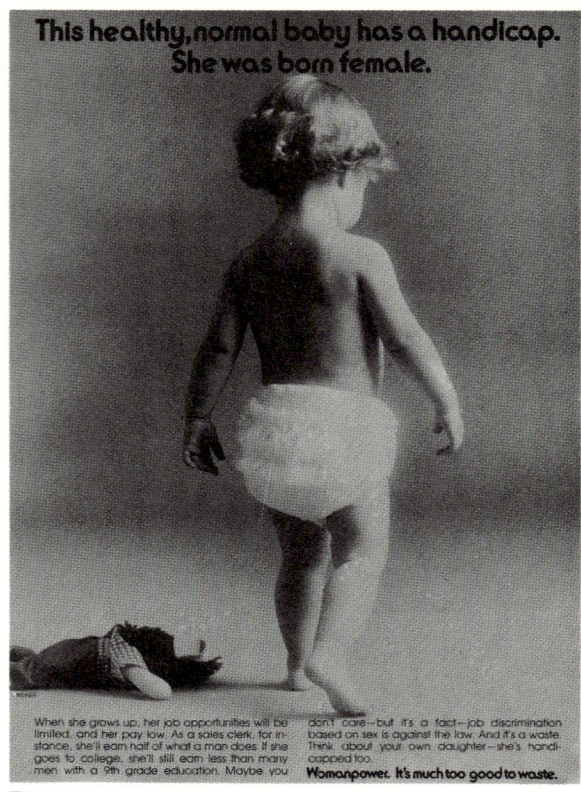

The National Organization for Women makes a case.

At this point the civil rights and peace movements offered models for "women's power." They helped train women in direct action tactics. They revealed also that many male activists were chauvinists who expected women to wash dishes and cook the meals while others "manned" the barricades. The position of women in the struggle for racial justice, Carmichael had sneered, should be prone. Friedan explained, "the absolute necessity for a civil rights movement for women had reached such a point of subterranean explosive urgency by 1966, that it took only a few of us to get together to ignite the spark—and it spread like a chain reaction." With others she helped form the National Organization for Women in 1966. Soon NOW and other more militant groups were employing the same aggressive tactics—sit-ins, demonstrations, protest meetings—that had inspired activists for other causes.

These feminists battled for a variety of goals: exposing "sexism" in families, repealing antiabortion statutes, starting "consciousness-raising" courses, seeking sexual freedom. The majority of the feminists focused on the need for equal treatment. These women worked hard for an equal rights amendment to the Constitution, a dream of militant feminists since 1920. Like

Median annual earnings, by sex and occupation: 1962 to 1972
(In current dollars. Covers persons 14 years old and over as of March of following year. Earnings are for year-round full-time workers)

OCCUPATION GROUP	1962		1966		1970 [a]		1972 [a]	
	MALE	FEMALE	MALE	FEMALE	MALE	FEMALE	MALE	FEMALE
Total earnings	5,754	3,412	6,856	3,946	8,966	5,323	10,202	5,903
Professional, technical, kindred workers	7,621	4,840	9,203	5,779	12,255	7,850	13,542	8,744
Teachers, primary and secondary	6,584	5,183	7,629	5,910	9,883	7,856	11,310	8,706
Managers, officials, proprietors	6,907	3,744	8,826	4,472	11,665	6,369	13,486	7,024
Clerical and kindred workers	5,613	3,826	6,542	4,315	8,652	5,539	9,716	6,054
Salesworkers	6,225	2,607	7,553	3,066	9,765	4,174	11,610	4,445
In retail trade	4,956	2,573	6,150	3,002	7,633	3,874	8,254	4,137
Other Salesworkers	7,137	(B)	8,294	4,153	10,853	5,967	12,838	5,775
Craftsmen, foremen, and kindred workers	6,249	(B)	7,161	4,213	9,253	4,955	10,413	5,545
Foremen	7,350	(B)	8,104	4,250	10,531	5,223	11,497	5,972
Craftsmen	6,056	(B)	6,981	4,161	9,051	4,772	10,196	5,317
Operatives and kindred workers	5,335	3,156	6,135	3,387	7,644	4,465	8,747	5,004
Manufacturing	5,422	3,260	6,219	3,467	7,580	4,559	8,754	5,114

[a]Data may not be strictly comparable with those of previous years. (B) Not computed; base less than minimum required for reliability.
SOURCE: Adapted from *Statistical Abstract of the United States*, 1974, p. 351

blacks and ethnics, the activists crusaded for recognition of their past accomplishments, for courses in women's history, and for coeducation in sex-defined courses, such as woodworking for boys and home economics for girls. They made especially effective use of the prohibition of discrimination on grounds of sex in Title VII of the 1964 Civil Rights Act. This title had been added by segregationists who had hoped to weaken support for the entire bill. Once passed, it enabled women to employ the full force of the government in the struggle against discrimination in federally assisted employment and education.

For a variety of reasons, "women's liberation" did not prove so frightening in the 1960s as the related movement for black power. Women, after all, were already working in large numbers: to give them equal rights was only reasonable. The growth in female white-collar employment may also have altered traditional concepts of masculinity and blurred sex roles. If men were not ready for Unisex, they were prepared at least to admit that not all women must languish at home. Most important, the movement for women's liberation was nonviolent, and it was led by middle-class people. For all its vehemence, it was not likely to overturn society.

By 1968 traditionalists could take further comfort in the fissures that divided the movement. From the beginning most black women devoted their energies to the cause of civil rights for black men. Women's liberation, they insisted, was a diversion. Working-class women objected that the Equal Rights Amendment, which proposed to wipe out sex-oriented laws, would deprive them of protective labor legislation. Such splits were hardly surprising, for women comprised 51 percent of the population. Nor were they entirely new—similar divisions had weakened the feminist cause since the nineteenth century. Still, they permitted opponents of "women's lib" to anticipate further disagreements in the 1970s.

But these cracks in the movement could not hide the fact that the new feminism was more widespread than campaigns earlier in the century. Even women who called themselves moderates were free in criticizing the glorification of marriage and domesticity. For militant women, as for blacks and other minorities, agitation and turmoil were to be welcomed if they accelerated social change. For traditionalists, therefore, the "new" women seemed threatening. To such conservatives, the future of the nation seemed to hinge on the forthcoming electoral campaign of 1968.

The incredible campaign of 1968

On January 3, 1968, Senator Eugene McCarthy of Minnesota surprised the pundits by announcing he would challenge President Johnson on an antiwar platform. In many ways he seemed ill-suited to such a formidable task. A devout Catholic who had seriously considered becoming a monk and an intellectual who numbered the poet Robert Lowell among his advisers, he was hardly a typical representative of American politics. But for many people his stand on the war and his courage in challenging an incumbent president were qualifications enough. And when the Vietcong blasted American installations (including the embassy at Saigon) during the daring Tet offensive beginning January 31, the bankruptcy of Johnson's policies became painfully obvious. With thousands of student volunteers making campaign arrangements, McCarthy came close to beating Johnson in the New Hampshire primary on March 12. He seemed likely to win the next important confrontation, in Wisconsin on April 2. Johnson's awareness of McCarthy's popularity helped to precipitate his startling announcement on March 31 that he would not run for renomination.

Though McCarthy won with ease in Wisconsin, he immediately faced challenges within the Democratic party. Centrists in the Democratic coalition, including many labor leaders, leaned toward Vice-President Hubert H. Hum-

Above, Senator Eugene McCarthy and youthful supporters, 1968. Below, fervent Wallace supporters, 1968.

phrey. Right-wingers flocked to Governor George Wallace of Alabama, who was antiintellectual, openly racist, and hawkish on the war. No one doubted that Wallace commanded widespread support among segregationists in the South and among advocates of escalation. But he displayed much more than a sectional appeal. By denouncing the counter culture, the New Left, and the eastern Establishment, he appealed to many "middle Americans," ethnics, and blue-collar workers. His impressive showings in northern primaries—34 percent in Wisconsin, 30 percent in Indiana, 43 percent in Maryland—suggested that backlash was widespread indeed.

As the campaign progressed McCarthy also demonstrated his lack of appeal to blacks. In the best of times this weakness would have been a liability for a prospective Democratic candidate. But after April 4 it became doubly serious. On that day James Earl Ray, a white exconvict, shot and killed Martin Luther King on the balcony of a Memphis motel. Outraged blacks responded immediately by rampaging through ghettos in Chicago, Washington, and other American cities. McCarthy was naturally appalled by the assassination. But most blacks continued to regard him as the candidate of the white student elite—which in large part he was. Someone else would have to be found who could unite the black masses and antiwar activists and appeal to the center as well.

That someone was Robert Kennedy, who announced his candidacy after the New Hampshire primary. His belated entry earned him few plaudits for courage, and McCarthy supporters abused him for his opportunism. But Kennedy possessed useful assets. He was rich, intelligent, highly organized, and charismatic. More than all other candidates in 1968, he aroused passionate support among·blacks, Chicanos, and many Catholics and blue-collar workers. By calling for deescalation of the war he gradually cut into McCarthy's support among the white student Left. Though he lost to McCarthy in a primary in Oregon, he won impressively everywhere else. He peaked on June 4 when he won the biggest test of all in California.

Whether he could have gone on to win the nomination is hard to judge. Perhaps not, for the Johnson loyalists hated him. But, in any case, he never got the chance. On the night of the California primary, as he walked down a kitchen corridor in a Los Angeles hotel, he was shot and killed by Sirhan Sirhan, a crazed Jordanian immigrant. To millions of blacks and poor people his assassination, following so closely on the murder of King, was the ultimate tragedy. It was also "proof" of the violence and divisions that rent American society.

Kennedy's death eliminated the last chance for the triumph of the antiwar forces at the Democratic convention in Chicago. McCarthy stayed in to the end, but his defeat in California exposed his limitations as a vote getter. Kennedy partisans tried to make a candidate of Senator George McGovern, an antiwar liberal from South Dakota. At that late date, however, McGovern excited little enthusiasm. After bitter struggles over the seating of delegates, the party regulars excluded most of the insurgents. They then chose Hum-

A demonstrator confronts a National Guardsman at the 1968 Democratic national convention in Chicago.

phrey by a margin of more than two to one over McCarthy and McGovern and balanced the ticket by naming liberal-leaning George Muskie, a senator from Maine, as the vice-presidential nominee. As in most Democratic conventions since the 1920s, the slightly left-of-center coalition within the party had triumphed.

These nominations seemed almost worthless as a result of the tumult that convulsed Chicago. As the convention opened, left-wing protesters moved into the city. Most of them were nonviolent whites working for McCarthy. Others, however, were determined to provoke confrontations with Mayor Richard Daley, who had earned notoriety after King's assassination by ordering his police to "shoot to kill" arsonists and to "shoot to maim" looters. Daley erected chain-link fences and barbed wire to protect the convention site and surrounded it with police. Some of the activists responded by taunting and insulting the "pigs," who then charged wildly into crowds, clubbing and gassing passersby as well as demonstrators. The "police riot," as the Walker Report later described it, shattered what hope had remained for rapprochement between the Democratic center and the youthful Left. For Humphrey, "beneficiary" of this police activity, the convention was a disaster.

Richard Nixon, the Republican nominee, seemed certain to profit from this Democratic disarray. His victory at the GOP convention was a triumph of ambition, persistence, and party loyalty. After losing to Kennedy in 1960, he had failed in a race for the governorship of California in 1962. Tired and petulant in defeat, he had told reporters, "You won't have Nixon to kick around any more, because, gentlemen, this is my last press conference." Thereafter, he had been a conscientious party worker, supporting Goldwater in 1964 and traveling widely for GOP congressional candidates in 1966. His smooth performance during the preconvention campaign outflanked right-wingers who had supported California governor Ronald Reagan and liberals who had favored governors Nelson Rockefeller of New York and George Romney of Michigan. It also misled many who had disliked him in the past. "The Nixon of 1968," said Theodore White, chronicler of presidential elections, "was so different from the Nixon of 1960 that the whole personality required reexplanation. . . . There was . . . a total absence of bitterness, of the rancor and venom that had once colored his remarks."

As the campaign developed, Nixon failed to generate enthusiasm. Despite his appeals for "law and order," a rightist slogan, it was clear that George Wallace, running as the presidential candidate of the American Independence party, would capture much of the right-wing vote. Nixon also waffled on Vietnam. In 1966 he had proclaimed, "we believe this is a war that has to be fought to prevent World War III." By early 1968 he was saying that America must "end the war," but refusing to say how or when he would do it. And many people, remembering his partisan, Red-baiting past, refused to believe there was a "new Nixon." As if these were not handicaps enough, he yoked himself to Governor Spiro Agnew of Maryland, his choice for vice-president. Inexperienced and maladroit. Agnew repeatedly insulted ethnic groups. He was one of the most ill qualified vice-presidential candidates in modern times.

Humphrey, meanwhile, labored earnestly to salvage what he could from the discord of the convention. Many union leaders, distrusting the GOP, gave him their support. So did some black spokesmen, who recalled his enthusiasm for civil rights as far back as the 1948 convention. Humphrey built bridges with the antiwar supporters by edging away, though much too slowly for McCarthy, from Johnson's policies. And he benefited from the energetic campaigning of Muskie, a Catholic who appealed to many ethnic voters. On October 31, when Johnson announced that he was stopping all bombing in North Vietnam, it seemed that Humphrey might have a chance.

Johnson's move came too late. Moreover, the South Vietnamese rejected his course of action, and the chances for peace quickly disappeared. On election day Nixon and Agnew triumphed over the Democrats. Considering the woeful state of the GOP in 1964, their victory was impressive. It suggested that voters were becoming much less partisan, indeed, more independent,

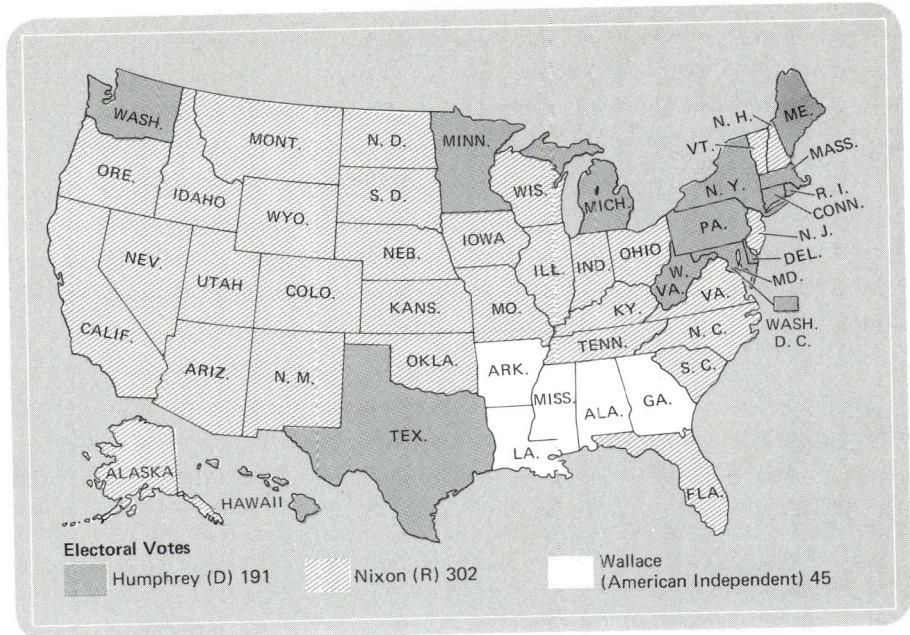

Election, 1968

Electoral Votes		
Humphrey (D) 191	Nixon (R) 302	Wallace (American Independent) 45

than they had been in the heyday of the Democratic coalition under Roosevelt.

The results, however, hardly gave Nixon much cause for rejoicing. In winning he got 31,770,222 votes, less than 1 percent more than Humphrey's 31,267,744. He took only 43 percent of the total vote, the smallest share for a victor since Wilson's in 1912. Like Eisenhower before him, he failed to dent the large Democratic majorities in Congress. Analysts concluded that a higher turnout among blacks would have given Humphrey the margin for victory, and that the Democratic coalition, though slipping, had not disappeared. Voters, they added, had not been attracted to Nixon. As in so many presidential elections since World War II, they had rejected the loser, not accepted the winner.

This negativism showed most clearly in the votes for Wallace and his warlike running mate, General Curtis LeMay. Although Wallace carried only five states (all in the Deep South), he won 9.9 million votes. This was 13.5 percent of the turnout, the highest for any third party candidate since Robert La Follette in 1924, and the highest ever for a candidate on the Right. Wallace's supporters included large numbers of northerners as well as southerners, young people as well as old, blue-collar workers (who defied union spokesmen) as well as wealthy conservatives. His appeal proved that a significant cross section was disgusted with the major parties, with radical youth, with liberalism generally. It showed also that millions still wanted to win the war, even if it meant adopting Le May's suggestion of bombing North Vietnam into the Stone Age. For people such as these Nixon's victory over Humphrey was small consolation.

The Left was even more discouraged than was the Right by the campaign of 1968. Nixon had campaigned on the slogan of "Bring Us Together Again." But he had shown little discernible longing to include in his happy circle the antiwar activists, the blacks, or young people generally. He had denounced the liberal Supreme Court, talked threateningly (though vaguely) about restoring "law and order," and hinted (again vaguely) about cutting back Great Society programs. Given the frustration, indeed the fury, felt by many activists, his victory did not augur well for social peace in the years ahead.

The dissatisfaction of both Right and Left should presumably have comforted the center. To a degree it did. Moderates considered it cause for congratulation that the American people had gone peaceably to the polls and had authorized without protest a transfer of great political power from one party to the other. As so often in the American past, the two-party system had helped to undermine extremes and to preserve the legitimacy of elected officials. This stability was impressive amid such turbulent events.

But thoughtful analysts also asked: stability for what? In being forced to choose between two middle-of-the-road candidates (Wallace was never a plausible winner) the voters had been given no real opportunity to express themselves. And in remaining so vague, Nixon had done little to enlighten them. Millions probably voted for him because of the violence they associated with the radicals in the Democratic party. But did they want Nixon to dismantle the Great Society? Polls suggested not. Millions also supported him because they were tired of "Johnson's war." But did that mean they expected Nixon to stop the fighting or to escalate it? Here the polls were disturbing, for they showed that Americans were frustrated and confused by the war. McCarthy's supporters, for instance, included many who wanted to end the conflict by moving in with the full force of American military power.

This confusion and ambiguity was the most unsettling feature of the campaign of 1968. Far from toning down the discord of the previous three years, it frustrated reactionaries as well as radicals and reduced even the center to apprehensiveness and uncertainty. As Americans were shortly to discover, the stability they had bought by letting Nixon "Bring Us Together Again" was to be short-lived indeed.

Suggestions for reading

Useful starting points for understanding Johnson's foreign policy are Philip L. Geyelin, *Lyndon B. Johnson and the World* (1966); and Richard J. Barnet, *Intervention and Revolution: U. S. and the Third World** (1969), a far-ranging analysis. For the intervention in the Dominican Republic see Theodore Draper, *Dominican Revolt** (1968); and Jerome Slater, *Intervention and Negotiation* (1970). Vietnam policy is covered in Townsend Hoopes, *Limits of Intervention** (1973); Chester Cooper, *Lost Crusade*

(1971); and Seymour Hersh, *My Lai* (1970). See especially Frances Fitzgerald, *Fire in the Lake** (1972), which exposes the impact of war on Vietnamese culture.

Books on domestic unrest include the Report of the National Advisory Commission on Civil Disorders* (1968); and the report of the Scranton Commission on Campus Violence* (1970). Hugh Davis Graham and Ted Gurr, *Violence in America** (1969), provides some historical background. See also Robert Fogelson, *Violence as Protest* (1971); and Robert Conot, *Rivers of Blood, Years of Darkness** (1968), which deals with the riot in Watts. Two eye-witness books by Norman Mailer are *Armies of the Night** (1968) on the demonstration at the Pentagon in 1968; and *Miami and the Siege of Chicago** (1968) on protest at the national conventions.

Among the many books on young people in the 1960s are Kenneth Keniston, *Young Radicals** (1968); Lewis Yablonsky, *Hippie Trip* (1968); Lewis Feuer, *The Conflict of Generations* (1969); and Seymour Lipset, *Rebellion in the University* (1972). Books read widely at the time are Theodore Roszak, *Making of a Counter Culture** (1969); and Charles Reich, *Greening of America** (1970). Paul Goodman, *Growing Up Absurd** (1960), is a lucid account of what alienated young people. Charles Silberman, *Crisis in the Classroom** (1970); and David Riesman and Christopher Jencks, *The Academic Revolution* (1969), cover their subjects thoroughly. Paul Jacobs and Saul Landau, eds., *New Radicals** (1966), is a useful anthology. Books dealing with left-wing ideology include Peter Clecak, *Radical Paradoxes: Dilemmas of the American Left, 1945–1970* (1973); Edward Baccioco, *The New Left: Reform to Revolution* (1974); and Irwin Unger, *The Movement: A History of the American New Left, 1959–1972** (1974). See also John Diggins, *The American Left in the Twentieth Century** (1973).

For the attitudes of militant blacks in the 1960s see James Baldwin, *The Fire Next Time** (1963); Malcolm X, *Autobiography** (1965); Stokeley Carmichael and Charles Hamilton, *Black Power** (1967); and Julius Lester, *Look Out Whitey* (1968). Peter Coleman, *The Death and Life of Malcolm X* (1973), is excellent. E. U. Essien-Udom, *Black Nationalism** (1962), describes the Black Muslims. Surveys of other minorities include Matt Meier and Feliciano Rivera, *The Chicanos** (1972); Stan Steiner, *La Raza** (1970); and Oscar Lewis, *La Vida** (1966), on Puerto Ricans. Michael Novak, *Rise of the Unmeltable Ethnics* (1970), describes the failure of the melting pot.

Books that help in understanding the rise of feminism are Robert Lifton, ed., *The Woman in America** (1965); Lois Banner, *Women in Modern America** (1974); and the book by William Chafe cited in chapter 6. Important feminist statements are Betty Friedan, *The Feminine Mystique** (1963); and Germaine Greer, *The Female Eunuch** (1972).

For politics, especially in 1968, consult the thorough account by Lewis Chester, et. al., *An American Melodrama** (1970). Theodore White, *Making of a President, 1968** (1969), is useful. Marshall Frady, *Wallace** (1970), is entertaining and provocative. David Halberstam, *The Unfinished Odyssey of Robert Kennedy* (1968); and Jeremy Larner, *Nobody Knows: Reflections on the McCarthy Campaign of 1968* (1970), add insights. Richard Scammon and Ben Wattenberg, *The Real Majority* (1970), is a well-written, balanced account of recent electoral trends.

15

The unsettled 1970s

In his first inaugural President Nixon repeated the "bring us together" note he had sounded during his campaign. "We are torn by division," he said. "To a crisis of the spirit, we need an answer of the spirit. And to find that answer, we need only look within ourselves. . . . We cannot learn from one another until we stop shouting at one another—until we speak quietly enough so that our words can be heard as well as our voices. For its part, government will listen."

No leader relishes the thought of presiding over a fractured society, and Nixon was no exception. He took extreme measures in his effort to impose "unity" on the nation. But except for an interlude in 1972, when he triumphed spectacularly in his quest for reelection, the goal of consensus eluded him. Indeed, his own failings did much to divide the country. So it was that Gerald Ford of Michigan, who replaced Nixon in 1974, assumed leadership of a worried country. It remains to be seen whether subsequent presidents can resolve or reduce the conflicts inherited from Nixon and whether the nation can harness the modernizing forces that have transformed American life in the twentieth century. Can the United States extend economic and social progress, curb the military-industrial complex, and find the sense of purpose and idealism appropriate to the future?

Limited advances, 1969–1973

There were some slight grounds for optimism even during the first few years of Nixon's tumultuous presidency. Racial unrest seemed to subside. Contrary to expectations, the ghettos had quieted in the summer of 1968, and they stayed relatively peaceful throughout the early 1970s. Some people attributed the calm to prosecutions that had driven militants like Carmichael and Rap Brown into jail or exile. Others concluded that blacks had come to doubt the wisdom of destroying their own property. As one Watts leader put it, "the rioting phase, where we burn down businesses in our own areas, is over. The whole movement is in another direction—toward implementing black power and finding our own dignity as a people."

To a limited extent blacks achieved these aims. Thanks to the Supreme Court, which ruled in 1969 *(Alexander* v. *Holmes)* that school desegregation must proceed "at once," the percentage of blacks in formerly all-black schools fell from 68 percent to 18 percent between 1968 and 1970. Statistics revealed that blacks, though still failing to capture a larger share of the national income, were developing a sizeable middle class: the proportion of employed blacks who earned $10,000 or more increased from 5 percent to 28 percent during the 1960s. The number who attended college rose between 1966 and 1970 by 85 percent—to 434,000. And blacks began to make use of the vote. By 1971 there were 13 black congressmen, 81 mayors, 198 state legislators, and 1,567 black local office-holders. These advances were significant. Few people in 1960 could have predicted them. Nevertheless, discrimination still plagued the nation. The controversy over busing in the schools, perhaps the most acrimonious domestic issue of the early 1970s, showed that many white Americans still refused to accept residential integration or to go much beyond tokenism in the schools.

Feminists, too, made modest gains in the 1970s. Writers like Robin Morgan, author of *Sisterhood Is Powerful* (1970), and Germaine Greer, author of the *Female Eunuch* (1971), advanced the economic, psychological, and physiological justifications for women's liberation. Others, including self-proclaimed lesbians like Kate Millett, led a growing campaign for sexual freedom. In 1972 activists founded *Ms,* the first militant feminist magazine to attract a sizeable circulation. In the same year Congress approved legislation banning sex discrimination in colleges and universities receiving federal aid. In 1973 the Supreme Court (*Doe* v. *Bolton, Roe* v. *Wade*) ruled against state laws prohibiting abortions, and both houses of Congress approved the Equal Rights Amendment, which feminists had been seeking for fifty years. A total of twenty-two states—of thirty-eight needed—ratified the amendment the same year.

Thereafter, feminism suffered reverses. Many black women continued to oppose the movement. So did large numbers of married working women—who were too intent on keeping their jobs (or on earning enough money to

Feminists on the march, New York City.

return to the home) to spend time on campaigns for women's rights. NOW moderates complained that lesbians and sexual radicals exposed the movement to distortion and ridicule. Other articulate women led a countermovement. One of their most forceful leaders, Phyllis Schlafly, was a conservative whose idols were Thomas Edison, Elias Howe (inventor of the sewing machine), and Clarence Birdseye, all of whom had promoted comforts of domesticity. "A man's first significant purchase," she said, "is a diamond for his bride, and the largest financial investment of his life is a home for her to

The women's movement promises to affect radically the life of virtually everyone in America. Only a small part of the population suffers because it is black, and most people have little contact with minorities. Women are 51 percent of the population, and chances are that every adult American either is one, is married to one, or has close social or business relations with many.

The feminist revolution will overturn the basic premises upon which these relations are built—stereotyped notions about the family and the roles of men and women, fallacies concerning masculinity and femininity, and the economic division of labor into paid work and homemaking.

If the 1960s belonged to the blacks, the next ten years are ours.

Lucy Komisar, an activist for women's liberation, explains her goals (1970).

live in." Reflecting this attitude, Nixon vetoed a bill in 1973 that would have provided funds for day-care centers. Meanwhile, antifeminists campaigned against ratification of the ERA, which they said would destroy the "special place" of women in the home.

Yet feminists, like blacks, could take some comfort in the progress they had made since the early 1960s. Though NOW still had fewer than 40,000 members in 1975, it had grown steadily since its formation in 1966. A majority of women told pollsters that they approved the general goals of the movement. Of all the protest movements that started in the 1960s—for peace, for black power, for brown power—women's liberation seemed most durable.

Other reformers took limited pleasure in accomplishments of the Democratic Congresses between 1969 and 1972. The legislators voted increases in social security benefits and extended the life of the 1965 Voting Rights Law. They approved an act regulating campaign spending and authorized eighteen-year-olds to vote in federal elections. The Twenty-sixth Amendment to the Constitution, ratified in 1971, extended the voting rights of eighteen-year-olds to state and local elections. Though Congress fell far short of attacking the nation's festering urban and racial problems, it did increase funding for some domestic purposes. In part because of a recession that descended on the economy in 1969, spending for food stamps—to go to 11 million poor people—rose from $250 million in 1969 to $2.2 billion in 1971. Nonmilitary federal expenditures as a percentage of the GNP almost doubled between 1969 and 1972.

The lawmakers occasionally proved responsive to the pressures for environmental conservation applied constantly by Ralph Nader and others in the early 1970s. Among the important measures approved were the Water Quality Improvement Act, which attempted to control pollution caused by industry and power companies; the Clean Air Act, which called for changes in the manufacture of automobiles; and the Resource Recovery Act, which promoted recycling of solid wastes. Congress also refused funds for the Super Sonic Transport (SST), a huge, noisy airplane that the administration had strongly favored. In 1971 Congress created the Environmental Protection Agency and empowered it to bring suits against corporate or municipal leaders who violated federal standards. Despite these laws, many corporations (especially in the automobile industry) found ways to evade or to postpone stringent regulation. Careless oil drilling and pumping, which had ruined beaches and marine life off Santa Barbara in 1969, continued to cause damage. Most alarming, Americans continued to squander resources at an alarming rate. But as the birth rate approached the point of zero population growth, the hope remained that the nation could learn to exist without destroying its environment.

Nixon could claim little credit for these developments. Indeed, he was cool to legislation for social welfare or environmental protection. But many observers welcomed his apparent expertise in the realm of foreign affairs. Here he, like Kennedy, paid little attention to the State Department. Its secretary until late 1973, William Rogers, played an insignificant role in policy making. Nixon relied instead on Dr. Henry Kissinger, his national security adviser. Kissinger, a German emigré who had become a professor of government at Harvard, was a highly skilled negotiator and a persuasive exponent of power politics. The way to avoid nuclear catastrophe, he believed, was to seek détente with the Soviet Union and China. These powers, with Japan and western Europe, could cooperate with the United States to prevent brush fires from escalating into World War III.

Kissinger's policies did not work wonders in 1969–71. In the Middle East they failed to end tensions heightened by Israel's stunning victory over Arab countries in the Six-Day War of 1967. Nixon and Kissinger also did not deserve much credit for the limited détente that did develop with Russia and China by 1972. Rather, these communist powers, at odds with each other, assumed considerable initiative for developing better relations with the West. Still, the administration helped to defuse the Cold War and to reverse the tide of postwar American foreign policy. Nixon, once the cold warrior extraordinaire, had revealed his capacity for change.

The President even seemed to make progress toward deescalating the war in Vietnam. In 1969 he announced the Nixon Doctrine, which proclaimed that allies could expect American aid, but not troops, when confronted with internal revolt. He added that he would end the draft within two years. Encouraged by Secretary of Defense Melvin Laird, he propounded Vietnamization, as it became called. The United States, Nixon said, would build up the Vietnamese military so that it could stand on its own. To back up this policy the President began withdrawing American troops. In 1968 there had been 543,000; by September 1972 there were only 39,000. Though later developments revealed the serious limitations of Vietnamization, the troop withdrawals were a popular step toward disengagement.

The persistence of discord

From the beginning of Nixon's presidency, however, the discord of the Johnson years persisted. For the universities, in fact, the spring of 1969 was the most disruptive to date. Police moved in to restore order at Howard, Massachusetts, Pennsylvania State, and San Fernando State. Conflicts between black and white students erupted in violence at the University of Wisconsin and City College of New York. Harvard students invaded University Hall, rifled files, and were thrown out by state police. And at Cornell armed blacks seized the student union, leading the university president to capitulate to their demands. The backlash that followed such demonstrations—perpetrated by a small minority of students—was one of many forces that culminated in scanty funding for colleges and universities in the early 1970s.

Militant black students at Cornell University, 1969.

Economic divisions plagued society at large. The 1970s were for public service employees what the 1930s had been for industrial workers. Teachers, nurses, policemen, garbage collectors, firemen, and transit employees formed militant unions, picketed city hall, and staged walkouts that would have seemed revolutionary in Calvin Coolidge's day. A strike of postal workers tied up the nation's mails for a week and forced the national guard to take charge in New York City. Despairingly, Congress established an independent postal service that was expected to soften discontent. Inflation stemming from a war-heated economy accounted for much of this conflict. So did new visions of the "good life" and meaningful work. White-collar and service workers in the 1970s, like so many Americans in the prosperous postwar years, were joining the revolution of rising expectations.

Continuing violence was particularly frightening. In early 1970 bombs tore up the Manhattan offices of IBM, General Telephone and Electronics Corporation, and Mobil Oil. Antiwar revolutionaries claimed credit for the explosions. Shortly thereafter two black militants, followers of Rap Brown, were killed when one of their homemade bombs went off prematurely. And in March 1970 three young radicals, one of them a socially prominent young woman who had recently graduated from Swarthmore, were blown to pieces in their "bomb factory" in Greenwich Village. Two other revolutionaries, cut and bleeding, fled from the scene.

These were but the most striking manifestations of apparent social upheaval in the years after 1968. In New York City bomb threats averaged 1000 a month in 1969–70. Within fifteen months 368 bombs actually exploded. In 1970 the FBI reported 35,202 assaults on policemen, four times the number in 1960. People were not even safe in the air: skyjacking diverted seventy-one planes in 1969 alone. The drug traffic seemed particularly frightening. When rock stars Jimi Hendrix and Janis Joplin died from overdoses, some of the worst fears seemed confirmed.

The most shocking violence of the early 1970s took place in prisons, many of which were breeding grounds for racial confrontations between convicts and authorities. One such outbreak occurred in August 1971 at San Quentin prison, where George Jackson, one of the three black "Soledad brothers" (actually not related), was caged for allegedly having killed a white guard at Soledad prison a year earlier. Using a smuggled pistol, Jackson broke out of his cell and demanded the release of twenty-seven prisoners. He then murdered three white guards and two trusties before falling in a rain of shots himself. Militants, outraged by his death, dressed him in a black panther uniform and gave him a martyr's funeral.

Jackson's death helped to trigger the most bloody prison riot in American history. This occurred at Attica, New York State, home of 2,254 convicts, 75 percent of whom were black or Puerto Rican. All the 383 guards were white, and racial incidents were common. In September 1971 angry blacks staged a rebellion that was quickly joined by more than 1200 inmates. They grabbed 39 hostages, seriously hurt a guard, barricaded themselves in a cell block, and issued demands on the warden. When the prisoners threatened to cut the throats of their hostages, the authorities waited no longer. In the assault which followed, police gunfire killed 30 prisoners and 10 guards. To some observers, like *The New York Times*'s Tom Wicker, the Attica riot displayed the urgent need for prison reform. To many others it was "proof" of the savagery of the criminal population—especially of blacks—and of the need for "law and order."

NIXON AT BAY, 1969–1971

Nixon, of course, was not to blame for such violence. But to many Americans—progressives, college activists, blacks—he was an unsympathetic figure. Between 1969 and mid-1971 they grew increasingly hostile to the President. They focused on four themes: his personal style, his domestic policies, his "southern strategy," and Vietnam.

Objections to Nixon's style ranged from the frivolous to the profound. Americans who had looked to the White House for cultural leadership disliked his patronage of pro football, middlebrow music, and Norman Vincent Peale. Others considered him banal, hypocritical, and sanctimonious. People wondered about his close friendships with C. G. ("Bebe") Rebozo, a wealthy real estate operator, and with Robert H. Abplanalp. a businessman, who helped

Nixon finance the purchase of property worth $600,000 at Key Biscayne, Florida, and San Clemente, California. Nixon's taste for regal living, it was revealed later, cost the government $10 million in improvements and security measures. To his critics, "Tricky Dick" was becoming "King Richard."

Nixon's style was above all secretive and suspicious. Extremely sensitive to criticism, he avoided contacts with the press. Faced with important decisions, he frequently slipped off to the presidential retreat at Camp David, Maryland, or to one of his tightly guarded compounds in Florida and California. There he would summon up the courage to act. Even his cabinet found him remote and nonsupporting. Two of the more popular among his appointees, Secretary of the Interior Walter Hickel and HEW Secretary Robert Finch, left or were fired by the end of 1970. Like reporters, they complained that Nixon surrounded himself with a much-expanded White House staff of ambitious, unscrupulous young lawyers, public relations men, and advertising executives. Among them were attorneys John Dean and Charles Colson, and Jeb Stuart Magruder, a young businessman. Nixon's closest domestic advisers, H. R. Haldeman and John R. Erlichman, had no experience in government. Tough, cold, and utterly devoted to their boss, they excluded visitors, insulted important politicians, and narrowed the circle of decision-making. Not even Lyndon Johnson at his most highhanded had seemed so inaccessible as Nixon.

The President's economic policies aroused special concern. Some of his angriest critics, suprisingly enough, were conservatives. When Nixon proclaimed, in January 1971, "I am now a Keynesian," they were appalled. They were equally shocked to discover that the budget deficit for the 1970–71 fiscal year amounted to more than $23 billion, only $2 billion less than the record set during Johnson's last year in office. Nixon's endorsement of unbalanced budgets provided added evidence of his flexibility (critics said of his lack of principle), and of the political clout enjoyed by pressure groups.

Conservatives had other complaints about Nixon's domestic policies. They resented Hickel's rigorous enforcement of the laws protecting the environment. They grumbled especially about the influence of Daniel Patrick Moynihan, a Harvard professor whom Nixon named to head the newly created Urban Affairs Council. Under Moynihan's persistent coaching Nixon endorsed the controversial Family Assistance Plan, which would have guaranteed an income of $1600 a year (plus food stamps valued at $800 or more) to a family of four. The plan promised cash payments to the hitherto neglected working poor. Michael Harrington, a socialist, termed FAP "the most radical idea since the New Deal." But Democrats in Congress ultimately sidetracked the measure—in part because they demanded more generous benefits, in part because they disliked Nixon, in part because the President (to gain conservative support) appeared to threaten able-bodied heads of households with loss of benefits if they failed to register for job training or to accept work. Congress's rejection of the measure meant that America's creaking welfare "system" staggered on.

Most criticism of the President's domestic policies came from liberals. They recognized that Nixon, like Kennedy, was primarily interested in foreign affairs. Indeed, Nixon once commented, "I've always thought this country could run itself domestically without a President." He added, "all you need is a competent cabinet to run the country at home." This attitude antagonized reformers, most of whom could not get past the "Berlin Wall" erected by Haldeman and Erlichman. Congress objected also to presidential pressure in 1969 for the funding of antimissile (ABM) development. Though Nixon won that fight, by one vote, it cost him what little chance he had had of working harmoniously with the Democratic Congresses of his administration. Long before Congress counterattacked in 1973–74, many of its most influential members were barely on speaking terms with the White House.

The liberals were particularly critical of Nixon's handling of the economy, which grew ragged and unstable between 1969 and 1972. The administration's tight money policy, they claimed, harmed investment and impeded construction. The failure to set forth price and wage guidelines encouraged round after round of inflationary settlements between management and labor. A $2.5 billion tax cut, which Nixon signed in December 1969, further fed inflation. By 1971 the country was experiencing the worst of all possible worlds: inflation (5.3 percent in 1970) and recession (6 percent unemployment) at the same time. At fault, said Democratic party chieftain Lawrence O'Brien, were "Nixonomics." O'Brien explained, "All the things that should go up—the stock market, corporate profits, real spendable income, productivity—go down, and all the things that should go down—unemployment, prices, interest rates—go up."

NIXON'S SOUTHERN STRATEGY

Most objectionable of all to progressives was the administration's "southern strategy." In its broad outlines this reflected the argument of Kevin Phillips, a Justice Department aide who wrote *The Emerging Republican Majority* in 1969. To Phillips the preeminent need of the GOP was to outflank men like Governor Wallace by 1972. This meant securing the votes of "middle Americans"—southern whites, blue-collar workers, Catholic ethnics, suburbanites, conservatives. It meant stressing the theme of "law and order," discrediting activist students, and paying relatively little attention to the wishes of blacks, Hispanic-Americans, and others who were predominantly Democratic anyway.

This southern strategy helps to explain Nixon's civil rights policies. These were a mixture of forward and backward movements. To assist blacks Nixon instituted the so-called Philadelphia Plan, which required unions working on federal projects to accept quotas of blacks as apprentices and to admit them when training was completed. To secure black support he named James Farmer, a leading activist, as an assistant secretary of HEW. He told Farmer that he wanted to do "what's right" for blacks. "I care," he added. "I just hope people will believe that I DO care."

During the two years that Farmer stayed with HEW, however, he was unable to penetrate the Berlin Wall. Like other advocates of civil rights, he confronted the influence of Attorney General John Mitchell, a Nixon law partner who emerged as the strongest figure in the new cabinet. Under Mitchell the Department of Justice attempted (unsuccessfully) to prevent extension of the voting rights act of 1965. He also brought suit to delay school desegregation guidelines in Mississippi. Outraged attorneys in the civil rights divisions of the Justice Department and HEW protested vigorously. Though the Supreme Court's ruling for desegregation "at once" foiled Mitchell's effort, he had shown the white South that the administration cared.

Mitchell's passion for "law and order" led him into several other blunders between 1969 and 1971. One was his attempt to prosecute antiwar demonstrators. Among the many activists he had arrested were the "Harrisburg Seven," the "Gainesville Eight," and others who were tried in groups. The trial of the "Chicago Seven," including the Yippies Jerry Rubin and Abbie Hoffman, degenerated into a shouting match between the unruly defendants and a judge so biased that his decision against them was later overruled. Capping efforts to stifle dissent, Mitchell brought suit in 1971 to stop publication of the so-called Pentagon papers, a forty-seven-volume, 2.5-million-word summary that documented the escalation of the war in Vietnam prior to 1969. The Supreme Court, however, ruled against prior restraint of publication in the press, and lesser courts sustained the antiwar demonstrators. The court decisions revealed the continuing independence of the judiciary from executive activity. They suggested also Mitchell's disregard for civil liberties. For a guardian of "law and order" it was an unedifying performance.

The southern strategy came gradually to dictate the administration's choice of justices to fill vacancies in the Supreme Court between 1969 and 1972. The first nominee, Warren Earl Burger of Minnesota, was a well-qualified moderate named to replace Chief Justice Warren, who retired after sixteen years on the bench. The Senate confirmed him quickly. Mitchell's next choice was Judge Clement F. Haynsworth, Jr., a South Carolinian. Union leaders, civil rights advocates, and progressives opposed him. Early supporters wavered when they learned of conflict-of-interest charges marring Haynsworth's judicial record. In November 1969 the Senate, including seventeen Republicans, rejected him.

The Senate's action infuriated Nixon, who called the attacks on Haynsworth "brutal, vicious . . . and unfair." His temper high, he carelessly nominated Mitchell's next choice, G. Harrold Carswell, a Floridian who served on the court of appeals. Suspecting Nixon's political motives, opponents produced evidence to show Carswell's racial bias. Law professors throughout the country exposed his mediocrity as a judge. Accordingly, the Senate, including thirteen Republicans, rejected him in April 1970. Adhering to the southern strategy, Nixon burst out, "I understand the bitter feelings of millions of Americans who live in the South. They have my assurance that the day will come when judges like Carswell and Haynsworth can and will sit on the High Court."

After circulating the names of other mediocre candidates, Nixon finally searched for qualified nominees who could command congressional support. By 1972 he had named three. The first, Judge Harry Blackmun of Minnesota, held views that resembled Burger's. The second, Lewis F. Powell, Jr., had been a president of the American Bar Association. The third, Assistant Attorney General William H. Rehnquist, was a young Goldwater Republican who was developing a reputation as a thoughtful exponent of conservative jurisprudence. The Senate confirmed all three.

Nixon's actions enhanced his standing in the South. But they antagonized Congress. And they failed to produce a tractable Court. Though the four new appointees often voted together, they showed little disposition to reverse the decisions of the Warren Court, and they did not comprise a majority. In addition to the abortion and Pentagon papers cases—both of which annoyed the administration—the Burger Court voted unanimously in 1971 that busing was necessary and proper if other means failed to achieve school desegregation. Though later decisions concerning busing left the issue in doubt, it was clear that Burger and his associates would not block the movement for racial justice.

In the next few years the Court continued to antagonize conservatives. In 1972 it held, five to four, that state laws that authorized the death sentence were unconstitutional because they gave too much discretion to judges and juries. The decision did not outlaw the death sentence per se—thirty-two states passed new laws authorizing it by 1975—but it stopped executions for the time being, and it prompted renewed litigation that branded the death penalty unconstitutional "cruel and unusual punishment." The court also ruled that the government had to get a court order before employing wiretapping against suspected subversives. And in 1974 it ruled, eight to nothing, that Nixon must turn over damning tape recordings to a district court. The President, like many of his predecessors in the White House, experienced the rugged independence of the judicial branch.

Vietnam, Cambodia, and Laos

Nixon's most divisive policies before 1973 were in the realm where he had seemed so assured: foreign policy. His problem was simple: Vietnamization was not working. As American troops were withdrawn, the North Vietnamese and the Viet Cong proved more than a match for the forces of South Vietnam's Dictator Nguyen Van Thieu. To compensate, Nixon authorized unpublicized bombing raids on neighboring Cambodia, which the enemy was using as a sanctuary. These raids, some 3,600 beginning early in 1969, failed to stop the communists. Encouraged by the Joint Chiefs, Nixon then toyed with the idea of sending American troops into Cambodia. But such an attack could not be concealed, and Prince Norodim Sihanouk, Cambodia's ruler, would have objected. The President's hands were tied.

In March 1970 the situation changed suddenly. Lon Nol, a rightist, staged a successful coup against Sihanouk. With the way now open for invasion, Nixon wasted little time. On April 30 he appeared on television to announce that an attack was underway to destroy the North Vietnamese sanctuaries. He did not mention the failure of Vietnamization, and he said nothing about the secret bombing raids of the previous fourteen months. The fact that American soldiers were invading a neutral nation did not seem to trouble him. On the contrary, he spoke fiercely. "We will not be humiliated," he explained. "We will not be defeated. If when the chips are down the United States acts like a pitiful helpless giant, the forces of totalitarianism and anarchy will threaten free nations and free institutions throughout the world. It is not our power but our will that is being tested. . . ." He added that the invasion might make him a "one-term President . . . but I have rejected all political considerations in making this decision . . . I would rather be a one-term President than be a two-term President at the cost of seeing America become a second-rate power and see this nation accept the first defeat in its proud 190-year history."

Nixon miscalculated badly. In Cambodia the attack was of dubious merit. According to American estimates, the invasion succeeded in killing more than 11,000 soldiers and in capturing stores of food and ammunition. By

One of the victims shot by National Guardsmen at Kent State, 1970.

reducing some of the military pressure on Thieu's forces, it may have given Vietnamization a little more time. But allied casualties were 1,138 dead and 4,911 wounded. The invasion failed to drive the enemy out of Cambodia. Worst of all, the assault dragged Cambodia itself into full-scale civil war. Within five years Lon Nol's increasingly unpopular regime was to fall to a nationalistic form of communism.

INTENSIFICATION OF ANTIWAR SENTIMENT

At home Nixon's action prompted stirrings—at last—of independence in Congress, which repealed the 1964 Gulf of Tonkin resolution. The invasion also led to tragedy in Ohio. Two nights after Nixon announced his move students at Kent State University firebombed the ROTC building, causing Ohio Governor James Rhodes to call in the national guard. For a time it seemed that calm would return. But on May 4 students threw rocks and bottles at the guardsmen, who responded with tear gas. When the soldiers ran out of gas, they retreated nervously up a hillside. They were out of range of rocks, and in no danger. Some of the guardsmen then stopped, turned, and began to shoot. A girl screamed, "my God, they're killing us." When the firing stopped, four students lay dead, and eleven were wounded. The Justice Department, acting under Mitchell's orders, failed to call a federal grand jury to review the tragedy, and it was not until 1974 that eight guardsmen were

Kent State University, 1970.

indicted (and acquitted) on criminal charges of violating the students' civil rights.

The deaths at Kent State unleashed a torrent of protest, especially on the campuses, which erupted for the third consecutive spring. Within the month demonstrations disrupted more than 400 universities; more than 250 had to be closed down before the end of the semester. By May 9 weekend, some 100,000 students descended on Washington in protest. A week later at Jackson State College in Mississippi two black students were killed and eleven wounded when police fired indiscriminately into a dormitory. President William J. McGill of Columbia University commented accurately that it was the "most disastrous month of May in the history of American higher education."

Nixon's first reaction was to discredit the students. "These bums . . . blowing up the campuses," he said, " . . . burning up the books, storming about." After the bloodshed at Kent State he commented that the shootings should "remind us once again that when dissent turns to violence it invites tragedy." But the protests worried him, and before dawn on May 9 he got out of bed and stole off to talk to demonstrators camped near the Lincoln Memorial. He intended to be responsive, conciliatory, understanding. But the ensuing dialogue exposed the gulf that separated him from the demonstrators. To California students he talked about surfing; to those from Syracuse he posed questions about the college football team. When he left to eat breakfast in a Washington hotel, he had done nothing to placate his opposition.

The campus disorders also heightened the President's desire to curb dissent. Already he had arranged to tap the phones of thirteen top government officials whom he suspected of leaking stories about the bombings in Cambodia, and of four journalists who had published them. Now, in June 1970, he tried to form a special national security committee composed of top people from the CIA, FBI, and Defense Intelligence Agency, and headed by FBI chief J. Edgar Hoover. The committee would have the power to engage in electronic surveillance, stage break-ins, open mail, and infiltrate college campuses. Hoover, however, spiked the plan by refusing to serve. Though a staunch anticommunist, he wanted no part of illegal operations that would damage the reputation of the FBI. Disappointed, Nixon had to put the plan aside for a while.

Instead, he relied on the vitriolic rhetoric of his vice-president, Spiro Agnew, who outdid himself during the congressional campaigning of 1970. Dissidents, Agnew said, were "parasites of passion," "ideological eunuchs," an "effete corps of impudent snobs who characterize themselves as intellectuals." The press was an "unelected elite," a "tiny and closed fraternity of privileged men . . . enjoying a monopoly sanctioned and licensed by the government." Agnew's assaults dovetailed neatly with the southern strategy and appealed to "middle Americans" who disliked the radical students and the "metromedia" of the eastern seaboard. But Agnew was practically threatening the media with censorship. Not since the days of the sedition and espionage acts during World War I had an administration acted so menacingly toward its opponents.

Perhaps for this reason, the Nixon-Agnew strategy backfired politically. In the election of 1970 the GOP gained two seats in the Senate but lost twelve in the House. They dropped eleven governorships, to trail twenty-nine to twenty-one nationwide. That winter a Gallup poll showed that only 49 percent of Americans, a new low, approved of the administration. Maine's Democratic Senator Edmund Muskie, who had made an extraordinarily effective election-eve broadcast, moved ahead of the President, 47 percent to 39 percent. It seemed possible that Nixon would be a one-term president.

During the first six months of 1971 Nixon did little to better his fortunes. The economy continued to skid. Inflation mounted. The nation faced an unfavorable balance of trade for the first time since the depression year of 1893. The press carried alarming stories of drug addiction, desertion, and mutiny among the troops in Vietnam. Courting further confrontations with antiwar spokesmen, Nixon intervened on behalf of Lieutenant William Calley, Jr., whom the army had convicted of murdering twenty-two civilians at My Lai in 1968. The President had him removed from the stockade pending appeal and promised personally to review the case. He also had charges of stealing government property brought against Daniel Ellsberg, a McNamara protégé and Rand Corporation employee who had released the Pentagon papers to the press. Some of Nixon's aides even drew up an "enemies list." It included such threats to the state as James Reston, Jane Fonda, Barbra Streisand, Paul Newman, and many others.

Nixon compounded his difficulties with yet another adventure in Southeast Asia. This was an invasion of Laos by South Vietnamese troops in February. Its aim, like the assault on Cambodia in 1970, was to cut off sanctuaries and supply routes winding into Vietnam. The incursion was also to display the fighting capacity of the South Vietnamese, who were to go it alone this time. When the attack was over in April, Nixon announced proudly, "tonight I can report that Vietnamization has succeeded." Press accounts showed otherwise. The enemy inflicted 50 percent casualties—3800 South Vietnamese killed and 4500 wounded—in six weeks. Only heavy bombing by the United States—again in a neutral country—prevented still more shocking losses.

Predictably, the invasion of Laos provoked demonstrations. This time the universities were relatively quiet—perhaps because students remembered Kent State, perhaps because protest on the campuses had seemed ineffective in the past. Instead, students and antiwar veterans—by then a growing lobby—headed for Washington. Their protests were orderly, and Washington police made no attempt to harass them. But the arrival in late April of the so-called Mayday tribe changed the situation. Though these activists, perhaps 15,000 strong, were nonviolent, they vowed to "stop the government." They threw trash into streets, abandoned cars at intersections, and milled about. This was too much for Mitchell, who sent in police, national guardsmen, and army troops. Using truncheons and tear gas, they arrested 12,614 people in four days and penned them in open spaces like Robert F. Kennedy Memorial Stadium. Mitchell said that the government had "stopped a repressive mob from robbing the rights of others." The courts, appalled, threw out the arrests as violations of civil rights. Once again the Nixon administration, which had promised to bring the nation together, had helped to drive it apart.

The great turnabout, 1971–1972

In mid-1971 the administration began a turnabout that dramatically improved its fortunes. Nixon began it in July by announcing that he would visit the People's Republic of China early in 1972. Critics grumbled that the proposed trip was a public relations stunt. Others complained that Chiang Kai-shek was being abandoned—indeed, the General Assembly of the United Nations voted three months later to seat Mao Tse-tung's regime. Still others pointed out that Red China, which felt threatened by the Soviet Union, was simply using the United States, and that the visit would poison American relations with Japan, the most highly industrialized nation in Asia. But most Americans were as pleased as they were surprised by Nixon's announcement. Kissinger's efforts for détente with the great powers were apparently paying off. The Cold War was thawing at last.

A month later Nixon made an equally dramatic announcement: the New Economic Policy. To improve the nation's balance of payments, he said, the United States would permit the dollar to find its own level—to "float" in the international exchange markets. He also called for a 10 percent tax on many imports, the repeal of important excise taxes, and tax breaks for industries that undertook new investment. To bring inflation to a halt, wages, prices, and dividends would be frozen for ninety days, and controlled (in so-called Phase II) thereafter.

Many of Nixon's critics refused to credit him with these policies. His new Secretary of the Treasury John Connally, a Democrat, seemed the more likely initiator. Still, the changes were startling. Permitting the dollar to float in its weakened condition was largely the same as devaluing it. To many Americans this was a rude shock. Establishing controls seemed even more incredible, for Nixon, who had served unhappily as a young lawyer with the Office of Price Administration in World War II, had adamantly rejected such a policy earlier in the year. But if Americans were surprised, they were pleased by the administration's show of resolve—and by the gains that appeared to follow. As the dollar declined in value (eventually by about 9 percent), American exports became cheaper, and the balance of trade seemed to improve. Controls temporarily slowed down the rate of inflation. Stock prices jumped encouragingly, until the Dow Jones industrial average broke 1000 for the first time in history, in November. The President's amazing turnabout was literally paying off.

In the next few months Nixon's economic policy seemed less assured. Even before the introduction of Phase II in November, the government's wage and price commissions began to give way before the pressure of unions and of business interests. Inflation, which controls had checked, began to accelerate again. Disgruntled, the AFL-CIO refused to cooperate any longer in March 1972. For the rest of the year—indeed for the next few years—the rising cost of living became an increasingly vital concern.

But Nixon's pyrotechnic diplomacy in early 1972 helped conceal the faults of his economic policies. His visit to China in February 1972, though accomplishing little that was concrete, was elaborately staged for the American television audience. It greatly enhanced his stature. Kissinger's handling of Moscow was even more dazzling. When North Vietnam mounted an offensive on March 30, Nixon responded by bombing the north for the first time in three years, and by dropping mines in the harbor of Haiphong, a provocative step that not even Johnson had dared to take. Yet the Soviet Union, anxious not to drive the United States and China closer together, posed no objections. On the contrary, it welcomed Nixon with open arms when he visited Moscow in May. In an amiable series of meetings the President and Brezhnev agreed to collaborate on space exploration, to limit deployment of antiballistic missiles, and to freeze offensive missiles for the next five years. The trips to Moscow and Peking marked the high points of the Nixon-Kissinger foreign policy.

By this time the President's campaign for reelection was well underway. Here he took no chances. In 1971 he had already formed the Special Investigations Unit, which placed on its payroll such security "experts" as G. Gordon Liddy, a former Treasury employee, and ex-CIA operatives E. Howard Hunt, Jr., and James McCord, Jr. These "plumbers," outfitted illegally by the CIA, burglarized the office of Daniel Ellsberg's psychiatrist in an unsuccessful attempt to find compromising evidence. In 1971 Nixon had also formed the Committee to Re-elect the President. CREEP disbursed funds for "dirty tricks" aimed at embarrassing potential opponents like Wallace and Muskie. It arranged to tap the phone of the secretary of Lawrence O'Brien, chairman of the Democratic National Committee. And it collected a record $60 million, much of it in violation of existing laws against corporate contributions to political campaigns.

In mapping out his campaign the President had more than the usual amount of luck. Senator Edward Kennedy of Massachusetts, once the most popular Democratic challenger, had seriously harmed his chances in 1969 when he had driven his car off a bridge on the island of Chappaquiddick near Martha's Vineyard. The crash caused the death by drowning of a passenger, Mary Jo Kopechne. Senator Edward Muskie, the front-runner early in 1972, was damaged politically by his tearful response to a letter contrived by a "dirty trickster" in the employ of CREEP and published during the New Hampshire primary. George Wallace, who scored well in Democratic primaries in the North as well as in the South and seriously threatened Nixon's chances in November, was shot on May 15 by a deranged white youth, Arthur H. Bremer. Though Wallace survived, the shots paralyzed him for life and removed him from the presidential race. As it turned out, Wallace's withdrawal practically guaranteed Nixon the election.

As if charmed, the President benefited from disarray within the Democratic party. With Muskie and Wallace out of the race, the two remaining contenders, Senators Hubert Humphrey of Minnesota and George McGovern of South Dakota, traded damaging accusations in the crucial California primary in early June. Though McGovern won, thereby assuring himself the nomination, Humphrey argued persistently that McGovern's economic program—which included giving $1000 to every American—was both costly and tough on the middle class. The charges proved useful to the GOP in the election campaign.

The Democratic convention added to McGovern's problems. Based on a quota system that favored blacks, women, and young people while discriminating against labor unions, urban political machines, congressional leaders, and ethnic groups, the convention alienated the traditional support of the Democratic party and exposed McGovern to the charge that he (like Goldwater in 1964) was the candidate of a lunatic fringe. As if to ensure McGovern's defeat, the delegates nominated as his running mate Senator Thomas Eagleton of Missouri. Eagleton, young, liberal, articulate, then disclosed that he had twice been hospitalized for psychiatric care. Under enormous pressure to reject Eagleton, McGovern at first proclaimed his support of the vice-presidential candidate, only to reverse himself and secure Eagleton's withdrawal. R. Sargent Shriver, a Kennedy brother-in-law who had headed the Peace Corps and the war on poverty, took Eagleton's place. McGovern, whose integrity had been a major asset, now struck many people as indecisive and self-righteous.

In an effort to redeem himself, McGovern moved to the attack. He criticized Nixon's handling of the war, which had caused 15,000 deaths since January 1969. He rapped the administration's economic policies. He charged the President with dropping an antitrust suit against ITT in return for a campaign contribution of $400,000. And he tried to implicate Nixon in a burglary on June 17 of the Democratic National Committee headquarters in Washington's Watergate Hotel.

The Watergate affair, as it became known, deeply worried Nixon, who knew of CREEP's involvement in it. Citing national security reasons, he got Haldeman to stop the FBI from investigating the incident. Later in the campaign he authorized payments of more than $460,000 in hush money to keep Hunt and some of his collaborators from implicating higher-ups in the administration. Publicly, he and other ranking Republicans disclaimed any involvement in the affair. Nixon said inaccurately in late August that his counsel, John Dean, had conducted a "complete investigation" that showed that "no one in the White House staff, no one in this administration, presently

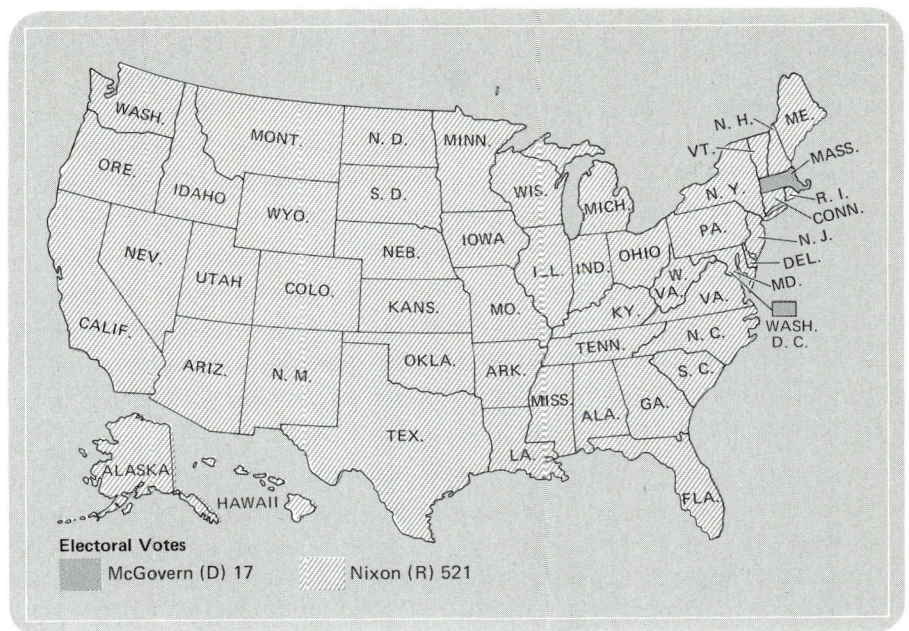

Electoral Votes

McGovern (D) 17   Nixon (R) 521

Election, 1972

employed, was involved in this very bizarre incident." He concluded: "what really hurts in matters of this sort is not the fact that they occur, because over-zealous people in campaigns do things that are wrong. What hurts is if you try to cover them up."

Americans apparently believed such protestations of innocence. Indeed, they had little choice, for the Democrats lacked evidence at the time to implicate the White House. The voters were also impressed with Nixon's conduct of foreign policy. Despite the failures of Vietnamization, troop withdrawals were continuing, and casualty lists, which had shown around 300 American deaths per week in late 1968, totaled near zero by September 1972. A month later, on October 26, Kissinger held a televised press conference to announce a breakthrough in the negotiations he had been conducting with the enemy in Paris. "Peace," he declared grandiloquently, "is at hand."

Kissinger's misleading announcement clinched victory for the team of Nixon and Agnew, which took 47 million votes to 29 million for McGovern and Shriver. This was 60.7 percent of the vote, the highest percentage in modern American history except for that won by Johnson in 1964. Nixon carried every state except Massachusetts and the District of Columbia, for a margin in the electoral college of 521 to 17. Representative John G. Schmitz of California, who headed the American party after Wallace was shot, got only 1.1 million—one-ninth of the total Wallace had received four years earlier. Dr. Spock, who ran on the People's party ticket, won but 74,000. Nixon's critics bravely explained that turnout had been low and pointed out that Democrats still held wide margins in Congress. But it was impossible to deny that the voters had endorsed the President. At least for the time being Nixon was a resounding political success.

Acrimony again, 1973–1975

INTERNATIONAL PROBLEMS

Those who hoped for harmony after the election were immediately disillusioned. Kissinger's forecast of peace, it developed, was inaccurate, primarily because General Thieu refused to agree to the deals the United States and North Vietnam were making without his knowledge. By mid-December the prospects for peace seemed as remote as ever.

Nixon, safely reelected, reacted sharply by authorizing the most savage bombing of North Vietnam in the twelve-year history of American involvement in the war. General Alexander Haig, Kissinger's deputy, described it aptly as the "brutalizing" of the north. Some of the bombs hit a hospital in Hanoi; others damaged a camp holding American prisoners of war. The enemy, better defended than in the past, shot down fifteen B-52 planes (each costing $8 million) and captured ninety-eight American airmen in two weeks.

The resumption of bombing may have achieved its aim: two weeks after starting it Nixon announced peace negotiations would soon resume. At the same time, he stopped the raids. More important in North Vietnam's attitude may have been pressure to settle from Russia and China, both of whom were tired of the war. In any event, the negotiations succeeded in establishing a cease-fire beginning January 28. An agreement signed by the United States, North Vietnam, South Vietnam, and the Vietcong's Provisional Revolutionary Government (PRG) decreed that in the next sixty days America would remove its 23,700 remaining troops, and the enemy would return 509 prisoners of war. The future of Vietnam—left vague—was to be determined by negotiations, not by force.

The agreement brought to an end, after twelve years, the presence of western combat troops in Vietnam. In that time the dead included 56,000 Americans, 5200 allied soldiers, 184,000 South Vietnamese, and an estimated 925,000 North Vietnamese. Approximately five times these numbers were wounded. The total of refugees, and of civilian deaths, in Vietnam, Laos, and Cambodia could only be guessed at—undoubtedly in the millions. In the face of such statistics it is not surprising that many Americans, relieved at the prospect of withdrawal, accepted Nixon's statement that he had bought "peace with honor."

Thoughtful observers knew better. In part because Nixon had secretly assured Thieu of military support in the event of communist gains, South

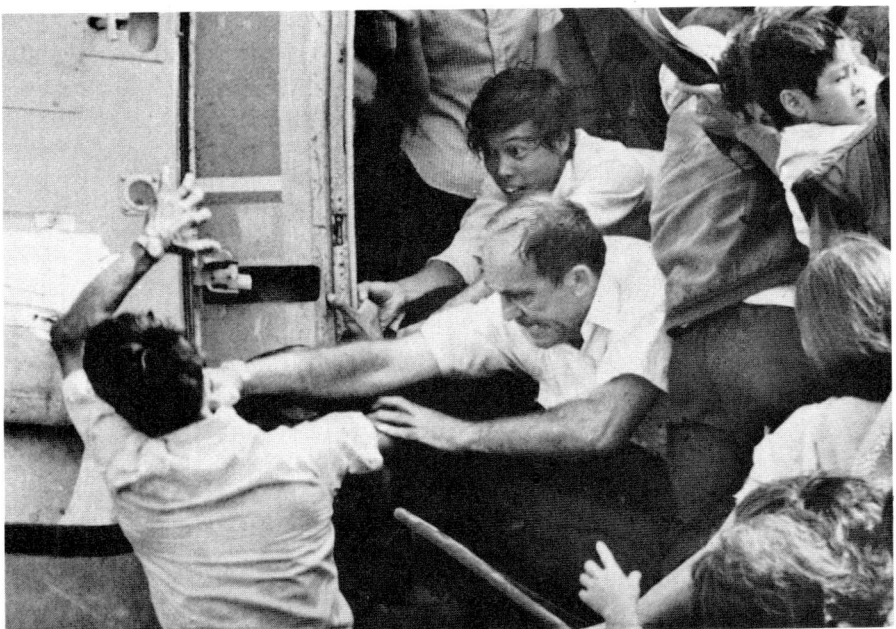

Desperate Vietnamese refugees try to board an American evacuation plane at Da Nang, April 1975.

Vietnam refused from the start to recognize the PRG, to consider communist participation in a coalition government, or to work earnestly to restrain its combat forces. Faced with this all-or-nothing attitude, the PRG and North Vietnam pressed on for a military solution, and fighting ravaged the country again. In response America dispatched bombing raids over Laos, propped up the deteriorating regime of Lon Nol in Cambodia, and sent billions more in military equipment to sustain Vietnamization. For a time in early 1973 Nixon even considered resuming saturation bombing of North Vietnam, refraining only for fear of domestic turmoil. Russia and China, meanwhile, aided Hanoi and the Vietcong. Knowledgeable onlookers suspected Nixon's secret understanding with Thieu and knew that the unpopular, repressive regime in Saigon would collapse without American support.

Whether America learned the correct "lessons" from the war also remains to be seen. World War I, after all, had taught the "virtues" of noninvolvement; World War II had encouraged globalism. By 1973 Americans seemed fairly sure about two things: first, that they could not protect the whole world; and second, that Southeast Asia should fight its own civil wars. Holding to such views, Congress forbade the President to undertake any military action whatever in Indo-China after August 15, 1973. It also approved, over Nixon's veto, the War Powers Act of 1973. Henceforth the White House would have to give Congress a full explanation within forty-eight hours for the dispatch of

America's mood:
the public's view of the most important
problem facing the country,
according to Gallup Poll results,
1969–1974

1969	Vietnam
1970	Reducing crime
1971	Inflation
1972	Vietnam
1973	High cost of living
1974	Energy crisis

SOURCE: Irish and Frank, *U. S. Foreign Policy*, p. 107

American troops abroad. Presidents must withdraw such troops within sixty days unless Congress specifically authorized them to stay. In 1975, when the administration wanted to intervene again in Cambodia and Vietnam, the War Powers Act stood in its way. As in 1919, the presidential excesses prompted a resurgence of congressional will.

It was too much to expect, however, that the withdrawal of American troops would bring an end to the nation's problems. On the contrary, continuing deficits in the balance of payments resulted in further devaluation of the dollar—this time of 10 percent—by February 1973. Rising inflation forced Nixon to reintroduce price controls, first on petroleum products and meat, and then (in June) on all retail prices. The controls lasted sixty days. On the moral plane, militant Indians on the Oglala Sioux reservation in South Dakota reminded Americans of injustice at home. Rising in anger at Wounded Knee, site of a massacre of Indians eighty-three years before, they seized eleven hostages and demanded redress of their grievances. Federal authorities responded by surrounding the Indians and blocking the flow of food. Before the siege ended eleven weeks later, outbreaks of shooting had killed one Indian and wounded one FBI man. The protracted confrontation settled nothing of consequence.

Withdrawal from Vietnam also failed to deliver the nation from overseas involvements. These became obvious in October 1973, when Israel and the Arab states went to war again. As in 1948, 1956, and 1967, the Israelis showed their military superiority. But this time the Arabs inflicted costly losses on their enemies, and it became clearer than ever that the future of Israel depended on continuing American support. In the next two years Kissinger, who became secretary of state in October 1973, shuttled back and forth to the Middle East in an effort to promote some understanding between the antagonists. Though he made progress with Egypt, he found Israel reluctant at first to return territory gained in the 1967 war. He also could not placate the Palestine Liberation Organization, which represented the million-plus Arabs displaced from their lands in Israel. Meanwhile the Soviet Union continued to provide arms to the Arabs and to persecute Jews at home. Soviet-American détente was quite obviously limited.

The Middle East war had the further effect of drawing the often quarrelsome Arab states closer together. Using oil as a weapon, they cut back on shipments of oil to their enemies, including the United States. Thereafter, they hiked their prices. These actions dramatically exposed the dependence of the industrialized nations on oil—the great powers, one observer cracked, were now the United States, Russia, Saudi Arabia, Kuwait, and Abu Dhabi. The increase in oil prices also caused the most frightening wave of inflation to date throughout the industrialized noncommunist world. Nixon called for voluntary restraint in the use of gasoline and heating oil. But he refused to impose rationing, to investigate high oil company profits, or to develop a long-range policy for the conservation of energy resources. Inflation continued to mount, the stock market to plummet, and the economy to stagnate.

A popular president might have been able to act resourcefully against these problems. But a host of revelations in 1973–74 combined to undermine Nixon's standing. One showed that the CIA had been involved in a military coup in September 1973 that overthrew Chile's Salvador Allende, the Western Hemisphere's first popularly elected Marxist leader. Though the CIA denied

A militant Indian at Wounded Knee, South Dakota, heads through bitter cold to church, March 1973.

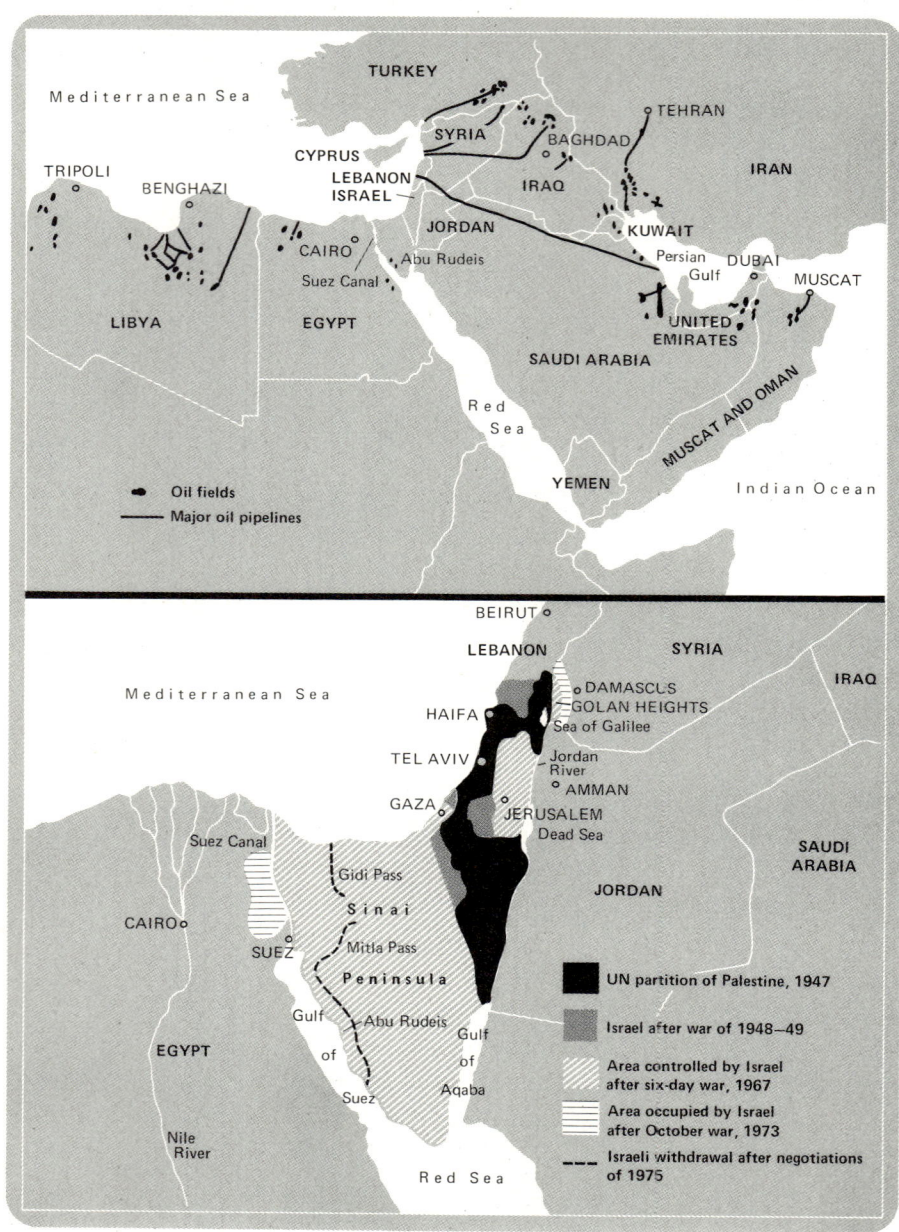

Middle East, 1947–1975

THE UNSETTLED 1970s

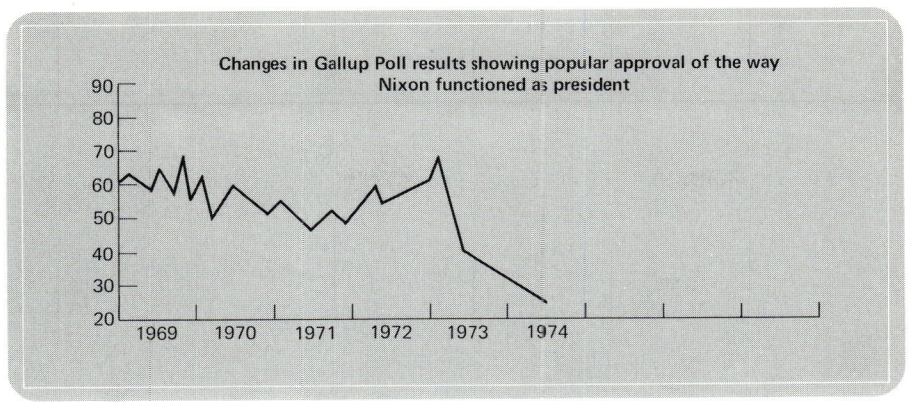

Changes in Gallup Poll results showing popular approval of the way Nixon functioned as president

SOURCE: Adapted from Irish and Frank, *U.S. Foreign Policy*, p. 104, anc *Gallup Opinion Index*, no. 111, Sept. 1974, p. 11

Nixon's popularity peaked in late 1969 and early 1973 when 68 percent of respondents approved of his handling the presidency and reached a low of 24 percent shortly before he resigned in 1974.

the charges, other rumors about the agency's excesses placed it also on the defensive. (One such rumor, that the CIA had hired Mafiosi to kill Fidel Castro in 1961, was later confirmed.) Nixon and Kissinger, like most of America's postwar leaders, wanted satellites in the Western Hemisphere.

WATERGATE

Charges of corruption further harmed the administration in 1973–74. In October 1973 Vice-President Agnew, champion of law and order, had to resign when it was revealed that he had cheated on his income taxes and had taken more than $100,000 in payoffs from contractors between 1966 and 1972. The IRS then disclosed that Nixon himself owed more than $400,000 in back taxes and penalties. Other critics showed that CREEP had solicited huge corporate campaign contributions, illegal under the 1972 campaign financing law, that the government had spent millions on improvements to the presidential properties in Florida and California, and that the administration had raised subsidies to milk producers, who thereupon contributed $527,500 to the Republican campaign chest. The trail of corruption surrounding the election was winding dangerously close to the Oval Office.

The President's major problem was the Watergate burglary. Though he did his best to cover up his involvement in the affair, hard-working reporters from the *Washington Post* and other papers gave him no rest. Neither did the Senate Select Committee on Campaign Practices headed by folksy Sam Ervin of North Carolina. Judge John Sirica of the United States district court of the

District of Columbia, which heard the cases of the burglars in early 1973, was perhaps the most persistent of all. Imposing stiff sentences on Hunt, Liddy, McCord, and four others in March, he read a letter from McCord that stated that higher-ups in the administration were involved.

A series of disclosures between April and July of 1973 sustained Sirica's point of view. On April 27 Patrick Gray, who had been acting chief of the FBI since Hoover's death a year earlier, resigned after admitting that he had burned incriminating documents concerning Watergate and related matters. Three days later evidence linking the White House to the cover-up forced the resignations of Haldeman and Erlichman. In May the revelation that the FBI had tapped Daniel Ellsberg's phone conversations in 1969–70 caused the dismissal of the government's case against him involving the Pentagon papers. In June, John Dean, who had turned against his White House associates, testified that the President himself had been involved in the cover-up. And a month later a White House aide revealed that Nixon had taped many of the conversations concerning the affair. This disclosure set off a year-long war in which the Senate, Judge Sirica, and federal prosecutors fought the President for access to the tapes.

Nixon claimed to be appalled by these revelations. On April 30 he appeared on prime time TV to announce the resignations of Haldeman and Erlichman and to emphasize his diligent quest for the facts. Next to him as he spoke were a picture of his family and a bust of Abraham Lincoln. "The easiest course," he explained, "would be for me to blame those to whom I delegated the responsibility to run the campaign. But that would be a cowardly thing to do. . . . In any organization the man at the top must bear the responsibility. . . . I accept it. . . . There can be no whitewash at the White House. . . . I love America. . . . God bless America and God bless each and every one of you."

In an attempt to promote public confidence in his conduct the President brightened the image of his administration. To head the FBI he picked William Ruckelshaus, an Indianan who then headed the Environmental Protection Agency. To run the Justice Department, the prosecuting arm of the government, he named Elliot Richardson, his secretary of defense. Both men had reputations for courage and integrity. The President even accepted Richardson's choice for a special Watergate prosecutor. This was Archibald Cox, a Harvard law professor. Cox, Nixon said, would have full cooperation from the White House.

When Cox insisted on going to court for the tapes, however, Nixon demanded that Richardson fire him. Claiming executive privilege, the President added that he would personally edit a summary of the transcripts. Richardson, refusing to do Nixon's bidding, resigned in late October. Ruckelshaus, who had become Richardson's deputy, agreed with Richardson, and was fired. The solicitor general, next in command at the Justice Department, then discharged Cox. In the ensuing uproar, Nixon felt compelled to yield some of the tapes, to name a new special prosecutor, Leon Jaworski of Texas, and to tell the public over TV, "I am not a crook." But he refused to give up all the tapes, and Jaworski, as tenacious as Cox, kept up the legal struggle in late 1973 and early 1974.

During this time the President continued to profess his innocence. On April 29, 1974 he appeared on TV again to announce that he was releasing transcripts of the tapes. These, he said, "will at last, once and for all, show that what I knew and what I did with regard to the Watergate cover-up were just as I described them to you from the very beginning." On other occasions he angrily blamed the press for his dilemma and insisted that impeachment, which the House Judiciary Committee began considering seriously in May 1974, would "jeopardize" world peace and endanger the American political system. As if to prove his indispensability, he toured the Middle East and Moscow in June and July. Though he attracted sizeable crowds, he accomplished little, in part because the Watergate affair was undermining his effectiveness abroad as well as at home. "Every negotiation," Kissinger said later, "was getting more and more difficult because it involved the question of whether we could, in fact, carry out what we were negotiating."

By this time the pressure on Nixon to release all the tapes was overwhelming. But Nixon had good reason to refuse such requests, because between

The cartoonist Herblock comments on Watergate, 1973.

May 5 and 7, 1974, he had listened carefully to them himself. He knew then, if not long before, that they proved his obstruction of justice. Accordingly, he cited "executive privilege" and national security as his reasons for keeping the recordings. His lawyers, none of whom were told the facts, were instructed to resist Jaworski's requests for the tapes and to appeal the matter to the Supreme Court.

On July 24 a unanimous Court gave its answer. It agreed that a president could withhold "military, diplomatic, or sensitive national security material." To this extent executive privilege gained explicit judicial sanction for the first time. But the judges went on to insist that the Court, not the president, had the right to "say what the law is," and that the Watergate affair, a criminal proceeding, did not involve "national security." The claim for executive privilege, therefore, had to "yield to the demonstrated, specific need for

I have discovered that according to a secret tape of June 23, 1972, I AM a crook.

evidence in a pending criminal trial," and the President must turn over "forthwith" the sixty-four recordings demanded by his foes. Judge Sirica could listen to the tapes and release relevant portions to Jaworski, who would be free to give them to Congress.

A few days later the House Judiciary Committee acted against the President by voting to impeach him on three counts. The first, passed twenty-seven to eleven, charged him with obstruction of justice. Nixon, the committee said, had made or caused to be made false statements, withheld relevant and material evidence, interfered with investigations by the FBI, the Justice Department, special prosecutors, and Congress, approved the payment of hush money to witnesses, and lied to the American people. The second charge, approved twenty-eight to ten, accused Nixon of abusing his presidential authority by resorting to illegal wiretapping and by using the FBI, CIA, and Internal Revenue Service against American citizens. A third charge hit him for refusing to turn over the tapes, after receiving a congressional subpoena, to the committee.

Some of the President's friends were consoled by the failure of the committee to approve two other articles of impeachment. One concerned his secret bombing of Cambodia in 1969–70; the other accused him of enriching himself with public funds while president. But most observers recognized that the three other charges were damaging enough to Nixon's standing. The committee, indeed, had deliberated long and responsibly, and its concluding debates, carried on radio and TV, did much to restore faith in Congress as an institution. There was little doubt that the House would endorse the committee's conclusions by wide margins. If the Senate could corral a two-thirds majority for conviction—and that seemed entirely possible—Nixon would have to leave office.

After these developments, some of Nixon's supporters called on him to resign immediately. His opponents feared that he would try to destroy the tapes rather than turn them over to Sirica. Nixon followed neither course. Instead, he procrastinated until August 5, when he finally released the tapes that proved his involvement in the cover-up. He admitted that he had concealed them, even from his own lawyers, but insisted that he had done nothing to warrant conviction by the Senate.

The Senate clearly disagreed. So did the American people, who felt betrayed by the President's lies over the previous twenty-six months. In the next few days Republicans as well as Democrats indicated they would vote for conviction. Deprived of support, the President resigned on August 9, 1974. Vice-president Gerald Ford of Michigan, whom Nixon had appointed to succeed Agnew earlier in the year, was immediately sworn in as the next president.

Nixon's resignation, while welcomed by many people at home and abroad, enabled him to avoid the Senate trial that might have established clearly the extent of his involvement in the Watergate affair. Worse, it left many questions unanswered. What self-incriminating documents had the administration hoped to steal at Watergate? Also, suppose Nixon had never taped the conversations? Having done so, suppose he had destroyed the tapes, along with logs that showed what they contained? What if some future president, having committed some egregious act, concealed such misconduct by claiming executive privilege based on the existence of "military, diplomatic, or sensitive national security material?" Such questions suggested that future presidents might still find ways of acting above the law. The imperial presidency, which the founding fathers had feared—and which twentieth-century chief executives from TR on had done so much to create—might again endanger constitutional processes and lead to paralysis of the state.

Subsequent disclosures did little to dispel such fears. These disclosures revealed a new kind of corruption. The men around Grant, Harding, and other scandal-stained presidents had acted primarily for financial gain. Many of Nixon's criminal subordinates, however, truly believed that their ends—defined as everything from reelection of the President to the maintenance of world peace—justified the means. They had no qualms about subverting democratic institutions and civil liberties. Colson, Nixon's counsel, had exclaimed, "for the President I would walk over my grandmother if necessary." Liddy added that Watergate was "an intelligence-gathering operation of one group of persons who were seeking to retain power against another group of persons who were seeking to acquire power. That's all it was. It's like brushing your teeth. It's basic." Defending the cover-up, CREEP director Magruder added that "after the Democrats nominated Senator McGovern, we felt that we were protecting the honorable peace that the President was bringing to Vietnam. . . . We were not covering up a burglary, we were safeguarding world peace." He concluded, "we wanted to win the election and we wanted to win it big. Just as a corporation wants to dominate its market, our reelection committee wanted to dominate that year's election. . . . We were past the point of halfway measures or gentlemanly tactics."

In the aftermath of Watergate

The resignation of Nixon brought to the fore problems that excitement over Watergate had helped to obscure. Most of the afflictions that had troubled the nation in the twentieth century—racial injustice, urban blight, economic inequality, sex discrimination, oppression of Indians and Hispanic-Americans—remained serious. Still more pressing at the time were inflation, which was increasing at the rate of 14 percent per year in late 1974, recession, which caused the GNP to fall 9 percent in the last quarter of 1974, instability in the Middle East, and the collapse—which became complete in April 1975—of the regimes of Lon Nol and General Thieu. The fall of Phnom Penh, Cambodia's capital, took place as President Ford and 100,000 others commemorated the

President Gerald Ford delivers his first state of the union address to Congress, January 1975. Vice-President Nelson Rockefeller sits behind him.

battles of Lexington and Concord 200 years earlier. The shots that had been heard 'round the world were losing their force.

Americans worried about the capacity of their new leaders to deal with these problems. In his lengthy political career Ford had shown little interest in fighting urban or racial problems. He was largely uninformed concerning fiscal policy. Confronted with recession, he insisted at first on tax increases and other deflationary measures that would have worsened the situation. He was handicapped also by his lack of a popular mandate. Both he and his new vice-president, former Governor Nelson Rockefeller of New York, were Republicans facing the most aroused and self-assertive Democratic Congresses in recent memory. Thanks to the Twenty-fifth Amendment (1967), which authorized presidents to nominate (and Congress to confirm) vice-presidents, both men were nonelective officials. The United States, which had done so much to advance the cause of political democracy 200 years earlier, would have to wait more than 2 years before being governed by a president chosen by popular vote.

President Ford then compounded doubts about his ability by pardoning his predecessor. He did so, he said, because he wanted people to forget the recent past and because Nixon had suffered enough. A few weeks later, when Nixon almost died after an operation on his leg for phlebitis, Ford's compassion seemed appropriate. Whether the pardon was proper was another matter. Men like Erlichman, Haldeman, Mitchell, Dean, and Magruder—and many lesser officials—were either in jail or appealing convictions for crimes ranging from perjury to obstruction of justice. These people, like many Americans, wondered about the fairness of a system that punished the little fish while the shark escaped scot-free. Americans found it equally impossible to forget the deceit and hypocrisy that had contaminated governmental institutions since the mid-1960s. As one magazine phrased it earlier, the United States seemed to have swung half circle in the 200 years of its existence: "from George Washington, who could not tell a lie, to Richard Nixon, who could not tell the truth."

As if to register their alienation, the voters showed little interest in the off-year elections of 1974. Democrats gained throughout the nation. But only 45 percent of eligible voters cast their ballots. In a nation supposedly governed by popular majorities, this was hardly encouraging. The turnout of youth was especially poor: only 21 percent of people aged eighteen to twenty bothered to vote. Students, indeed, seemed amazingly quiescent in contrast to a few years earlier. With the economy deteriorating they worried about finding jobs or getting into graduate schools, and seldom engaged in sustained protest. The historian C. Vann Woodward commented, "Rarely in history has publicized activism been replaced so rapidly by apparent apathy, student dissent by silence."

Many Americans in the mid-1970s shared the students' worries about the future. Though the nation was calmer than it had been in the turbulent years of the late 1960s, no one could be confident that domestic tranquility would last. Some observers feared that the approach of zero population growth, for the first time in American history, signaled not only the end of economic expansion but also a more general loss of confidence. The last frontiers, it appeared, had been conquered; it was time to consolidate and pull back. Others, lamenting the continuing coexistence of inflation and recession, foresaw increasing government control over a stagnant economy. Robert Lekachman, a respected economist, wrote, "I think we are entering a long period of slower growth. I take seriously the resource scarcities. We've reached the end of cheap energy. . . . The prospects for improvement in the American standard of life thus are much less than they've been."

Reflecting these doubts, many observers concluded that the nation was becoming a "business civilization" like that of the 1920s: materialistic, hollow, lacking in securely held values or sense of purpose beyond individual self-aggrandizement. The rise of such a society, critics said, exposed the mixed blessings of modernization, which had unleashed a revolution in expectations along with economic growth and technological progress. Restless, cranky, divided, Americans seemed psychologically unfulfilled and impossible to satisfy.

American foreign policy gave special cause for concern. In 1975 the United States operated a defense budget of $104 billion—an increase of $15 billion over the amount needed during the years of involvement in Vietnam in 1972–74. America also sold arms to more than 130 countries and maintained military commitments with forty nations. Most of these forty were NATO or Latin American countries. Other commitments included South Korea, a repressive dictatorship, Japan, Taiwan, the Philippines, Australia, and New Zealand. Two danger zones, West Berlin and Israel, were not covered by treaty, but appeared to be integral parts of America's worldwide defense perimeter. With naval vessels circling the globe, planes ever in the air, 8500 strategic nuclear weapons in full deployment, and more than 400,000 troops stationed overseas in the cause of Pax Americana, the once uncommitted United States ran the risk of constant military involvement.

The Ford administration quickly showed its readiness to use part of this formidable arsenal. In May 1975 Cambodia captured the *Mayaguez,* an American merchant vessel sailing near its shores. When the anti-American government of Cambodia was slow to answer United States protests, Ford authorized an attack by 350 marines on Koh Tang, a nearby island where the crew was wrongly believed to be held. The assault, accompanied by bombing in Cambodia, marked a heavy overreaction to a minor incident. It cost the United States fifteen dead, three missing, and fifty wounded. It was probably unnecessary, for Cambodia was in the process of returning both ship and crew at the time. But many Americans exulted in Ford's show of steel. The incident suggested that they cared little for consultation, that they had learned almost nothing from ten years of trauma over Vietnam, and that deep down they were a little like schoolyard bullies—afraid, uncertain, and insecure.

It was nonetheless possible in the mid-1970s to contemplate the future with guarded optimism. Whatever the President's faults, he appeared honest and open. Some people hailed him as a Republican Harry Truman. Ford also proved willing to compromise. When Congress rebuffed his conservative economic policies in late 1974, he reversed himself to favor a multibillion-dollar tax cut, an increase in unemployment benefits, and a thoroughly Keynesian budget that envisaged a deficit of $52 billion. His turnabout did little to arrest inflation—it may in fact have made it a little worse—and it failed to end the worst recession since the 1930s. Unemployment, hovering at around 9 per cent in 1975 (affecting more than eight million people) had not been so high since 1940. Still, Ford's flexibility relieved observers who had feared a return to Hooverism. Congress acted quickly to expand on his proposals.

Americans with a sense of history also recognized that the strife of the immediate past had brought progress as well as pain. Indeed, it may be that conflict necessarily accompanies progressive social change. The forces of technology, industrialization, and economic growth had made the nation incomparably richer than it had been in 1776, or—more to the point—than in 1940 or 1960. The civil rights revolution had brought the most impressive gains

It's just that they don't consider us a practical purpose.

for blacks since emancipation. Supreme Court decisions had broadened the civil rights and civil liberties of the people. The Cold War, with its attendant threat of nuclear catastrophe, had softened. The country's political institutions, apparently so flawed, had remained stable under pressure of war, assassinations, and incomparable presidential abuse. The virtues of a free press, an independent judiciary, and an alert Congress had rarely been so clearly revealed. For all the nation's problems, it had withstood a public airing of its deficiencies that would have disrupted many other countries in the world. For these and some other blessings the United States could take cautious pride.

Suggestions for reading

Books on Richard Nixon include Earl Mazo and Stephen Hess, *Nixon: A Political Portrait** (1968); Jules Witcover, *The Resurrection of Richard Nixon* (1970), which covers the years of 1960–68; Gary Wills, *Nixon Agonistes** (1970); Bruce Mazlish, *In Search of Nixon** (1971), a psychological inquiry; and Rowland Evans and Robert Novak, *Nixon in the White House** (1971), the best account of the first two years of his presidency. Other books that deal with politics and policies of the 1970s are Leonard Silk, *Nixonomics** (1972); Jules Witcover, *White Knight: The Rise of Spiro Agnew* (1972); Robert S. Ansom, *McGovern* (1972); Richard Harris, *Decision* (1971), on the Carswell nomination; and Daniel Moynihan, *Politics of a Guaranteed National Income** (1973).

Important books on political trends include Walter Dean Burnham, *Critical Elections and the Mainstream of American Politics** (1972), a stimulating analysis of twentieth-century developments; Walter De Vries and V. L. Torrance, *The Ticket Splitters* (1972); Samuel Lubell, *The Hidden Crisis in American Politics** (1970); Frederick G. Dutton, *The Changing Sources of Power* (1971); and David S. Broder, *The Party's Over** (1972). See also Theodore White, *Making of a President, 1972** (1973); Kevin Phillips, *The Emerging Republican Majority** (1969); and Richard Scammon and Ben Wattenberg, *The Real Majority** (1970). Among the books on Watergate are Carl Bernstein and Bob Woodward, *All the President's Men** (1974), a devastating account by two *Washington Post* reporters; and Raoul Berger, *Impeachment: The Constitutional Problems* (1974).

Sources for foreign policy include Henry Brandon, *The Retreat of American Power* (1973); David Landau, *Kissinger* (1972); R. W. Tucker, *The Radical Left and American Foreign Policy** (1971); and Arthur Schlesinger, Jr., *The Imperial Presidency* (1973), which narrates the impact of foreign policy on the executive branch. See also V. Brodine and Mark Seldon, eds., *Open Secret: The Nixon-Kissinger Doctrine in Asia* (1972); Lloyd Gardner. ed., *The Great Nixon Turnaround* (1973); Morton Halperin, *Defense Strategies for the Seventies* (1971); Leonard Mosley, *Power Play* (1973), on oil companies in the Middle East; and Adam Yarmolinsky, *The Military Establishment: Its Impact on American Society* (1971).

Domestic unrest in the 1970s is the subject of many books, including J. A. Michener, *Kent State: What Happened and Why* (1973); I. F. Stone, *Killings at Kent State* (1971); George Jackson, *Soledad Brother: The Prison Letters of George Jackson* (1970); Tom Wicker, *A Time to Die* (1975), on the Attica riot; Ramsey Clark, *Crime in America* (1970); and Robert C. Wood, *The Necessary Majority: Middle America and the Urban Crisis* (1972). An important book dealing with the growth of corporate power is J. K. Galbraith, *The New Industrial State** (1971).

Among the books that focus on environmental issues are Paul Erlich, *Population Bomb** (1968); Barry Commoner, *The Closing Circle** (1971); Garrett De Bell. ed., *The Environmental Handbook* (1970); and R. F. Buckhorn, *Nader: The People's Lawyer* (1972). See also Emma Rothschild, *Paradise Lost: The Decline of the Auto-Industrial Age* (1973).

Unrest among American Indians is the subject of: A. M. Josephy, ed., *Red Power** (1971); Stan Steiner, *The New Indians** (1968); and Sar Levitan and Barbara Hetrick, *Big Brother's Indian Programs** (1971).

The Constitution of the United States of America

We the people of the United States, in Order to form a more perfect Union, establish Justice, insure domestic Tranquility, provide for the common defence, promote the general Welfare, and secure the Blessings of Liberty to ourselves and our Posterity, do ordain and establish this Constitution for the United States of America.

ARTICLE I

Section 1. All legislative Powers herein granted shall be vested in a Congress of the United States, which shall consist of a Senate and House of Representatives.

Section 2. The House of Representatives shall be composed of Members chosen every second Year by the People of the several States, and the Electors in each State shall have the Qualifications requisite for Electors of the most numerous Branch of the State Legislature.

No Person shall be a Representative who shall not have attained to the Age of twenty-five Years, and been seven Years a Citizen of the United States, and who shall not, when elected, be an Inhabitant of that state in which he shall be chosen.

[Representatives and direct Taxes shall

The Constitution and all amendments are shown in their original form. Parts that have been amended or superseded are bracketed and explained in the footnotes.

be apportioned among the several States which may be included within this Union, according to their respective Numbers, which shall be determined by adding to the whole Number of free Persons, including those bound to Service for a Term of Years, and excluding Indians not taxed, three fifths of all other Persons.][1] The actual Enumeration shall be made within three Years after the first Meeting of the Congress of the United States, and within every subsequent Term of ten Years, in such Manner as they shall by Law direct. The Number of Representatives shall not exceed one for every thirty Thousand, but each State shall have at Least one Representative; and until such enumeration shall be made, the State of New Hampshire shall be entitled to chuse three, Massachusetts eight, Rhode Island and Providence Plantations one, Connecticut five, New-York six, New Jersey four, Pennsylvania eight, Delaware one, Maryland six, Virginia ten, North

[1]Modified by the Fourteenth and Sixteenth amendments.

Carolina five, South Carolina five, and Georgia three.

When vacancies happen in the Representation from any State, the Executive Authority thereof shall issue Writs of Election to fill such Vacancies.

The House of Representatives shall chuse their Speaker and other Officers; and shall have the sole Power of Impeachment.

Section 3. The Senate of the United States shall be composed of two Senators from each State, [chosen by the Legislature thereof,][2] for six Years; and each Senator shall have one Vote.

Immediately after they shall be assembled in Consequence of the first Election, they shall be divided as equally as may be into three Classes. The Seats of the Senators of the first Class shall be vacated at the Expiration of the second Year, of the Second Class at the Expiration of the fourth Year, and of the third Class at the Expiration of the sixth Year, so that one-third may be chosen every second Year; [and if Vacancies happen by Resignation, or otherwise, during the Recess of the Legislature of any State, the Executive thereof may make temporary Appointments until the next Meeting of the Legislature, which shall then fill such Vacancies].[3]

No Person shall be a Senator who shall not have attained to the Age of thirty Years, and been nine Years a Citizen of the United States, and who shall not, when elected, be an Inhabitant of that State in which he shall be chosen.

The Vice-President of the United States shall be President of the Senate, but shall have no vote, unless they be equally divided.

The Senate shall chuse their other Officers, and also a President pro tempore, in the absence of the Vice-President, or when he shall exercise the Office of the President of the United States.

The Senate shall have the sole Power to try all Impeachments. When sitting for that purpose, they shall be on Oath or Affirmation. When the President of the United States is tried, the Chief Justice shall preside. And no person shall be convicted without the Concurrence of two thirds of the Members present.

Judgment in Cases of Impeachment shall not extend further than to removal from Office, and disqualification to hold and enjoy any Office of honor, Trust, or Profit under the United States: but the Party convicted shall nevertheless be liable and subject to Indictment, Trial, Judgment, and Punishment, according to Law.

Section 4. The Times, Places and Manner of holding Elections for Senators and Representatives, shall be prescribed in each state by the Legislature thereof; but the Congress may at any time by Law make or alter such Regulations, except as to the Places of Chusing Senators.

The Congress shall assemble at least once in every Year, and such Meeting shall [be on the first Monday in December,][4] unless they shall by Law appoint a different Day.

Section 5. Each House shall be the Judge of the Elections, Returns and Qualifications of its own Members, and a Majority of each shall constitute a Quorum to do Business; but a smaller number may adjourn from day to day, and may be authorized to compel the Attendance of absent Members, in such Manner, and under such Penalties, as each House may provide.

Each House may determine the Rules of its Proceedings, punish its Members for disorderly Behavior, and, with the Concurrence of two thirds, expel a Member.

Each House shall keep a Journal of its Proceedings, and from time to time publish the same, excepting such Parts as may in their Judgment require Secrecy; and the Yeas and Nays of the Members of either House on any question shall, at the Desire of one fifth of those Present, be entered on the Journal.

Neither House, during the Session of Congress, shall, without the Consent of the other, adjourn for more than three days, nor to any other Place than that in which the two Houses shall be sitting.

[2]Superseded by the Seventeenth Amendment.
[3]Modified by the Seventeenth Amendment.

[4]Superseded by the Twentieth Amendment.

Section 6. The Senators and Representatives shall receive a Compensation for their Services, to be ascertained by Law, and paid out of the Treasury of the United States. They shall in all Cases, except Treason, Felony, and Breach of the Peace, be privileged from Arrest during their Attendance at the Session of their respective Houses, and in going to and returning from the same; and for any Speech or Debate in either House, they shall not be questioned in any other Place.

No Senator or Representative shall, during the Time for which he was elected, be appointed to any civil Office under the Authority of the United States, which shall have been created, or the Emoluments whereof shall have been increased, during such time; and no Person holding any Office under the United States shall be a Member of either House during his continuance in Office.

Section 7. All Bills for raising Revenue shall originate in the House of Representatives; but the Senate may propose or concur with Amendments as on other bills.

Every Bill which shall have passed the House of Representatives and the Senate, shall, before it become a Law, be presented to the President of the United States; If he approve he shall sign it, but if not he shall return it, with his Objections, to that House in which it shall have originated, who shall enter the Objections at large on their Journal, and proceed to reconsider it. If after such Reconsideration two thirds of that House shall agree to pass the bill, it shall be sent, together with the objections, to the other House, by which it shall likewise be reconsidered, and if approved by two thirds of that House, it shall become a Law. But in all such Cases the Votes of both Houses shall be determined by Yeas and Nays, and the names of the Persons voting for and against the Bill shall be entered on the Journal of each House respectively. If any Bill shall not be returned by the President within ten Days (Sundays excepted) after it shall have been presented to him, the Same shall be a Law, in like Manner as if he had signed it, unless the Congress by their Adjournment prevent its Return, in which Case it shall not be a Law.

Every Order, Resolution, or Vote to which the Concurrence of the Senate and House of Representatives may be necessary (except on a question of Adjournment) shall be presented to the President of the United States; and before the Same shall take Effect, shall be approved by him, or being disapproved by him, shall be repassed by two thirds of the Senate and House of Representatives, according to the Rules and Limitations prescribed in the Case of a Bill.

Section 8. The Congress shall have Power To Lay and collect Taxes, Duties, Imposts and Excises, to pay the Debts and provide for the common Defence and general Welfare of the United States; but all Duties, Imposts and Excises shall be uniform throughout the United States;

To borrow money on the credit of the United States;

To regulate Commerce with foreign Nations, and among the several States, and with the Indian Tribes;

To establish an uniform Rule of Naturalization, and uniform Laws on the subject of Bankruptcies throughout the United States;

To coin Money, regulate the Value thereof, and of foreign Coin, and fix the Standard of Weights and Measures;

To Provide for the Punishment of counterfeiting the Securities and current Coin of the United States;

To establish Post Offices and post Roads;

To promote the Progress of Science and useful Arts, by securing for limited Times to Authors and Inventors the exclusive Right to their respective Writings and Discoveries;

To constitute Tribunals inferior to the Supreme Court;

To define and punish Piracies and Felonies committed on the high Seas, and Offenses against the Law of Nations;

To declare War, grant Letters of Marque and Reprisal, and make Rules concerning Captures on Land and Water;

To raise and support Armies, but no Appropriation of Money to that Use shall be for a longer Term than two Years;

To provide and maintain a Navy;

To make Rules for the Government and Regulation of the land and naval forces;

To provide for calling forth the Militia to execute the Laws of the Union, suppress Insurrections and repel Invasions;

To provide for organizing, arming, and disciplining the Militia, and for governing such Part of them as may be employed in the Service of the United States, reserving to the States respectively, the Appointment of the Officers, and the Authority of training the Militia according to the discipline prescribed by Congress;

To exercise exclusive Legislation in all Cases whatsoever, over such District (not exceeding ten Miles square) as may, by Cession of particular States, and the acceptance of Congress, become the Seat of the Government of the United States, and to exercise like Authority over all Places purchased by the Consent of the Legislature of the State in which the Same shall be, for the Erection of Forts, Magazines, Arsenals, dock-Yards, and other needful Buildings;—And

To make all Laws which shall be necessary and proper for carrying into Execution the foregoing Powers, and all other Powers vested by this Constitution in the Government of the United States, or in any Department or Officer thereof.

Section 9. The Migration or Importation of such Persons as any of the States now existing shall think proper to admit shall not be prohibited by the Congress prior to the Year one thousand eight hundred and eight, but a tax or duty may be imposed on such Importation, not exceeding ten dollars for each Person.

The privilege of the Writ of Habeas Corpus shall not be suspended, unless when in Cases of Rebellion or Invasion the public Safety may require it.

No Bill of Attainder or ex post facto Law shall be passed.

[No capitation, or other direct, Tax shall be laid unless in Proportion to the Census or Enumeration herein before directed to be taken.][5]

[5]Modified by the Sixteenth Amendment.

No Tax or Duty shall be laid on Articles exported from any State.

No Preference shall be given by any Regulation of Revenue to the Ports of one State over those of another: nor shall Vessels bound to, or from, one State, be obliged to enter, clear, or pay Duties in another.

No Money shall be drawn from the Treasury, but in Consequence of Appropriations made by Law; and a regular Statement and Account of the Receipts and Expenditures of all public Money shall be published from time to time.

No Title of Nobility shall be granted by the United States: And no Person holding any Office of Profit or Trust under them, shall, without the Consent of the Congress, accept of any present, Emolument, Office, or Title, of any kind whatever, from any King, Prince, or foreign State.

Section 10. No State shall enter into any Treaty, Alliance, or Confederation; grant Letters of Marque and Reprisal; coin Money; emit Bills of Credit; make any Thing but gold and silver Coin a Tender in Payment of Debts; pass any Bill of Attainder, ex post facto Law, or Law impairing the Obligation of Contracts, or grant any title of Nobility.

No State shall, without the Consent of the Congress, lay any Imposts or Duties on Imports or Exports, except what may be absolutely necessary for executing its inspection Laws: and the net Produce of all Duties and Imposts, laid by any State on Imports or Exports, shall be for the Use of the Treasury of the United States; and all such Laws shall be subject to the Revision and Control of the Congress.

No State shall, without the Consent of Congress, lay any duty of Tonnage, keep Troops, or Ships of War in time of Peace, enter into any Agreement or Compact with another State, or with a foreign Power, or engage in War, unless actually invaded, or in such imminent Danger as will not admit of delay.

ARTICLE II

Section 1. The executive Power shall be vested in a President of the United States of

America. He shall hold his Office during the Term of four years, and, together with the Vice-President, chosen for the same Term, be elected, as follows:

Each State shall appoint, in such Manner as the Legislature thereof may direct, a Number of Electors, equal to the whole Number of Senators and Representatives to which the State may be entitled in the Congress: but no Senator or Representative, or Person holding an Office of Trust or Profit under the United States, shall be appointed an Elector.

[The Electors shall meet in their respective States, and vote by Ballot for two persons, of whom one at least shall not be an Inhabitant of the same State with themselves. And they shall make a List of all the Persons voted for, and of the Number of Votes for each; which List they shall sign and certify, and transmit sealed to the Seat of the Government of the United States, directed to the President of the Senate. The President of the Senate shall, in the Presence of the Senate and House of Representatives, open all the Certificates, and the Votes shall then be counted. The Person having the greatest Number of Votes shall be the President, if such Number be a Majority of the whole Number of Electors appointed; and if there be more than one who have such Majority, and have an equal Number of Votes, then the House of Representatives shall immediately chuse by Ballot one of them for President; and if no Person have a Majority, then from the five highest on the List the said House shall in like Manner chuse the President. But in chusing the President, the Votes shall be taken by States, the Representation from each State having one Vote; a quorum for this Purpose shall consist of a Member or Members from two-thirds of the States, and a Majority of all the States shall be necessary to a Choice. In every Case, after the Choice of the President, the Person having the greatest Number of Votes of the Electors shall be the Vice-President. But if there should remain two or more who have equal votes, the Senate shall chuse from them by Ballot the Vice-President.][6]

The Congress may determine the Time of chusing the Electors, and the Day on which they shall give their Votes; which Day shall be the same throughout the United States.

No person except a natural-born Citizen, or a Citizen of the United States, at the time of the Adoption of this Constitution, shall be eligible to the Office of President; neither shall any Person be eligible to that Office who shall not have attained to the Age of thirty-five years, and been fourteen Years a Resident within the United States.

[In Case of the Removal of the President from Office, or of his Death, Resignation, or Inability to discharge the Powers and Duties of the said Office, the same shall devolve on the Vice-President, and the Congress may by Law provide for the Case of Removal, Death, Resignation, or Inability, both of the President and Vice-President, declaring what Officer shall then act as President, and such Officer shall act accordingly, until the disability be removed, or a President shall be elected.][7]

The President shall, at stated Times, receive for his Services a Compensation, which shall neither be increased nor diminished during the Period for which he shall have been elected, and he shall not receive within that Period any other Emolument from the United States, or any of them.

Before he enter on the execution of his Office, he shall take the following Oath or Affirmation:—''I do solemnly swear (or affirm) that I will faithfully execute the Office of President of the United States, and will, to the best of my Ability, preserve, protect, and defend the Constitution of the United States.''

Section 2. The President shall be Commander in Chief of the Army and Navy of the United States, and of the Militia of the several States, when called into the actual Service of the United States; he may require the Opinion, in writing, of the principal Officer in each of the executive Departments, upon any subject relating to the Duties of their respective Offices, and he shall have Power to Grant Reprieves and

[6]Superseded by the Twelfth Amendment.

[7]Modified by the Twenty-fifth Amendment.

Pardons for Offenses against the United States, except in Cases of Impeachment.

He shall have Power, by and with the Advice and Consent of the Senate, to make Treaties, provided two thirds of the Senators present concur; and he shall nominate, and by and with the Advice and Consent of the Senate, shall appoint Ambassadors, other public Ministers and Consuls, Judges of the supreme Court, and all other Officers of the United States, whose Appointments are not herein otherwise provided for, and which shall be established by Law: but the Congress may by Law vest the Appointment of such inferior Officers, as they think proper, in the President alone, in the Courts of Law, or in the Heads of Departments.

The President shall have Power to fill up all Vacancies that may happen during the Recess of the Senate, by granting Commissions which shall expire at the End of their next Session.

Section 3. He shall from time to time give to the Congress Information of the State of the Union, and recommend to their Consideration such Measures as he shall judge necessary and expedient; he may, on extraordinary occasions, convene both Houses, or either of them, and in Case of Disagreement between them, with respect to the Time of Adjournment, he may adjourn them to such Time as he shall think proper; he shall receive Ambassadors and other public Ministers; he shall take Care that the Laws be faithfully executed, and shall Commission all the Officers of the United States.

Section 4. The President, Vice-President and all civil Officers of the United States, shall be removed from Office on Impeachment for, and Conviction of, Treason, Bribery, or other high Crimes and Misdemeanors.

ARTICLE III

Section 1. The judicial Power of the United States, shall be vested in one supreme Court, and in such inferior Courts as the Congress may from time to time ordain and establish. The Judges, both of the supreme and inferior Courts, shall hold their Offices during good Behaviour, and shall, at stated Times, receive for their Services, a Compensation, which shall not be diminished during their Continuance in Office.

Section 2. The judicial Power shall extend to all Cases, in Law and Equity, arising under this Constitution, the Laws of the United States, and treaties made, or which shall be made, under their Authority;—to all Cases affecting ambassadors, other public ministers and consuls;—to all cases of admiralty and maritime Jurisdiction;—to Controversies to which the United States shall be a Party;—to Controversies between two or more States;— [between a State and Citizens of another State;]—between Citizens of different States, —between Citizens of the same State claiming Lands under Grants of different States, and between a State, or the Citizens thereof, and foreign States, Citizens or Subjects.

In all Cases affecting Ambassadors, other public Ministers and Consuls, and those in which a State shall be Party, the supreme Court shall have original Jurisdiction. In all the other Cases before mentioned, the supreme Court shall have appellate Jurisdiction, both as to Law and Fact, with such Exceptions, and under such Regulations as the Congress shall make.

The trial of all Crimes, except in Cases of Impeachment, shall be by Jury; and such Trial shall be held in the State where the said Crimes shall have been committed; but when not committed within any State, the Trial shall be at such Place or Places as the Congress may by Law have directed.

Section 3. Treason against the United States, shall consist only in levying War against them, or in adhering to their Enemies, giving them Aid and Comfort. No Person shall be convicted of Treason unless on the Testimony of two Witnesses to the same overt Act, or on Confession in open Court.

The Congress shall have power to declare the Punishment of Treason but no Attainder of Treason shall work Corruption of Blood, or Forfeiture except during the Life of the Person attainted.

---

[8]Modified by the Eleventh Amendment.

ARTICLE IV

Section 1. Full Faith and Credit shall be given in each State to the public Acts, Records, and judicial Proceedings of every other State. And the Congress may by general Laws prescribe the Manner in which such Acts, Records and Proceedings shall be proved, and the Effect thereof.

Section 2. The Citizens of each State shall be entitled to all Privileges and Immunities of Citizens in the several States.

A Person charged in any State with Treason, Felony, or other Crime, who shall flee from Justice, and be found in another State, shall on demand of the executive Authority of the State from which he fled, be delivered up, to be removed to the State having Jurisdiction of the crime.

[No Person held to service or Labour in one State, under the Laws thereof, escaping into another, shall, in Consequence of any Law or Regulation therein, be discharged from such Service or Labour, but shall be delivered up on Claim of the Party to whom such Service or Labour may be due.]⁹

Section 3. New States may be admitted by the Congress into this Union; but no new State shall be formed or erected within the Jurisdiction of any other State; nor any State be formed by the Junction of two or more States, or parts of States, without the Consent of the Legislatures of the States concerned as well as of the Congress.

The Congress shall have Power to dispose of and make all needful Rules and Regulations respecting the Territory or other Property belonging to the United States; and nothing in this Constitution shall be so construed as to Prejudice any Claims of the United States, or of any particular State.

Section 4. The United States shall guarantee to every State in this Union a Republican Form of Government and shall protect each of them against Invasion; and on Application of the Legislature, or of the Executive (when the Legislature cannot be convened) against domestic Violence.

⁹Superseded by the Thirteenth Amendment.

ARTICLE V

The Congress, whenever two-thirds of both Houses shall deem it necessary, shall propose Amendments to this Constitution, or, on the Application of the Legislatures of two-thirds of the several States, shall call a Convention for proposing Amendments, which, in either Case, shall be valid to all Intents and Purposes, as part of this Constitution, when ratified by the Legislatures of three-fourths of the several States, or by Conventions in three-fourths thereof, as the one or the other Mode of Ratification may be proposed by the Congress; Provided that no Amendment which may be made prior to the Year One thousand eight hundred and eight shall in any Manner affect the first and fourth Clauses in the Ninth Section of the first Article; and that no State, without its Consent, shall be deprived of its equal Suffrage in the Senate.

ARTICLE VI

All Debts contracted and Engagements entered into, before the Adoption of this Constitution, shall be as valid against the United States under this Constitution as under the Confederation.

This Constitution, and the Laws of the United States which shall be made in Pursuance thereof; and all Treaties made, or which shall be made, under the Authority of the United States, shall be the supreme Law of the Land; and the Judges in every State shall be bound thereby, any Thing in the Constitution or Laws of any State to the Contrary notwithstanding.

The Senators and Representatives before mentioned, and the Members of the several State Legislatures, and all executive and judicial Officers, both of the United States and of the several States, shall be bound by Oath or Affirmation to support this Constitution; but no religious Test shall ever be required as a qualification to any Office or public Trust under the United States.

ARTICLE VII

The Ratification of the Conventions of nine States shall be sufficient for the Establishment of this Constitution between the States so ratifying the same.

Done in Convention by the Unanimous Consent of the States present the Seventeenth Day of September in the Year of our Lord one thousand seven hundred and Eighty seven, and of the Independence of the United States of America the Twelfth. In Witness whereof We have hereunto subscribed our Names.

Articles in Addition to, and Amendment of, the Constitution of the United States of America, Proposed by Congress, and Ratified by the Legislatures of the Several States, Pursuant to the Fifth Article of the Original Constitution.

AMENDMENT I[10]

Congress shall make no law respecting an establishment of religion, or prohibiting the free exercise thereof; or abridging the freedom of speech, or of the press; or the right of the people peaceably to assemble, and to petition the Government for a redress of grievances.

AMENDMENT II

A well regulated Militia, being necessary to the security of a free State, the right of the people to keep and bear Arms shall not be infringed.

AMENDMENT III

No Soldier shall, in time of peace, be quartered in any house, without the consent of the Owner, nor in time of war, but in a manner to be prescribed by law.

AMENDMENT IV

The right of the people to be secure in their persons, houses, papers, and effects, against unreasonable searches and seizures, shall not be violated, and no Warrants shall issue, but upon probable cause, supported by Oath or affirmation, and particularly describing the place to be searched, and the persons or things to be seized.

[10]The first ten amendments were passed by Congress September 25, 1789. They were ratified by three-fourths of the states December 15, 1791.

AMENDMENT V

No person shall be held to answer for a capital or otherwise infamous crime, unless on a presentment or indictment of a Grand Jury, except in cases arising in the land or naval forces, or in the Militia, when in actual service in time of War or public danger; nor shall any person be subject for the same offence to be twice put in jeopardy of life or limb; nor shall be compelled in any criminal case to be a witness against himself, nor be deprived of life, liberty, or property, without due process of law; nor shall private property be taken for public use, without just compensation.

AMENDMENT VI

In all criminal prosecutions, the accused shall enjoy the right to a speedy and public trial, by an impartial jury of the State and district wherein the crime shall have been committed, which district shall have been previously ascertained by law, and to be informed of the nature and cause of the accusation; to be confronted with the witnesses against him; to have compulsory process for obtaining witnesses in his favor, and to have the Assistance of Counsel for his defence.

AMENDMENT VII

In suits at common law, where the value in controversy shall exceed twenty dollars, the right of trial by jury shall be preserved, and no fact tried by a jury, shall be otherwise reexamined in any Court of the United States, than according to the rules of the common law.

AMENDMENT VIII

Excessive bail shall not be required, nor excessive fines imposed, nor cruel and unusual punishments inflicted.

AMENDMENT IX

The enumeration in the Constitution, of certain rights, shall not be construed to deny or disparage others retained by the people.

AMENDMENT X

The powers not delegated to the United States by the Constitution, nor prohibited by it to the States, are reserved to the States respectively, or to the people.

AMENDMENT XI (1798)[11]

The Judicial power of the United States shall not be construed to extend to any suit in law or equity, commenced or prosecuted against one of the United States by Citizens of another State, or by Citizens or Subjects of any Foreign State.

AMENDMENT XII (1804)

The Electors shall meet in their respective States and vote by ballot for President and Vice-President, one of whom, at least, shall not be an inhabitant of the same State with themselves; they shall name in their ballots the person voted for as President, and in distinct ballots the person voted for as Vice-President, and they shall make distinct lists of all persons voted for as President, and of all persons voted for as Vice-President, and of the number of votes for each, which lists they shall sign and certify, and transmit sealed to the seat of the government of the United States, directed to the President of Senate;—The President of the Senate shall, in the presence of the Senate and House of Representatives, open all the certificates and the votes shall then be counted;— The person having the greatest number of votes for President, shall be the President, if such number be a majority of the whole number of Electors appointed; and if no person have such majority, then from the persons having the highest numbers not exceeding three on the list of those voted for as President, the House of Representatives shall choose immediately, by ballot, the President. But in choosing the President, the votes shall be taken by states, the representation from each state having one vote; a quorum for this purpose shall consist of a member or members from two-thirds of the states, and a majority of all the states shall be necessary to a choice. [And if the House of Representatives shall not choose a President whenever the right of choice shall devolve upon them, before the fourth day of March next following, then the Vice-President shall act as President, as in the case of the death or other constitutional disability of the President.][12]—The person having the greatest number of votes as Vice-President, shall be the Vice-President, if such number be a majority of the whole number of Electors appointed, and if no person have a majority, then from the two highest numbers on the list, the Senate shall choose the Vice-President; a quorum for the purpose shall consist of two-thirds of the whole number of Senators, and a majority of the whole number shall be necessary to a choice. But no person constitutionally ineligible to the office of President shall be eligible to that of Vice-President of the United States.

AMENDMENT XIII (1865)

Section 1. Neither slavery nor involuntary servitude, except as a punishment for crime whereof the party shall have been duly convicted, shall exist within the United States, or any place subject to their jurisdiction.

Section 2. Congress shall have power to enforce this article by appropriate legislation.

AMENDMENT XIV (1868)

Section 1. All persons born or naturalized in the United States, and subject to the jurisdiction thereof, are citizens of the United States and of the State wherein they reside. No State shall make or enforce any law which shall abridge the privileges or immunities of citizens of the United States; nor shall any State deprive any person of life, liberty, or property, without due process of law; nor deny to any person within its jurisdiction the equal protection of the laws.

Section 2. Representatives shall be apportioned among the several States according to their respective numbers, counting the whole number of persons in each State, excluding Indians not taxed. But when the right to vote at any election for the choice of electors for President and Vice-President of the United States, Representatives in Congress, the Executive and Judicial officers of a State, or the members

[11]Date of ratification.

[12]Superseded by the Twentieth Amendment.

of the Legislature thereof, is denied to any of the male inhabitants of such State, being twenty-one years of age, and citizens of the United States, or in any way abridged, except for participation in rebellion, or other crime, the basis of representation therein shall be reduced in the proportion which the number of such male citizens shall bear to the whole number of male citizens twenty-one years of age in such State.

Section 3. No person shall be a Senator or Representative in Congress, or elector of President and Vice-President, or hold any office, civil or military, under the United States, or under any State, who, having previously taken an oath, as a member of Congress, or as an officer of the United States, or as a member of any State legislature, or as an executive or judicial officer of any State, to support the Constitution of the United States, shall have engaged in insurrection or rebellion against the same, or given aid or comfort to the enemies thereof. But Congress may by a vote of two-thirds of each House, remove such disability.

Section 4. The validity of the public debt of the United States, authorized by law, including debts incurred for payment of pensions and bounties for services in suppressing insurrection or rebellion, shall not be questioned. But neither the United States nor any State shall assume or pay any debt or obligation incurred in aid of insurrection or rebellion against the United States, or any claim for the loss or emancipation of any slave; but all such debts, obligations, and claims shall be held illegal and void.

Section 5. The Congress shall have the power to enforce, by appropriate legislation, the provisions of this article.

AMENDMENT XV (1870)

Section 1. The right of citizens of the United States to vote shall not be denied or abridged by the United States or by any State on account of race, color, or previous condition of servitude—

Section 2. The Congress shall have power to enforce this article by appropriate legislation.

AMENDMENT XVI (1913)

The Congress shall have power to lay and collect taxes on incomes, from whatever source derived, without apportionment among the several States, and without regard to any census or enumeration.

AMENDMENT XVII (1913)

The Senate of the United States shall be composed of two Senators from each State, elected by the people thereof, for six years; and each Senator shall have one vote. The electors in each State shall have the qualifications requisite for electors of the most numerous branch of the State legislatures.

When vacancies happen in the representation of any State in the Senate, the executive authority of such State shall issue writs of election to fill such vacancies: *Provided,* That the legislature of any State may empower the executive thereof to make temporary appointments until the people fill the vacancies by election as the legislature may direct.

This amendment shall not be so construed as to affect the election or term of any Senator chosen before it becomes valid as part of the Constitution.

AMENDMENT XVIII (1919)[13]

Section 1. After one year from the ratification of this article the manufacture, sale, or transportation of intoxicating liquors within, the importation thereof into, or the exportation thereof from the United States and all territory subject to the jurisdiction thereof for beverage purposes is hereby prohibited.

Section 2. The Congress and the several States shall have concurrent power to enforce this article by appropriate legislation.

Section 3. This article shall be inoperative unless it shall have been ratified as an amendment to the Constitution by the legislatures of the several States, as provided in the Constitution, within seven years from the date of the submission hereof to the States by the Congress.

[13]Repealed by the Twenty-first Amendment.

AMENDMENT XIX (1920)

The right of citizens of the United States to vote shall not be denied or abridged by the United States or by any State on account of sex.

Congress shall have power to enforce this article by appropriate legislation.

AMENDMENT XX (1933)

Section 1. The terms of the President and Vice-President shall end at noon on the 20th day of January, and the terms of Senators and Representatives at noon on the 3d day of January, of the years in which such terms would have ended if this article had not been ratified; and the terms of their successors shall then begin.

Section 2. The Congress shall assemble at least once in every year, and such meeting shall begin at noon on the 3d day of January, unless they shall by law appoint a different day.

Section 3. If, at the time fixed for the beginning of the term of the President, the President elect shall have died, the Vice-President elect shall become President. If a President shall not have been chosen before the time fixed for the beginning of his term, or if the President elect shall have failed to qualify, then the Vice-President elect shall act as President until a President shall have qualified; and the Congress may by law provide for the case wherein neither a President elect nor a Vice-President elect shall have qualified, declaring who shall then act as President, or the manner in which one who is to act shall be selected, and such person shall act accordingly until a President or Vice-President shall have qualified.

Section 4. The Congress may by law provide for the case of the death of any of the persons from whom the House of Representatives may choose a President whenever the right of choice shall have devolved upon them, and for the case of the death of any of the persons from whom the Senate may choose a Vice-President whenever the right of choice shall have devolved upon them.

Section 5. Sections 1 and 2 shall take effect on the 15th day of October following the ratification of this article.

Section 6. This article shall be inoperative unless it shall have been ratified as an amendment to the Constitution by the legislatures of three-fourths of the several States within seven years from the date of its submission.

AMENDMENT XXI (1933)

Section 1. The eighteenth article of amendment to the Constitution of the United States is hereby repealed.

Section 2. The transportation or importation into any State, Territory, or possession of the United States for delivery or use therein of intoxicating liquors, in violation of the laws thereof, is, hereby prohibited.

Section 3. This article shall be inoperative unless it shall have been ratified as an amendment to the Constitution by conventions in the several States, as provided in the Constitution, within seven years from the date of the submission hereof to the States by the Congress.

AMENDMENT XXII (1951)

No person shall be elected to the office of the President more than twice, and no person who has held the office of President, or acted as President, for more than two years of a term to which some other person was elected President shall be elected to the office of the President more than once.

But this Article shall not apply to any person holding the office of President when this Article was proposed by the Congress, and shall not prevent any person who may be holding the office of President, or acting as President, during the term within which this Article becomes operative from holding the office of President or acting as President during the remainder of such term.

AMENDMENT XXIII (1961)

Section 1. The District constituting the seat of Government of the United States shall appoint in such manner as the Congress may direct:

A number of electors of President and Vice-President equal to the whole number of Senators and Representatives in Congress to which the District would be entitled if it were a

State, but in no event more than the least populous State; they shall be in addition to those appointed by the States, but they shall be considered for the purposes of the election of President and Vice-President, to be electors appointed by the State; and they shall meet in the District and perform such duties as provided by the twelfth article of amendment.

Section 2. The Congress shall have power to enforce this article by appropriate legislation.

AMENDMENT XXIV (1964)

Section 1. The right of citizens of the United States to vote in any primary or other election for President or Vice-President, for electors for President or Vice-President, or for Senator or Representative in Congress, shall not be denied or abridged by the United States or any State by reason of failure to pay any poll tax or other tax.

Section 2. The Congress shall have power to enforce this article by appropriate legislation.

AMENDMENT XXV (1967)

Section 1. In case of the removal of the President from office or of his death or resignation, the Vice-President shall become President.

Section 2. Whenever there is a vacancy in the office of the Vice-President, the President shall nominate a Vice-President who shall take office upon confirmation by a majority vote of both Houses of Congress.

Section 3. Whenever the President transmits to the President pro tempore of the Senate and the Speaker of the House of Representatives his written declaration that he is unable to discharge the powers and duties of his office, and until he transmits to them a written declaration to the contrary, such powers and duties shall be discharged by the Vice-President as Acting President.

Section 4. Whenever the Vice-President and a majority of either the principal officers of the executive department or of such other body as Congress may by law provide, transmit to the President pro tempore of the Senate and the Speaker of the House of Representatives their written declaration that the President is unable to discharge the powers and duties of his office, the Vice-President shall immediately assume the powers and duties of the office as Acting President.

Thereafter, when the President transmits to the President pro tempore of the Senate and the Speaker of the House of Representatives his written declaration that no inability exists, he shall resume the powers and duties of his office unless the Vice-President and a majority of either the principal officers of the executive department or of such other body as Congress may by law provide, transmit within four days to the President pro tempore of the Senate and the Speaker of the House of Representatives their written declaration that the President is unable to discharge the powers and duties of his office. Thereupon Congress shall decide the issue, assembling within forty-eight hours for that purpose if not in session. If the Congress, within twenty-one days after receipt of the latter written declaration, or, if Congress is not in session, within twenty-one days after Congress is required to assemble, determines by two-thirds vote of both Houses that the President is unable to discharge the powers and duties of his office, the Vice-President shall continue to Discharge the same as Acting President; otherwise, the President shall resume the powers and duties of his office.

AMENDMENT XXVI (1971)

Section 1. The right of citizens of the United States, who are eighteen years of age or older, to vote shall not be denied or abridged by the United States or by any State on account of age.

Section 2. The Congress shall have power to enforce this article by appropriate legislation.

Presidential elections, 1900-1972

YEAR	NUMBER OF STATES	CANDIDATES	PARTIES	POPULAR VOTE (In thousands)	ELECTORAL VOTE	PERCENTAGE OF POPULAR VOTE[a]
1900	45	WILLIAM McKINLEY	Republican	7,218	292	51.7
		William J. Bryan	Democratic; Populist	6,356	155	45.5
		John C. Wooley	Prohibition	208		1.5
1904	45	THEODORE ROOSEVELT	Republican	7,628	336	57.4
		Alton B. Parker	Democratic	5,084	140	37.6
		Eugene V. Debs	Socialist	402		3.0
		Silas C. Swallow	Prohibition	258		1.9
1908	46	WILLIAM H. TAFT	Republican	7,675	321	51.6
		William J. Bryan	Democratic	6,412	162	43.1
		Eugene V. Debs	Socialist	420		2.8
		Eugene W. Chafin	Prohibition	253		1.7
1912	48	WOODROW WILSON	Democratic	6,296	435	41.9
		Theodore Roosevelt	Progressive	4,118	88	27.4
		William H. Taft	Republican	3,486	8	23.2
		Eugene V. Debs	Socialist	900		6.0
		Eugene W. Chafin	Prohibition	206		1.4
1916	48	WOODROW WILSON	Democratic	9,127	277	49.4
		Charles E. Hughes	Republican	8,533	254	46.2
		A. L. Benson	Socialist	585		3.2
		J. Frank Hanly	Prohibition	220		1.2
1920	48	WARREN G. HARDING	Republican	16,143	404	60.4
		James N. Cox	Democratic	9,130	127	34.2
		Eugene V. Debs	Socialist	919		3.4
		P. P. Christensen	Farmer-Labor	265		1.0
1924	48	CALVIN COOLIDGE	Republican	15,718	382	54.0
		John W. Davis	Democratic	8,385	136	28.8
		Robert M. La Follette	Progressive	4,831	13	16.6
1928	48	HERBERT C. HOOVER	Republican	21,391	444	58.2
		Alfred E. Smith	Democratic	15,016	87	40.9

SOURCE: Adapted from *Historical Statistics of the United States*, p. 682; *Statistical Abstract of the United States: 1974*, p. 422
[a]Candidates receiving less than 1 percent of the popular vote have been omitted. For that reason the percentage of popular vote given for any election year may not total 100 percent.

YEAR	NUMBER OF STATES	CANDIDATES	PARTIES	POPULAR VOTE (In thousands)	ELECTORAL VOTE	PERCENTAGE OF POPULAR VOTE"
1932	48	FRANKLIN D. ROOSEVELT	Democratic	22,809	472	57.4
		Herbert C. Hoover	Republican	15,758	59	39.7
		Norman Thomas	Socialist	881		2.2
1936	48	FRANKLIN D. ROOSEVELT	Democratic	27,752	523	60.8
		Alfred M. Landon	Republican	16,674	8	36.5
		William Lemke	Union	882		1.9
1940	48	FRANKLIN D. ROOSEVELT	Democratic	27,307	449	54.8
		Wendell L. Willkie	Republican	22,321	82	44.8
1944	48	FRANKLIN D. ROOSEVELT	Democrat c	25,606	432	53.5
		Thomas E. Dewey	Republican	22,014	99	46.0
1948	48	HARRY S. TRUMAN	Democratic	24,105	303	49.5
		Thomas E. Dewey	Republican	21,970	189	45.1
		J. Strom Thurmond	States' Rights	1,169	39	2.4
		Henry A. Wallace	Progressive	1,157		2.4
1952	48	DWIGHT D. EISENHOWER	Republican	33,936	442	55.1
		Adlai E. Stevenson	Democratic	27,314	89	44.4
1956	48	DWIGHT D. EISENHOWER	Republican	35,590	457	57.6
		Adlai E. Stevenson	Democratic	26,022	73	42.1
1960	50	JOHN F. KENNEDY	Democratic	34,227	303	49.9
		Richard M. Nixon	Republican	34,108	219	49.6
1964	50	LYNDON B. JOHNSON	Democratic	43,126	486	61.1
		Barry M. Goldwater	Republican	27,176	52	38.5
1968	50	RICHARD M. NIXON	Republican	31,785	301	43.4
		Hubert H. Humphrey	Democratic	31,275	191	42.7
		George C. Wallace	American Independent	9,906	46	13.5
1972	50	RICHARD M. NIXON	Republican	47,170	520	60.7
		George S. McGovern	Democratic	29,170	17	37.7

Index

Eisenhower, 392, 396, 401, 428; farm bloc in, 393; and FDR, 241, 260, 261, 264, 308; four-party government in, 389; and Harding, 174; and Hoover, 228–29; and Johnson, 428, 441; and Kennedy, 413, 414, 416–17, 428; 1935 public welfare legislation, 245, 248; and Nixon, 493, 495, 505–6; and pressure groups, 97, 440, 441; progressives in, 177; Republican majorities in, 134, 145, 367; southern bloc in, 133–34; and Taft, 95; and TR, 82, 83, 95; and Truman, 329, 330, 331, 332, 333, 334, 349, 368; and Wilson, 95, 96, 133, 134

Congress of Industrial Organization, 52, 248, 249, 252, 473; alliance with New Deal, 249, 260; Communist loss of strength in, 354; as interest group, 252; and sit-down strikes, 260; and unskilled workers, 251

Congress on Racial Equality, 319–20, 321, 417, 463

Connally, John, 500

Conner, Eugene ("Bull"), 417, 419

Conroy, Jack, *The Disinherited* by, 220

Conscientious objectors: in WW I, 137, 140; in WW II, 310

"Consciousness III," 469

Conservation, 5, 47, 82, 217, 471; Ballinger-Pinchot controversy, 89–91; and TR, 83, 85, 90

Conservatism, 19, 260, 429, 436; and holding company bill, 254, 255; in Supreme Court, 80; and wealth tax, 254, 255

Conservatives, 375, 465, 472, 492

Conspicuous consumption, 26

Constitution, 44, 80; Amendments: 16th (income tax), 88, 95; 18th (prohibition), 67; 19th, (women's suffrage), 59; 22nd, (limiting presidency to two terms), 337; 25th (authorizing president to name vice-president), 515; 26th (extending voting rights), 448; Bill of Rights, 141, 144, 388, 411; Equal Rights Amendment (proposed) 474, 476, 486

Construction industry, 158, 206, 209, 380

Consumer price index, 334

Consumerism, 165, 262, 332, 336, 470; consumer groups, 471; and credit, 383; demand for goods, 159, 332, 375; and growth of industries, 24, 159; and race riots, 453

Contraband, 118, 119

Contraceptive devices, state laws banning, 443. *See also* Birth control

Controlled Materials Plan, 313

Coolidge, Calvin, 163, 174, 175–76, 177, 178, 332, 490; election of, 177, 178; Mencken on, 17, 176

Cooper, Gary, 378

Copper mining, 1917 strike, 140

Coral Sea battle, 296

CORE. *See* Congress on Racial Equality

Corcoran, Thomas, 254

Cornell University black student takeover, 489, 490

Corporations, 24, 25, 38, 43, 69, 73, 98, 132, 162, 175, 209, 250, 263, 382, 383, 391, 415; bureaucratic, 379; concentration of, 84, 93, 162, 182; and crash (1929), 207; and Federal Trade Commission, 96; government regulation, 91, 95; influence on economy, 440–41; influence on foreign policy, 440; interlocking directorates, 96, 207; and Meany, 442; mergers, 25–26; pension fund investments, 441; and political campaign contributions, 501; and TR, 82, 83, 84, 85; and unions, 250–51; and wealth tax, 254, 255; WW I profits, 124, 126. *See also* Big business; Monopolies; Trusts

Corregidor defeat, 291

Corwin, Edward S., 278, 309, 388

Cost of living, 3, 23, 28, 48, 94, 501; WW I, 133

Cotton mills, child labor in, 54

Cotton picking, 27

Cotton price controls (WW I), 134

Coughlin, Charles, 252, 253, 254, 256, 257

Council of Economic Advisors, 210, 333, 442

Council of National Defense, 312

Counter culture, 213, 449, 467–72, 478; and backlash, 472; differences within, 471

Counts, George S., 214, 217;

Dare the School Build a New Social Order? by, 214

Cowley, Malcolm, 216, 218

Cox, Archibald, 510, 511

CPI. *See* Committee on Public Information

Crash (1929), 157, 173, 198–206, 226; causes, 207–10; repercussions, 211–22

Crane, Stephen, *Maggie—A Girl of the Streets* by, 42

Credibility gap, 463

Credit. *See* Installment buying

Creel, George, 137

CREEP (Committee to Reelect the President), 501, 509, 514; and Watergate, 502

Crime, 18, 183–84, 438–39; Crime Control and Safe Streets Act, 443; criminals, rights of, 443, 444

Cripple Creek miners' strike, 53

Cromwell, William, 108

Crosby, Ernest Howard, 103

Cuba, 102, 103, 115, 270; Bay of Pigs invasion, 421–22; and Castro, 403, 509; CIA in, 509; and Kennedy, 406–7; Soviet Missile Crisis, 422–24

Cubberly, Ellwood, 192

Culture: and behavior, 170; change, 40–41; High, 375, 376; inner-directed, 374, 375; and cultural misconceptions, 112; new era critics, 179–81, 183; other-directed, 374, 377; philistine, 375, 376

Currency, government control, 95. *See also* Banking

Czechoslovakia, 147, 188; Egyptian arms deal, 402; Hitler takeover, 273, 274, 275; Soviet communization, 254, 342

Daladier, Eduard, 274

Daley, Richard, 440, 479

Dance, 40; modern, 166, 167

Dance marathons, 211

Darlan, Jean, 303, 305

Darrow, Clarence, 37, 185

Daugherty, Harry, 175

Daughters of the American Revolution, 16, 19

Davis, Elmer, 310, 390

Davis, James J., 175

Davis, Jeff, 64

Davis, John W., 177, 178, 255

Day, Clarence: *Life with Father* by, 213; *Life with Mother* by, 213

Heflin, Thomas, 193

Heller, Walter, 442

Hell's Angels motorcycle gang, 469

Hemingway, Ernest, 181; *For Whom the Bell Tolls* by, 218, 220; *Old Man and the Sea* by, 220, 375; *To Have and Have Not* by, 218

Hendrix, Jimi, 491

Hepburn Act, 83, 84, 85–86

Herberg, Will, 382

Herskovitz, Melville, 170

Hewitt, Alexander, 68, 69

Hickel, Walter, 492

Hicks, Granville, 216

High Schools, 26, 169; enrollment during depression, 203–4

Highways, 160, 206; construction of, 22, 96, 97, 132, 395; federal act for, 394, 395

Hill, Napoleon, *Think and Grow Rich* by, 221

Hillman, Sidney, 52

Himmler, Heinrich, 296

Hirohito, 287

Hiroshima bombing, 292, 297, 300, 326, 327

Hippies, 467, 472

Hiss, Alger, 354

Hitler, Adolf, 149, 216, 269, 272, 276, 283, 292, 296, 303, 344; America and, 275–82, 342; European aggression in WW II, 273–75, 285; persecution of Jews, 269, 277, 283; Roosevelt and, 282–83; and Russia, 275, 281, 282

Hobby, Oveta Culp, 392

Ho Chi Minh, 400, 425, 426, 461

Hoffman, Abbie, 471, 472, 494

Hoffman, Dustin, 469, 472

Hofstader, Richard, 382

Holding companies, 162, 207, 208; control bill, 254, 255

Holland, German invasion of, 285

Holli, Melville, 68

Holmes, Oliver Wendell, Jr., 44, 46; *The Common Law* by, 44; on Espionage Act, 141

Home Owners Loan Corporation, 235

Homosexuality, 470

Hoover, Herbert, 165, 166, 171, 174, 182, 183, 226–30, 231, 232, 233, 234, 254, 267, 269, 368, 389, 408, 409; anti-interventionism of, 277; election of, 177; FDR on, 226; Food Administration, 133; and foreign affairs, 268–69; and government reorganization, 329; public works spending by, 263; as Secretary of Commerce, 175, 187

Hoover, J. Edgar, 143, 498, 509

Hoovervilles, 201

Hopkins, Harry, 235, 238, 242, 243, 244, 291, 304, 306

Horney, Karen, *The Neurotic Personality of Our Time* by, 215

House, Edward, 118, 120, 121, 145, 152

House Judiciary Committee, Nixon impeachment charges, 511, 513

House of Representatives, 79, 420; *Panay* incident, 274; un-American Activities Committee, 261; and WW I, 124, 126

House-Grey memorandum, 120

Housing: post WW II, 373, 380; public. *See* Public housing; suburban, 373

Houston, 6; race riot (1917), 134; suburban growth, 372

Howard University student demonstrations, 489

Howe, Frederic, 144–45

Howells, William Dean, 39

HUD. *See* Department of Housing and Urban Development

Huerta, Victoriano, 112, 113, 115

Hughes, Charles Evans, 96, 123, 172, 174, 175, 259

Hughes, Langston, 188, 190, 456

Hull, Cordell, 270, 272, 274, 286, 287, 291, 306

Hull House, 50, 51

Humphrey, George, 392, 393

Humphrey, Hubert H., 346, 348, 388, 389, 406, 430, 480; presidential candidate, 1968, 476, 478–79, 480, 481, 502

Hungarian revolution (1956), 397, 398, 401, 405

Hunt, E. Howard, 501, 502, 509

Hunter, Robert, *Poverty* by, 26, 28

Hutchins, Robert, 214–15

Hydrogen bomb, 386, 398

IBM. *See* International Business Machines

ICC. *See* Interstate Commerce Commission

Iceland, 282; U. S. occupation, 280

Ickes, Harold, 238, 258, 274, 312, 330

Immigration, 6, 15–20, 32, 37, 107; act (1924), 192; anti-immigrationists, 15–16, 19, 186; Chinese exclusion, 15; ethnic conflicts, 192–93; Japanese exclusion, 172; literacy tests, 15; and out-migration, 18; quotas, 15, 172, 337, 431; restrictions, 15–16, 20, 47, 49, 172, 178, 192; West Indian, 190, 191; and Wilson, 93, 97

Immigration Restriction League, 20, 47

Immigrants, 4, 5, 15–20, 74; in city machine politics, 10–11, 68, 69

Imperialism, 103–15; interventionist policy, 111, 112, 113, 172, 173, 268. *See also* Realpolitik; Roosevelt Corollary; Third World

Imports, 104, 500

Income, 383, 384; of blacks, 486; distribution, 209, 262, 316, 331, 338, 385, 414, 436, 437, 438; national, 158, 200, 262, 316; personal, 158; tax on, 26, 80, 83, 88, 95, 96, 97, 134, 309; and wealth tax, 254, 255, 262; widening gap between black and white, 446

Independents, 1936 election, 258

Indians. *See* American Indians

Indo-China: Geneva accord, 400; and Japan, 285, 286, 287, 292; U.S. aid to French in, 364, 400. *See also* Cambodia; Laos; Vietnam

Individualism, 9, 182, 210, 218, 332

Industrial Workers of the World, 53–55, 57; suppression of (WW I), 140, 142

Industrialization, 2, 21–32, 37, 74, 86, 517; impact on labor, 28, 31; and monopolies, 24, 25; and progressivism, 47; and urban growth, 6, 24

Infant mortality, 26

Inflation, 48, 462, 499, 506, 514, 517; labor–management settlements, 493; and oil prices, 507; and Phase II, 500, 501; post–WW II, 334, 337; price and wage controls, 500, 501; with recession, 493, 516; WW I, 133, 142, 154

Initiative, 49, 69, 70, 71, 72, 92

Installment buying, 160, 163, 198, 207

Insull, Samuel, 162, 207

Tonkin Gulf resolution, 282, 401, 457, 458; repeal, 497
Toqueville, Alexis de, 342
Tourist business, 204
Townsend, Francis, 252, 253, 254, 256
Trade: balance, 104; expansion act, 413; expansion of, 5; foreign, 105; restraint of, 81, 84
Transportation Department, 77
Treasury Department, 175
Treaties, 111; Washington Conference, 172–73
Triangle Shirtwaist company, 28, 52
Tripartite Pact (1940), 283, 286
Trotskyites, 56
Trucking industry, 132
Truman, Harry S., 308, 325–42, 367, 368, 392, 399, 415, 517; aid to France in Indo-China, 364; aid to Greece, 341; aid to Turkey, 341; Asian policy, 350–51, 363–64, 366; and China, 406; and civil liberties, 337; and civil rights, 337, 349; and Cold War, 339–46; and Congress, 329, 330, 331, 332, 333, 334, 336–38, 349, 368; Doctrine, 341, 342, 344, 345; domestic controversies, 329–36; and Eisenhower, 389, 392; election (1948), 348, 367; end of WW II, 326–29; Fair Deal of, 329, 337; and health insurance, 337, 349; and Hiroshima bombing, 326; Israel, recognition of, 402; and Korean War, 357–64, 368, 458, 461; and labor legislation, 337; and MacArthur, 361–64; and McCarthyism, 356; Nagasaki bombing, 326; New Dealers' support of, 338; and Pendergast machine, 325, 330; Point Four program of, 349, 350; at Potsdam conference, 339; and social problems, 396; and Stalin, 345; strike settlements by, 335–36
Trusts, 26, 40, 47, 69, 132; regulatory commissions, 91, 93, 96; and Taft, 89; and TR, 82, 83, 84, 91; and Wilson, 93, 96
Tugwell, Rexford, 170, 171, 227; in FDR brain trust, 232, 236, 239, 241
Turkey, 345; and Soviet Union, 338, 339, 343; U.S. military aid to, 336, 341; U.S. military bases in, 424

Turner, Frederick Jackson, 3, 5, 9, 32, 170, 219, 270
Tuskegee Institute, 63
Twenty-fifth amendment, 515
Twenty-second amendment, 337
Twenty-sixth amendment, 488
Tydings, Millard, 357

U-2 affair, 403–5
Underwood Simmons Tariff, 95, 97
Unemployment, 68, 227, 228, 262, 309, 493, 517; bonus army, 229; caused by technological advance, 162; and CCC, 235, 258; and CWA, 235; in depression, 200, 201, 203; and FERA, 235; in 1950s, 394; and PWA, 258; migrant workers, 203, 438; relief programs, 235, 242–45; RFC loans, 226; WPA, 242–45, 246, 258, 261, 308
Unemployment compensation, 245–46, 394
Union for Social Justice, 252, 256
Union party, 256, 257
Unions, 29–32, 81, 248, 249, 251, 262, 332, 440, 480; affluence of, 383; antiunion contracts, 226; and blacks, 32, 189, 383, 441, 493; closed shop, 32, 337; and collective bargaining, 236, 238; and Cold War, 398; company-run, 30, 248; craft, 32, 52, 248; on federal projects, 493; gain, 319; and immigrants, 30; industrial, 31, 52, 55, 248, 249–51; industrial clout of, 442; membership growth, 132, 249, 441; neglect of nonunion workers, 383; and Nixon's economy controls, 501; and noncommunist oaths, 337; and NLRB, 236, 248; and NRA, 248, 337; Philadelphia plan, 493; power of in Democratic party, 51; in presidential campaign, 480; public service workers, 490; restraint of trade by, 81; strikes by. See Strikes; and Taft-Hartley Act, 248, 337, 338, 349, 350, 383
Unisex, 475–76
United Auto Workers, 248, 251, 441
United Mine Workers, 335
United Nations, 304, 326, 342, 361, 462; Communist China seated, 500; Korean War sanc-

tion, 360; Middle East situation, 402; Russian seats in General Assembly, 305; Security Council of, 360
Universities: Anti-Semitism, 192; federal funding, 486, 489; leftist organizations, 213; sex discrimination ban, 486; student demonstrations, 464, 489, 498
University of Wisconsin, student violence at, 489
Unknown Soldier, 154
Updike, John, 375, 376; *Rabbit Run* by, 378
Uprising of the Twenty Thousand, 52
Urban life, 9–15
Urban reform, 67–69, 432, 439
Urban renewal, 432, 450
Urbanization, 6, 24, 32, 37, 74, 160, 382; and black ghettos, 61–62, 64–65; decrease, 316; increase, 316; in 1920s, 157, 181; and progressivism, 47; and reform, 67–69
U.S. Marines: in Nicaragua, 111, 112; in Santo Domingo, 112
U.S. Employment Service, 228
U.S. Steel, 25, 28, 85, 89, 128, 143, 162, 210, 250, 416
Utilities, 7, 162, 234, 254, 264; crash, 207; holding company bill, 254, 255; municipal ownership, 67, 68; state regulation, 69, 70
Utley, Freda, *Japan: Feet of Clay* by, 285

Vandenberg, Arthur, 234, 277, 278, 281, 292
Vanderbilt family, 26, 27
Vanzetti, Bartolomeo, 144, 181
Venezuela, 109, 403
Vardaman, James K., 64, 124
Vaughn, Harry, 330
Veblen, Thorstein, 44, 46, 379
Versailles peace treaty, 134, 145–53; ethnic group hostility to, 152; League of Nations incorporation in, 147; Paris conference, 145–49; Senate rejection, 149–53
Veterans, 229, 316, 332, 334
Vichy, France, 303
Vietcong, 459, 460; bleed-ins for, 462; National Liberation Government, 457, 561; Provisional Revolutionary Government, 504, 505; Tet offensive, 460, 464, 476

B
C
D
E
F
G   1
H   2
I   3
J   4